IMAGES
of America

KITTANNING

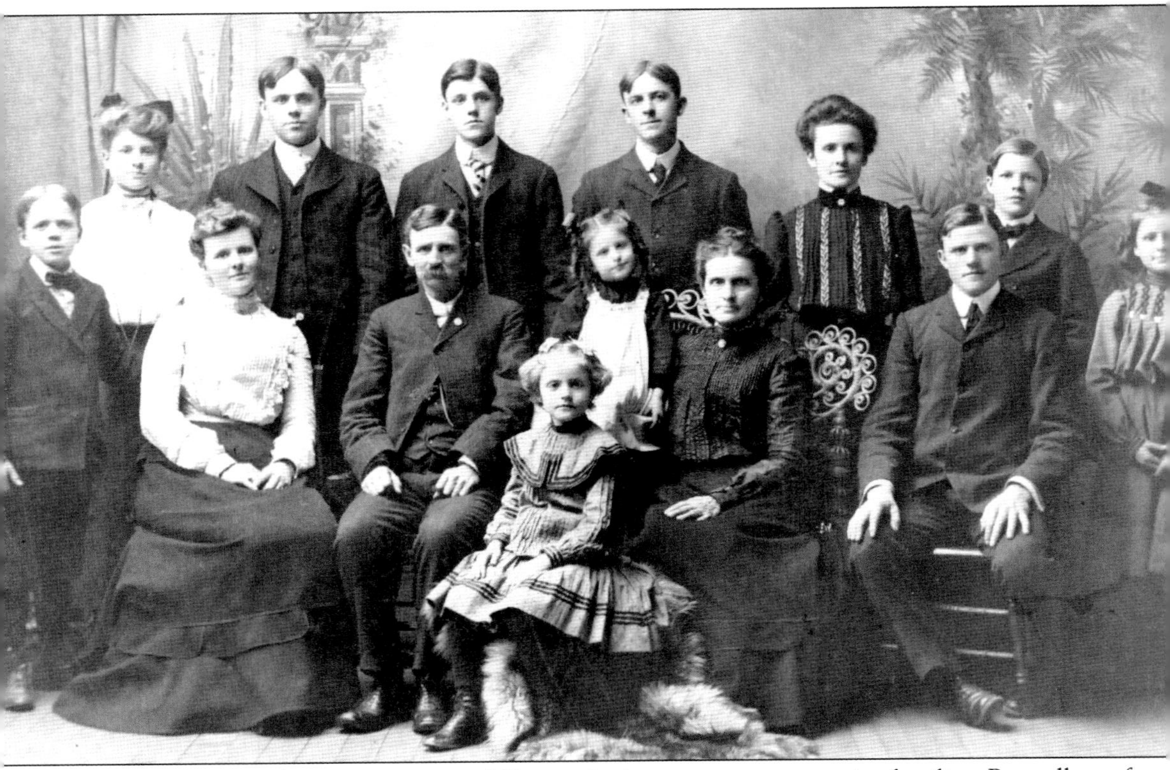

This photograph represents one of Kittanning's greatest resources, its families. Regardless of ethnicity or background, many of the town's residents came, planted roots, and grew here. Seven generations of the Blaney family, owners of Blaney's Meat Market, have called Kittanning home. Erwin and Clara Blaney are pictured here with their children in this family portrait. From left to right are (first row) Annie, Erwin (father), Louise, Jane, Clara (mother), and Turney; (second row) Edward, Harriett, William, Fred, Charles, Susan, Harry, and Clara. (Courtesy of Fred Blaney and family.)

On the cover: Not exactly looking dressed to kill, these apparently proud hunters, wearing ties and coats, pose with their trophies in front of Blaney's Meat Market in this 1917 photograph. Blaney's, a family owned business, butchered and sold a variety of meats that brought in regular clientele, week after week, year after year, in their shop located on Jefferson Street and then later on McKean Street. Pictured from left to right are Ellis Shaw, Walter Crim, George Burns, C. Smith, Bill Sedwick, Ed Blaney, Mert Schall, George King, Eli Smith, William "Bunker" Johnston, and Harry Walker. (Courtesy of the Armstrong County Historical Society.)

IMAGES
of America

KITTANNING

Diane Acerni for the Armstrong County
Historical Society

ARCADIA
PUBLISHING

ISBN 978-0-7385-6525-5

Published by Arcadia Publishing
Charleston, South Carolina

Printed in the United States of America

Library of Congress Control Number: 2008939959

For all general information contact Arcadia Publishing at:
Telephone 843-853-2070
Fax 843-853-0044
E-mail sales@arcadiapublishing.com
For customer service and orders:
Toll-Free 1-888-313-2665

Visit us on the Internet at www.arcadiapublishing.com

To my mother, Mary Etta Frampton Orris.

Contents

ACKNOWLEDGMENTS

This book is truly the collaborative effort of many. Without the initial referral to Jerry Roberts at Arcadia Publishing by Beth Milanak and Linda Cunningham, as well as the collective support of the Kittanning Public Library and the Armstrong County Historical Society, this book would not have materialized. The board of directors and members at large of both are also thanked. Special thanks are given to Anne Pepling, who was my staunchest cheerleader, as well as Lakota Ridinger, Debe Acierno Gamble, Sue Meyer, Cheryl Deel, Claire Ashe, Rose Altemus, Kate Nee, Pat Prentice, Kevin Holbein, and Pete Harmon for their hands-on help. A huge amount of indebtedness is owed to all of the people who took the time to entrust their stories and photographs with me. Unless otherwise noted, images are courtesy of the Armstrong County Historical Society.

Publication would never have been reality without the incredible support and expertise of Erin Vosgien of Arcadia Publishing, who has a history of her own, one of optimism and unending patience.

INTRODUCTION

Although the Delaware Nation no longer exists in western Pennsylvania, many places are still identified by their Delaware names.

Located along the Allegheny River, approximately 40 miles north of Pittsburgh, Kittanning takes its name from this Native American language.

A visit to this picturesque place explains the derivation of the town's name. And while there may be some discrepancies in scholarly interpretations, Kittanning, or Kit-han-ne, essentially means "at the great river."

This great river, the Allegheny, was recognized by the Delaware, or Lenni-Lenape, as they were also known, for its potential as a life source and its prime location for trade. Occupation of this site by the Delaware began around 1727, due to their migration from a more eastern area of Pennsylvania near the Susquehanna River. Many Delaware, as well as Shawnee, crossed the mountains of central and western Pennsylvania to help make Kit-han-ne the largest Native American village west of Shamokin.

The Kittanning Trail, as it became known, was an extensive path for travel in those days and proved to be even more vital of a trail when the French and English presence were later felt.

French traders documented visits to Kit-han-ne, or as they described it, "Kythenning River," as early as 1731. Dwellings were noted on both banks of the Allegheny River, with an estimation of 50 families and 150 men residing in Attique, the French name given to Kittanning.

The size of this important village, in all likelihood, grew at the onset of the French and Indian War. Other members of the Delaware and the Shawnee tribes who were hostile towards the British made Kit-tan-he their home base.

Because of the extensive network of the Kittanning Trail, its village namesake became a vital holding for the French and Native Americans and one that was coveted by the British.

Heading eastward, one could follow the Kittanning Trail to the Juniata River and into the Cumberland Valley. The trail also allowed connection with the Catawba Trail, which crossed Westmoreland and Fayette Counties and linked with the newly-made Braddock Road.

The Kittanning Trail granted access to essentially every British settlement in the area, and the hostile Native Americans were known to use it in attacks on these settlers. Specific reference to English colonists captured and held at Kittanning can be found as early as 1755.

As Delaware aggression towards these colonists mounted, a Native American considered friendly by the British was sent from the government council at Carlisle to investigate the reports of such activity. "Delaware Jo," as he was referred, validated the news with first-hand sightings of approximately 100 English prisoners from Virginia and Pennsylvania in captivity at Kit-han-ne.

The British command decided to take definite action by sending forces from their post in Fort Shirley, Huntingdon County, to Kittanning. They chose Lt. Col. John Armstrong, commander of the second battalion of the Pennsylvania Regiment, to lead the expedition.

Armstrong was born in Northern Ireland in 1725 and is believed to have arrived in Pennsylvania in his early 20s in the period between 1745 and 1748. Prior to his appointment as the commanding officer of this Kittanning-bound force, Armstrong was known for his involvement as a surveyor in the establishment of the town of Carlisle and opening the road from Carlisle to the Youghiogheny River for transportation of British general Edward Braddock's supplies.

Armstrong's force left Carlisle on August 30, 1756, to attempt to suppress Native American aggression towards British settlers, which had recently escalated. Some factors that contributed to this escalation have been offered by historians with perspectives from both sides of the conflict.

The British interactions with the original Pennsylvanians were not always characterized by such friction. In a letter dated August 18, 1681, William Penn, the Quaker son of English nobility who was granted the tract of land to be known as Pennsylvania, stated, "But I desire to enjoy it with your love and consent, that, we may always live together as neighbors and friends."

The following year, the Delaware Nation did give its consent to peaceful coexistence in a treaty made with Penn in northern Philadelphia. Although there appears to be no written record of this friendship pact of 1682, it was honored by both sides during Penn's lifetime.

However, after Penn's death in 1716, a different management of Penn's property by his heirs dramatically changed the way of life for the Delaware and Shawnee tribes. Penn's sons did not uphold their part of the agreement, using less than scrupulous methods to revoke parts of the treaty and take back what had been promised by their father.

The protests of the Delaware and Shawnee tribes fell on deaf ears, as the government of second-generation Penns would not deal with these native tribes. Only the Six Nations of New York State had the Penn government's ear. And it was at the order of fellow Native American chieftain Canassatego that the Delaware Nation was forced to leave its ancestral homes in the Delaware Valley.

This pilgrimage, which began in 1742, ultimately took this nation's people to the Indian Territory of Oklahoma. Ill-treatment of these people followed them along their way. Adding to their frustration were the unfair trading practices of white traders. In return for their hard earned, valuable furs, the Delaware and Shawnee tribes were usually given payment of rum and to a much lesser extent, gunpowder, clothing, and other goods.

Because the traders that the Delaware and Shawnee tribes encountered were primarily Frenchmen, they had no real affinity for the French. They even went so far as to refuse the initial partnership proposed by the governor of Duquesne. This "French Hatchet" was eventually accepted by the two tribes, who subsequently raided settlements in Virginia and Pennsylvania, returning to Kittanning with their plunder.

Kittanning and its inhabitants had become a force to be reckoned with by the time Armstrong and the 300 men assigned to him arrived in the area more than a week after their departure from Fort Shirley.

Although the village was not contained to one specific area, the majority of the battle of Kittanning was played out on Jacob's Hill, where Captain Jacobs, a chief of the Kit-han-ne Delaware tribe, resided. Although his given name was Tewea, Jacobs was commonly referred to by this Anglicized name, which came from a settler who thought that he resembled another colonist. Jacobs was in charge of Kit-han-ne in the absence of his superior, Chief Shingas, which happened to be the case at the time of Armstrong's arrival.

Jacobs was well known by the British command, especially Armstrong, for it was Jacobs who, only the month before, had led the raid on Fort Granville, setting fire to the fortification and killing many. Among the casualties was Lt. Edward Armstrong, Col. John Armstrong's brother.

On Monday, September 6, 1756, Armstrong's battalion was just 50 miles from their goal, having marched through present-day Huntingdon, Blair, Cambria, Indiana, and Armstrong

Counties. As these Pennsylvanian troops marched into the evening of September 7, some signs of Native American activity were noted in the area. Armstrong assigned 12 of his own men, under the leadership of Lt. James Hogg, to remain behind and monitor the situation to prohibit any further complications that a detached party of Native Americans could create.

By daybreak on September 8, 1756, the militiamen were poised for attack. The majority approached the town from its lower side, and the remainder defended the eastern slope above the village.

Jacobs and over 100 Native American fighters, along with a few French troops under the command of a French officer DeNormanville, were fortified in their log houses within Kit-tan-he. They displayed a show of force that held Armstrong's men at bay long enough for him and several others to sustain wounds and the battalion to also suffer casualties.

As each side held their ground, an event on the morning of September 9, 1756, decided the fate of Jacobs and Kit-han-ne. Jacobs's house was set afire, and the blaze ignited the large cache of gunpowder that was stored in the ground beneath the house. The explosion that resulted was so tremendous that those stationed in Fort Duquesne, approximately 40 miles away, were said to have heard the blast.

Jacobs and his family were supposedly killed by gunfire as they exited from their burning house. The majority of those that perished in the fighting were Lenni-Lenape, and for those Delaware that did survive, they faced capture by the British or life apart from their tribe of origin.

The Pennsylvania troops did suffer greatly with the loss of Hogg and several of his men, who were assigned duty away from the main battle. The suspected Native American activity that was discovered days before materialized in the form of combat with the Lenni-Lenape, leaving this small group hard-hit from the encounter.

To this day, a location just a few miles outside of Kittanning is still known as Blanket Hill because of the blankets and other equipment left behind by Armstrong's men in the aftermath of the battle.

Not only was the battle of Kittanning considered a decisive victory for Armstrong and the men of the Pennsylvania regiment, it was considered one of the most critical victories for the British in the French and Indian War.

One

Forts and Frontiers

Discord between British colonists and native Pennsylvanians did not end with the 1756 battle of Kittanning. Confrontation continued in settlements south of the Allegheny River. As a result, the decision was made to construct a fort, which became known as Fort Armstrong, named for Col. John Armstrong, the victorious commanding officer of the battle of Kittanning.

Gen. George Washington, in correspondence sent to Col. Daniel Brodhead early in 1779, outlined plans for the construction of this proposed fort. Three companies of militiamen were dispatched to Kittanning. Completion of Fort Armstrong was documented in a message sent from Brodhead to Washington, dated July 31, 1779, in which Brodhead succinctly states, "A complete stockade fort is erected at Kittanning and is now called Fort Armstrong."

Despite the perceived need for the protection that such a fortification could provide, Fort Armstrong's usage was uneventful, and its existence was short-lived. Not long after the orders were given to build this structure, which was located a few miles south of the original village of Kit-han-ne, orders were given for the troops at Kittanning to return to Fort Pitt. Fort Armstrong was abandoned before the close of 1779.

Only a few hardy colonists are known to have attempted permanent settlement in Kittanning during those last decades of the 18th century. James Claypoole is believed to be one of the very first settlers to locate his family in what was once Kit-han-ne, in 1791. The Claypoole family lived on a property believed to be near the northwest corner of present-day Arch and Water Streets. The arrival of the Claypooles did not prompt a warm welcome from area Native Americans, and approximately one year later, they fled to Pittsburgh to avoid an impending attack.

Robert Brown, Patrick Daugherty, and Andrew Hunter are also believed to have planted their roots in Kittanning in the late 1700s.

Since then, immigrants from many other countries and cultures have settled in Kittanning. Each successive group of newcomers has influenced the town that Kittanning is today. Their influence may not be as evident as that of the Delaware Nation, as no one has renamed this town, but all have contributed to Kittanning's second name, home.

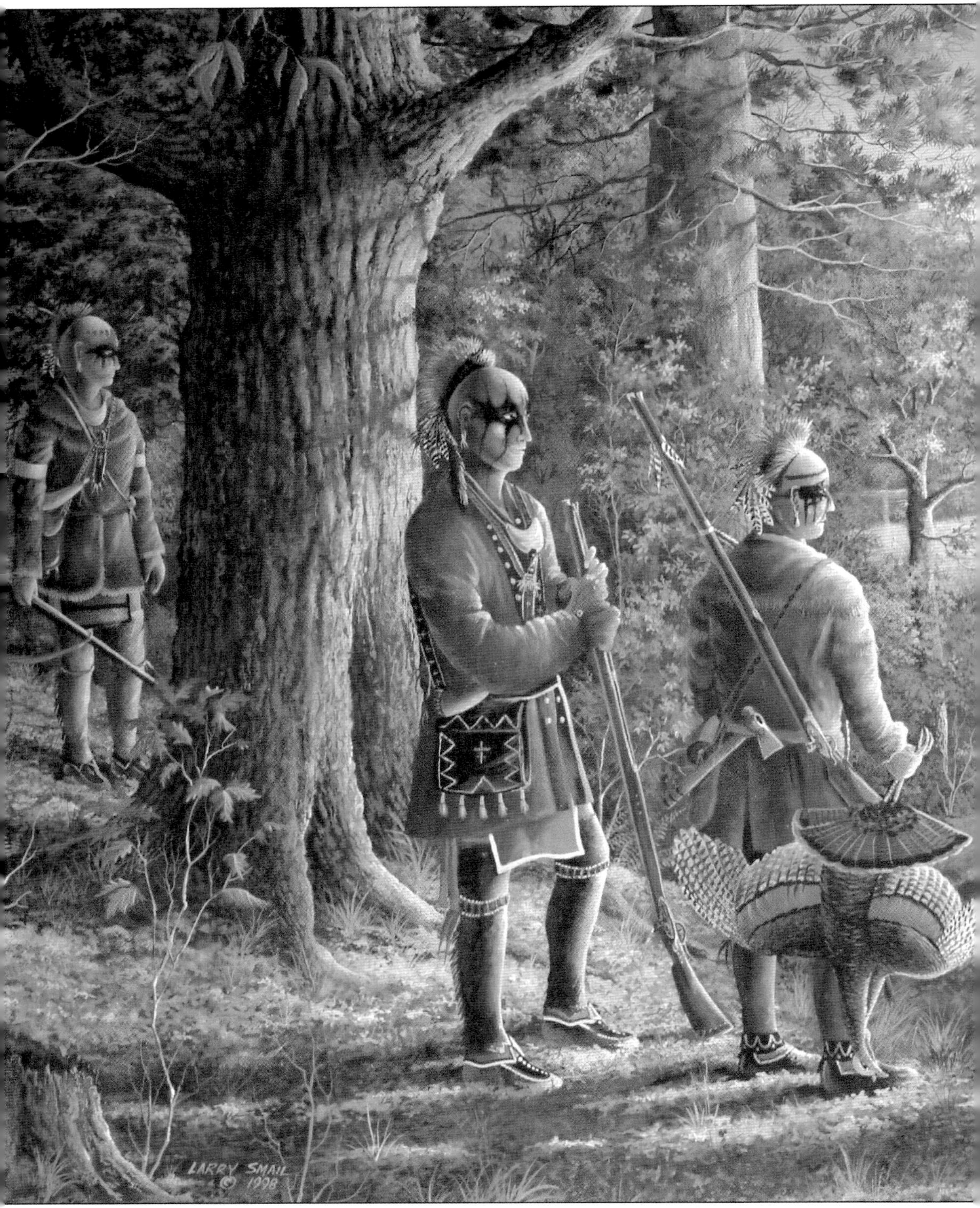

Home to Kit-han-ne is wildlife artist Larry Smail's second painting depicting Native Americans. In this work, Delaware Nation warriors return to the village of Kit-han-ne after a raid.

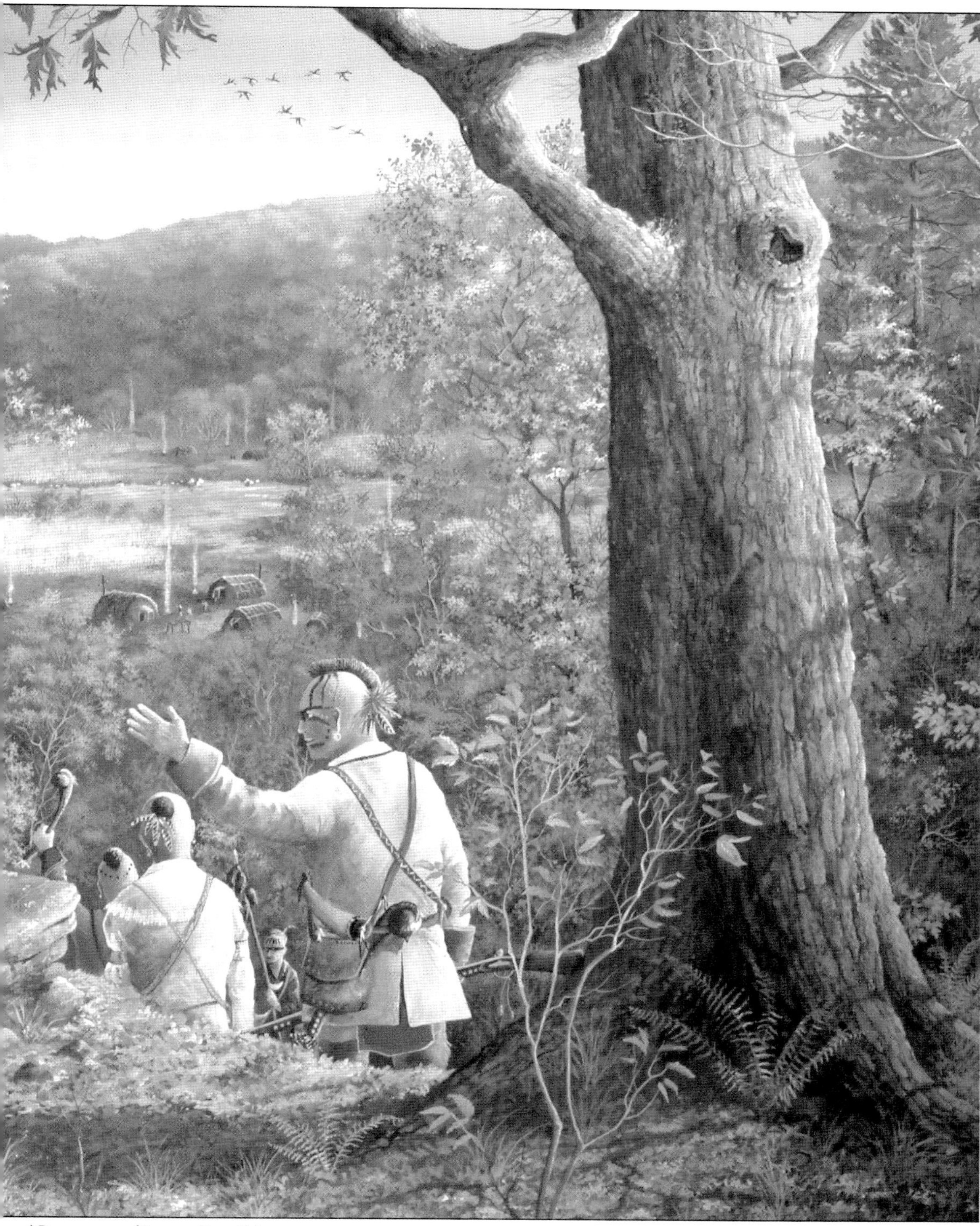

(Courtesy of Larry Smail.)

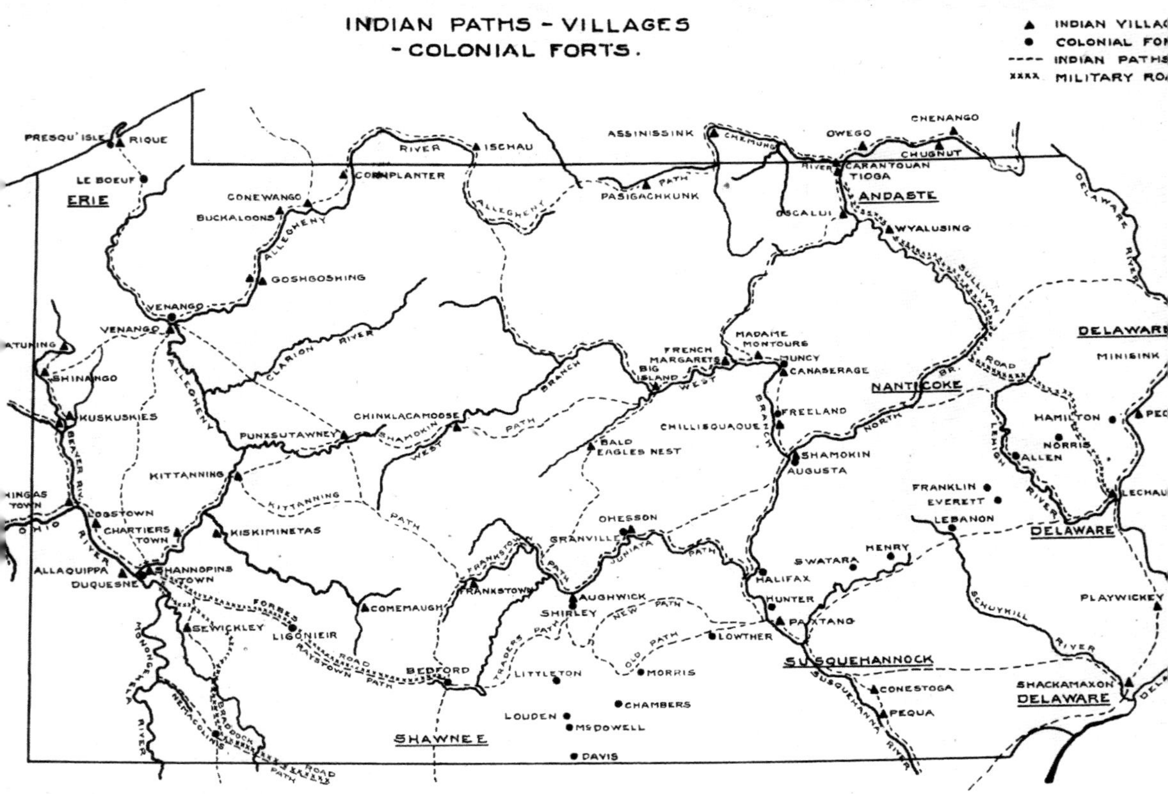

Although the perimeter of this map is recognizable as the commonwealth of Pennsylvania, the road markings are not. The network of Native American paths and military roads connected their villages such as Kit-han-ne to colonial forts such as Fort Shirley. All were critical in the early history of Kittanning.

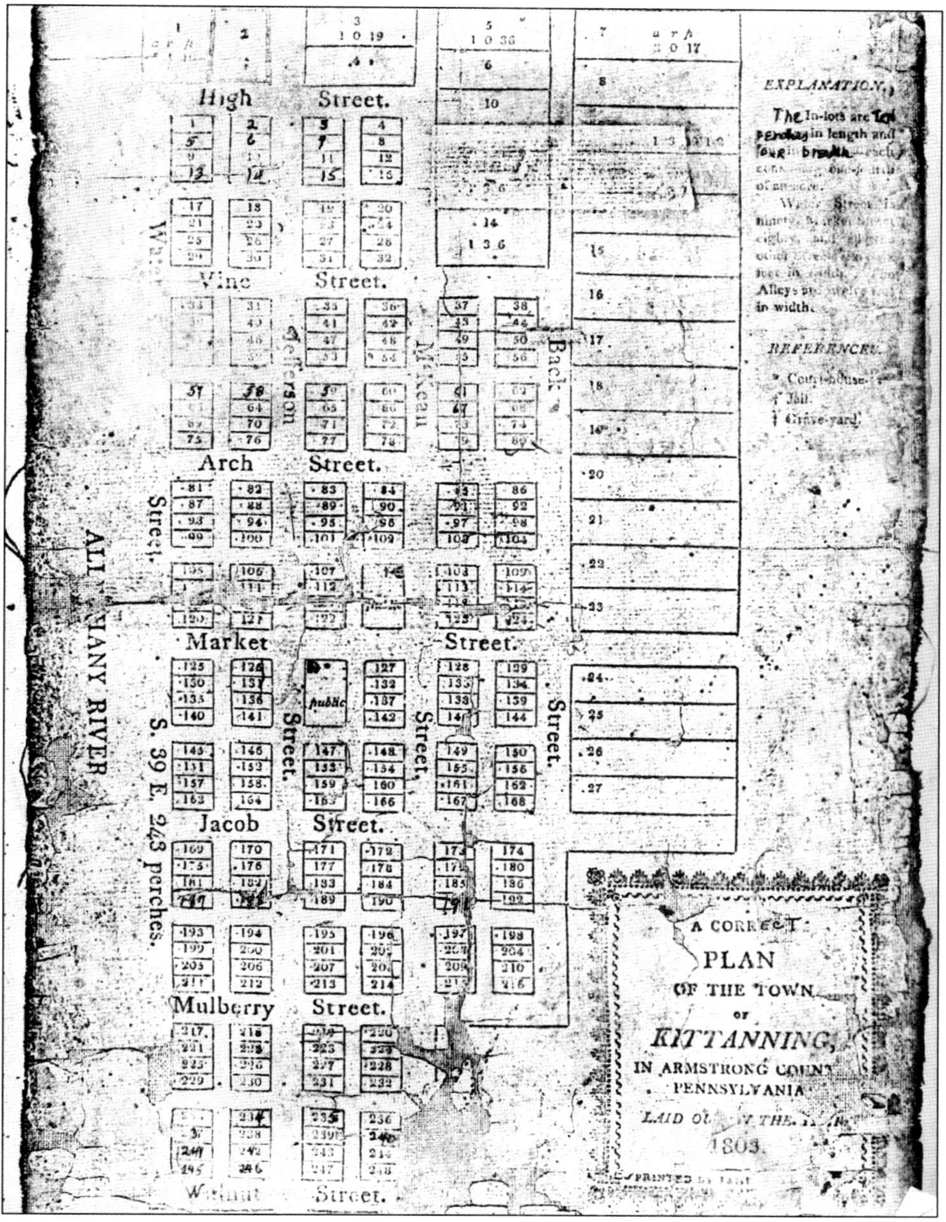

A *Correct Plan of the Town of Kittanning* illustrates the layout of the town in 1803. The ACT of March 12, 1800, subdivided many of Pennsylvania's original larger counties. Armstrong County was formed from 660 square miles of land that was named for Col. John Armstrong, leader of the British militia forces in the battle of Kittanning. Armstrong purchased 556.5 acres from Pennsylvania's provincial government, with the property survey dated 1771. The tract of land, which included Kittanning, was named Victory. After a distinguished military career, which included silver and bronze medals for bravery and the first brigadier general appointment by Congress, Armstrong was buried in the Carlisle Cemetery after his death in 1795. The heirs of Armstrong deeded 150 acres for what became Kittanning, contingent upon their receipt of half of the price of the 248 in lots and 27 out lots, which were sold at that time for $11.45 each.

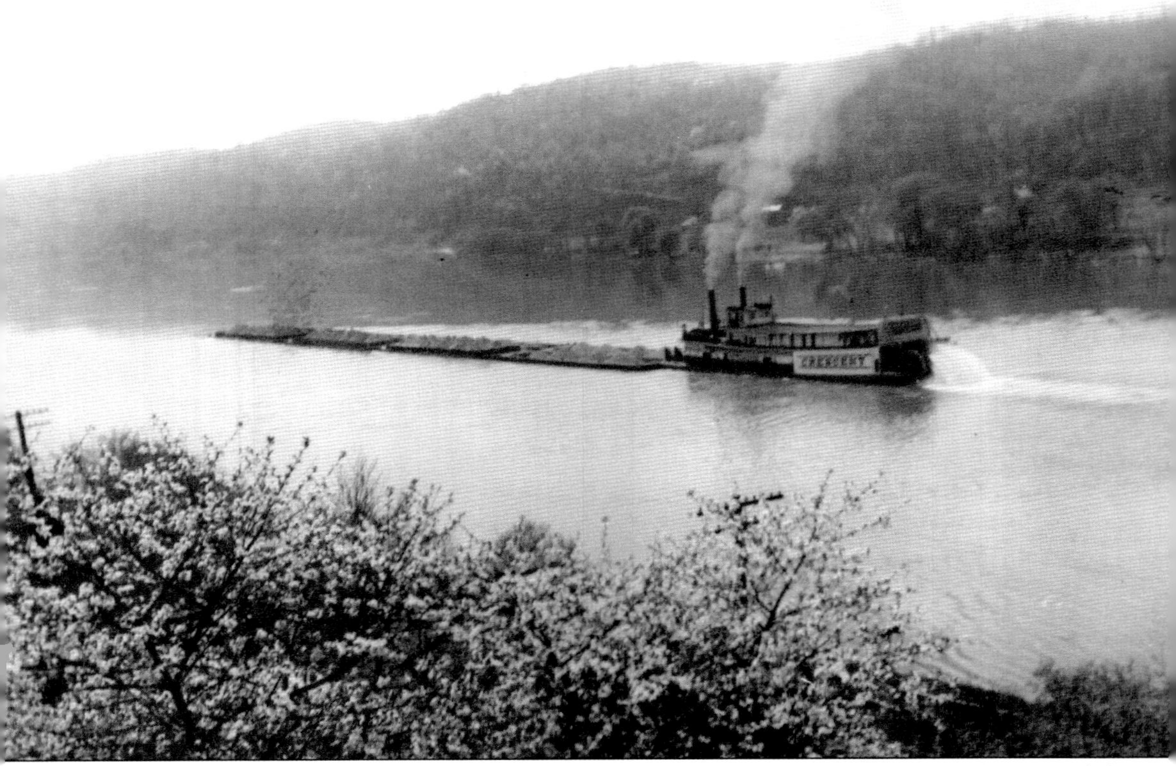

Riverboat travel became a major means of connecting Armstrong County to the rest of the world. A steam-powered barge is seen here on the Allegheny River in this photograph by P. D. Hileman. The steamboat credited as the first to come to Kittanning was the *Albion*, arriving from Pittsburgh in April 1827. Once docked, the *Albion* welcomed approximately 160 passengers (120 men and 40 women) aboard for a leisurely ride. The captain of the *Albion* then proceeded up the Allegheny River but returned quickly, due, in part, to what he described as exuberant gentlemen who were unable to contain their enthusiasm.

Two

FOUNDATIONS

A foundation forms the basis for all that is built upon it. Kittanning's history reflects a community that prioritized church and school as foundations for its success.

A mid-20th-century profile of the area relates a claim that Armstrong County had more churches per population than any other county in the United States. Whether this can be supported with precise figures is not known. What is known, however, is that a variety of Christian denominations and a Jewish community of worshipers called Kittanning home over the years. Kittanning was incorporated as a borough in 1821, with a population of 325. By 1837, Presbyterian, Episcopal, Methodist, Lutheran, and associate Presbyterian congregations worshiped in Kittanning, the first three meeting in their own church buildings.

The first school, housed in a log building located on property between Water and Jefferson Streets, opened in 1805. The school later relocated to a space in the new county jail. Adam Elliot was the school's first teacher.

The Kittanning Teachers' Institute was a prime example of this town's commitment to its youth. Records exist of annual conferences that this group held. The 34th annual gathering of the Kittanning Teachers' Institute took place December 24–28, 1900, in the Armstrong County Courthouse. Superintendent of schools at that time was J. O. Wolfe. Nearly 300 educators were enrolled to attend this event, which drew speakers from all across Pennsylvania and out-of-state. The written program that attendees received highlighted the lectures and speeches that were given during this symposium. Superintendent James M. Coughlin of Wilkes Barre expressed the opinion that was common to most of his professional peers. Coughlin posed the question of what constituted a good education and then offered a simple answer that was agreed upon by many, teaching character.

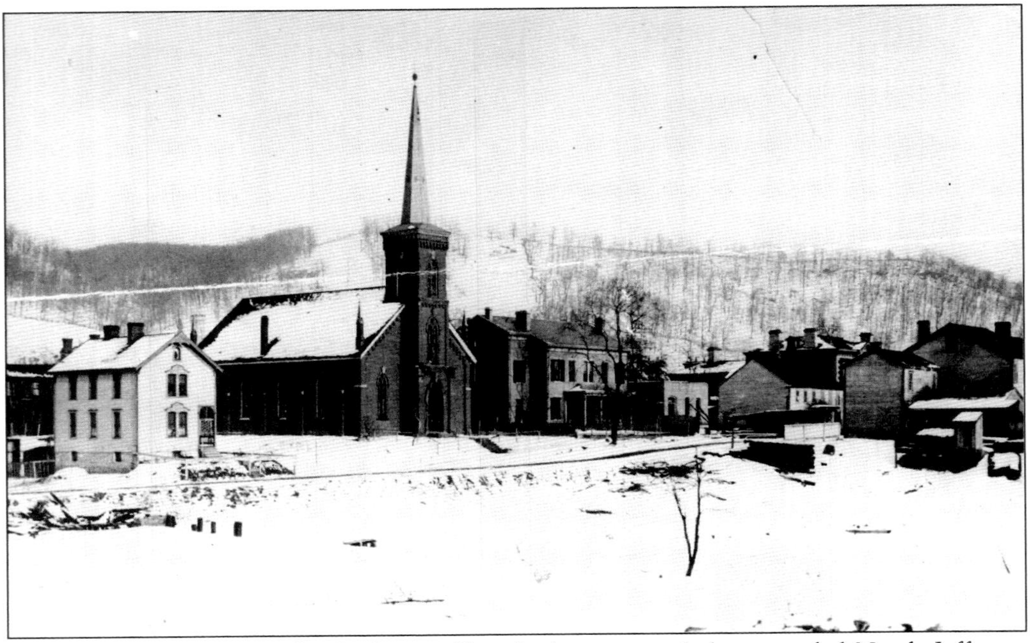

This photograph of St. John Lutheran Church shows a much less crowded North Jefferson Street. This property on North Jefferson Street was bought from Aaron Shoop for $900 in 1866. The cornerstone for the new church was laid on August 8, 1867. The building was dedicated September 28, 1873. (Courtesy of the Dave Lindeman family.)

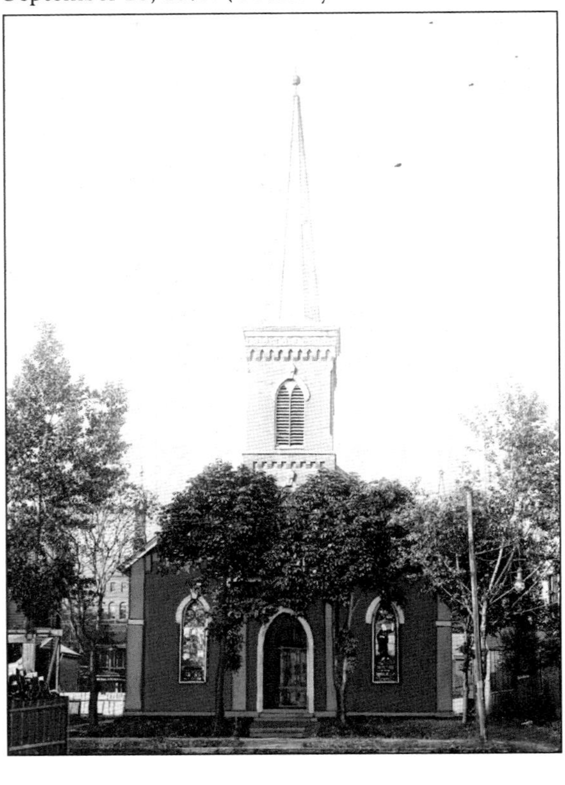

This Furnee and Kennerdell rendering of St. John Lutheran Church includes details of its stained-glass windows and recessed doorway. A Mohler tracker organ was purchased for the church with money donated by Andrew Carnegie and was installed in 1904. (Courtesy of the Dave Lindeman family.)

The Methodist Episcopal Church of Kittanning, one of the first congregations to have a home for its worship services, still uses this sanctuary, located on the corner of North Jefferson and Vine Streets. (Courtesy of the Methodist Episcopal Church.)

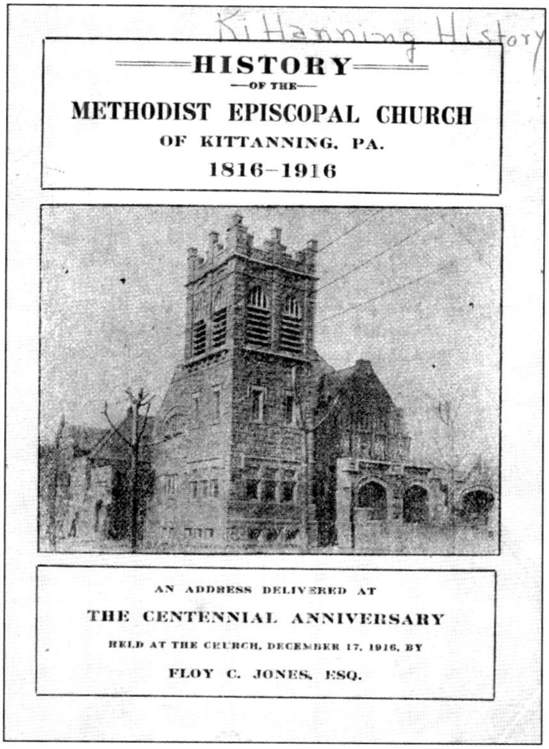

Kittanning History

HISTORY
—OF THE—
METHODIST EPISCOPAL CHURCH
OF KITTANNING, PA.
1816–1916

AN ADDRESS DELIVERED AT
THE CENTENNIAL ANNIVERSARY
HELD AT THE CHURCH, DECEMBER 17, 1916, BY
FLOY C. JONES, ESQ.

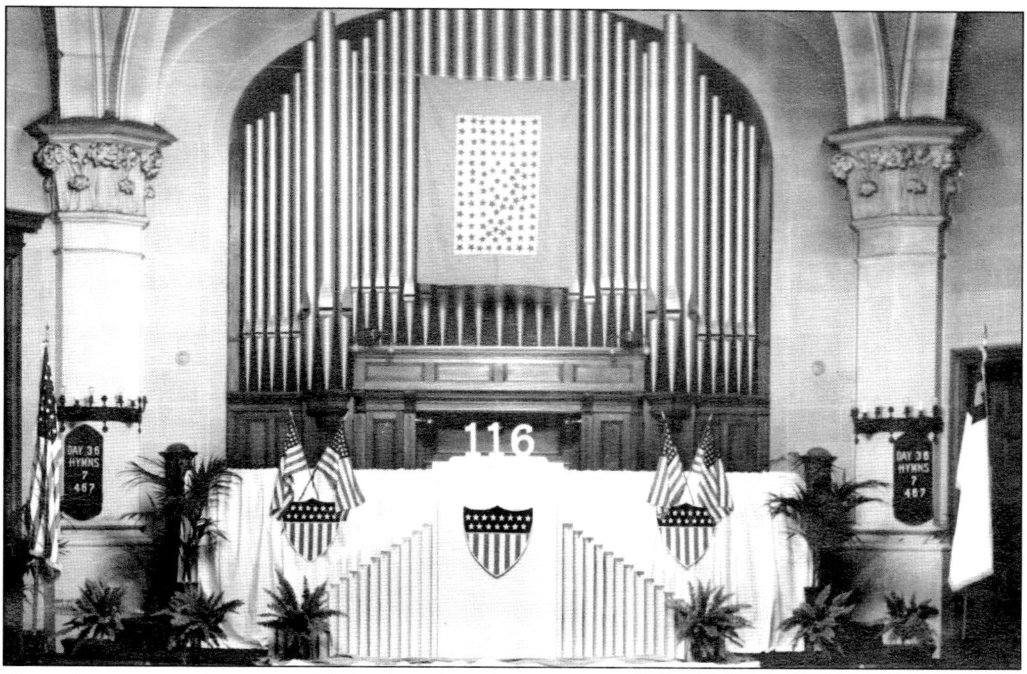

This photograph shows the Methodist church's commemoration of World War II servicemen, known as an honor roll. The church's pipe organs and alter are adorned with stars, stripes, flags, banners, and a multitude of lit candles.

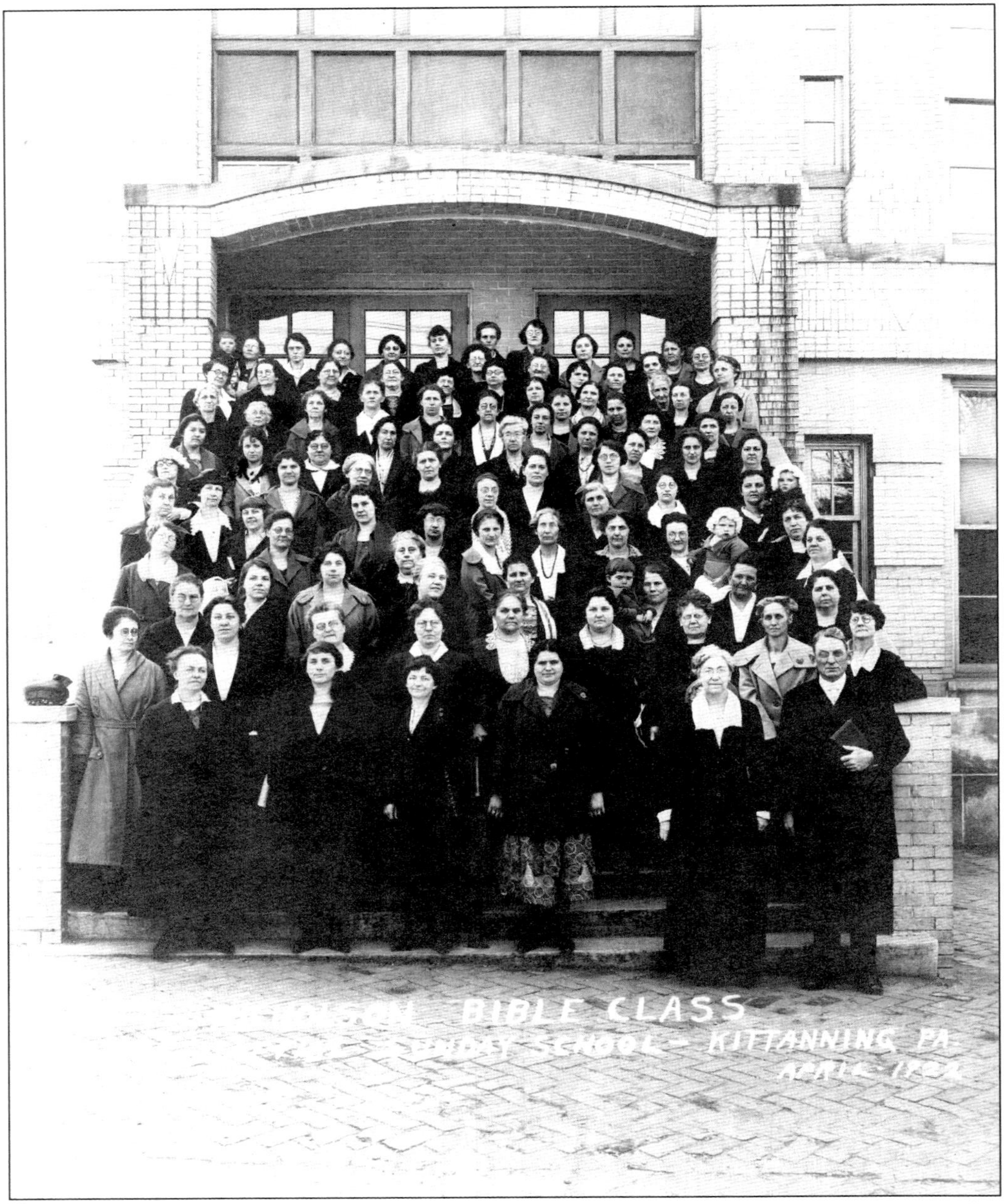

The 1922 Nicholson Bible class of the First Baptist Church's Sunday school gathers for this photograph. Over 60 women were instructed by W. A. Nicholson, who is pictured holding a Bible at the far right.

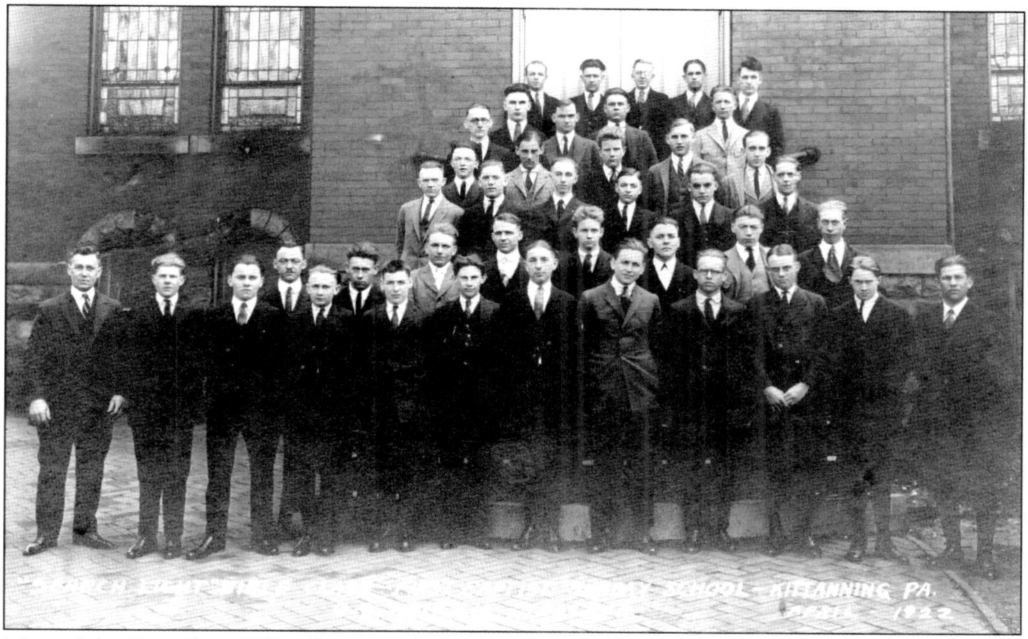

Men of the First Baptist Sunday school were instructed by O. C. Rairigh in 1922. Known as the Search Light Bible Class, nearly 40 men are seen in attendance in this photograph. The only gentlemen identified are Alfred Hawk (third row, fourth from left) and John A. Mechling (top row, second from left).

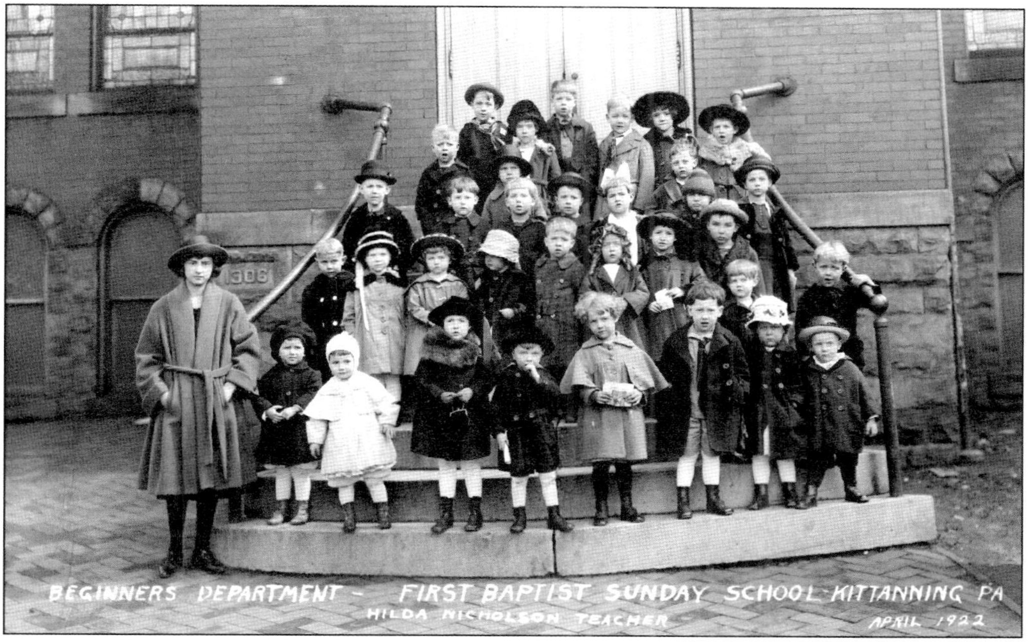

Clad in their "Sunday-go-to-meeting" attire, these adorable children were members of the beginners department of the First Baptist Sunday school in 1922. Hilda Nicholson, daughter of H. M. Nicholson, was not only a Sunday school teacher at First Baptist Church but was also an elementary school teacher in Kittanning.

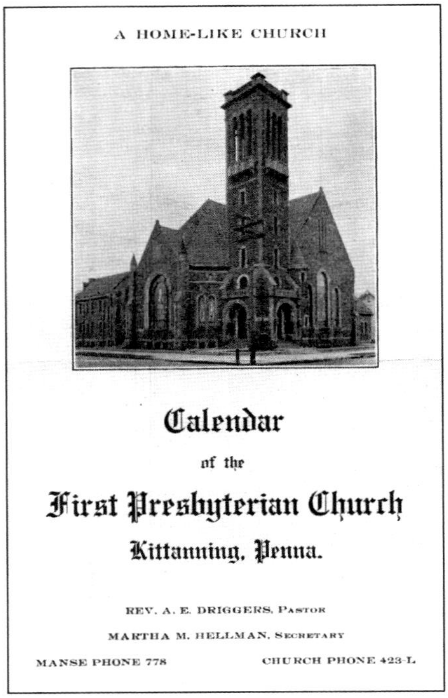

A HOME-LIKE CHURCH

Calendar

of the

First Presbyterian Church

Kittanning, Penna.

REV. A. E. DRIGGERS, PASTOR

MARTHA M. HELLMAN, SECRETARY

MANSE PHONE 778 CHURCH PHONE 423-L

This weekly bulletin from the November 10, 1929, Sunday services of the First Presbyterian Church depicts this congregation as a "Home-Like Church." The church was home to Rev. A. E. Driggers at that time. Its slogan was, "Every member present at all of the services during the month." Morning services were held at 10:00 a.m., and evening services were at 7:00 p.m.

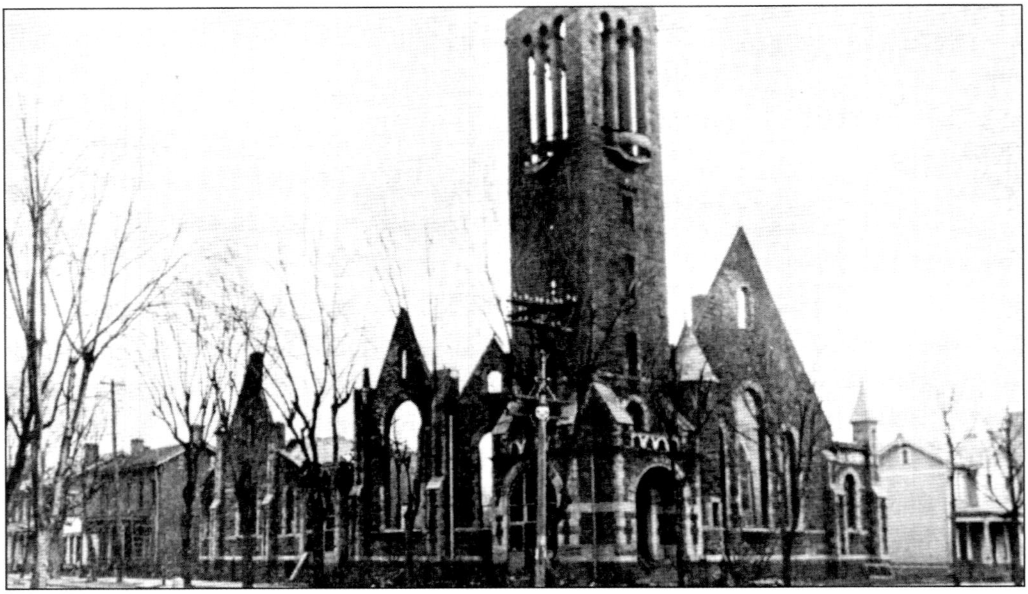

Kittanning's largest Presbyterian congregation built its third church structure, dedicated in June 1890, to accommodate a growing membership, which reached 859 in 1907. Located on the corner of Arch and Jefferson Streets, it was enjoyed only for a short time, as a fire destroyed it in the spring of 1909. Most of the building was lost in this tragedy; however, a zealous effort to rebuild began in 1910. The larger church that stands today on the same property used the bell tower and walls that survived the fire as its anchor. Grace Presbyterian Church was dedicated on April 2, 1911, and included a series of memorial windows with biblical themes designed by Louis Tiffany. (Courtesy of Jeanne Ashe.)

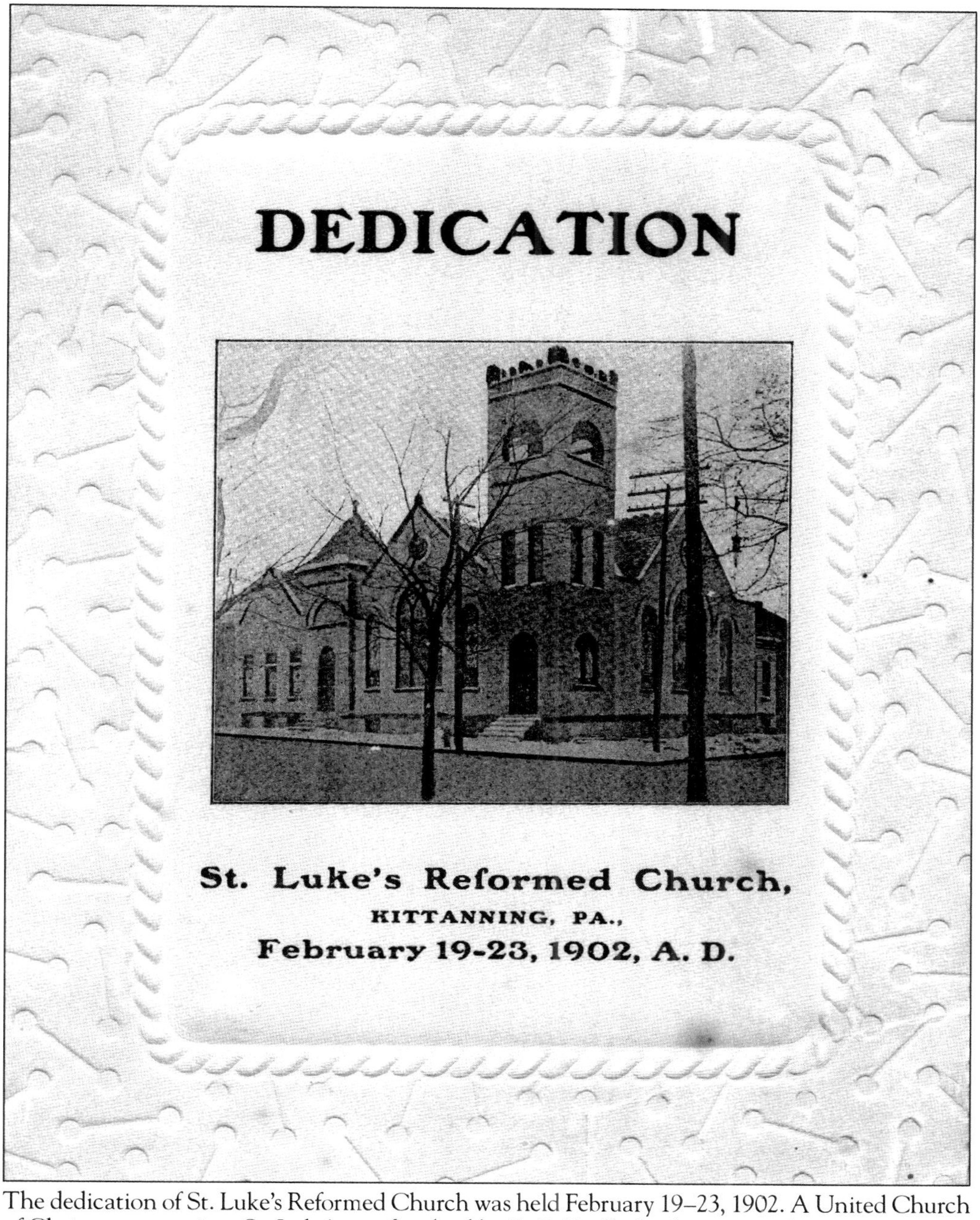
DEDICATION

St. Luke's Reformed Church,
KITTANNING, PA.,
February 19-23, 1902, A. D.

The dedication of St. Luke's Reformed Church was held February 19–23, 1902. A United Church of Christ congregation, St. Luke's was first lead by D. S. Dieffenbacher, pastor from 1873 to 1885, and Robert C. Bowling, pastor from 1885 to the time of dedication.

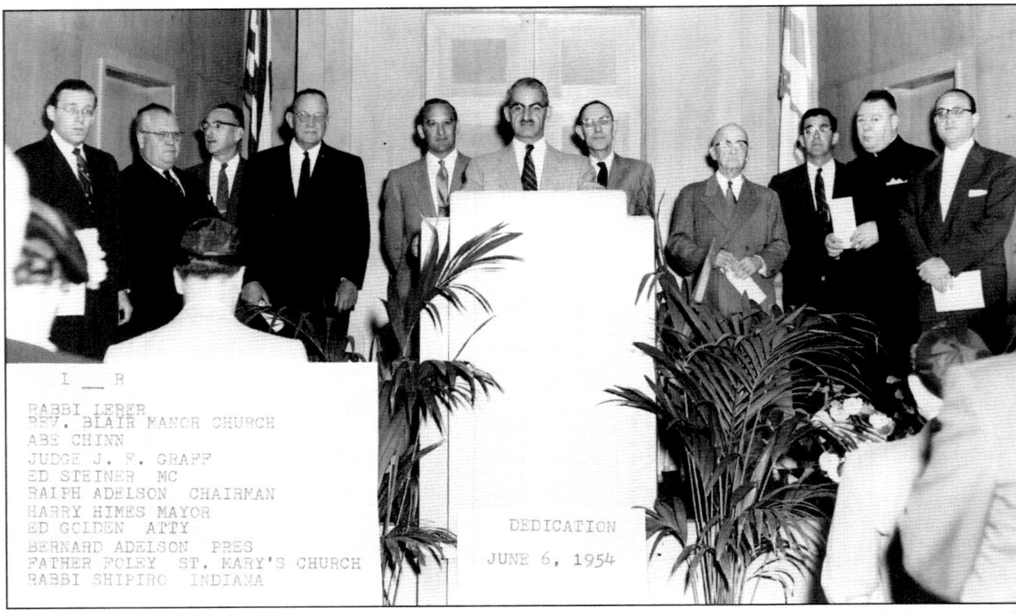

Various dignitaries are seen in this photograph of the June 6, 1954, dedication of the Kneseth Israel Congregation, the only Jewish house of worship in Kittanning. Pictured from left to right are Rabbi Lerer, Rev. Blair Manor, Abe Chinn, Judge J. F. Graff, Ed Steiner, Ralph Adelson, Harry Himes, Ed Golden, Bernard Adelson, Father Foley of St. Mary's Church, and Rabbi Shipiro Indiana.

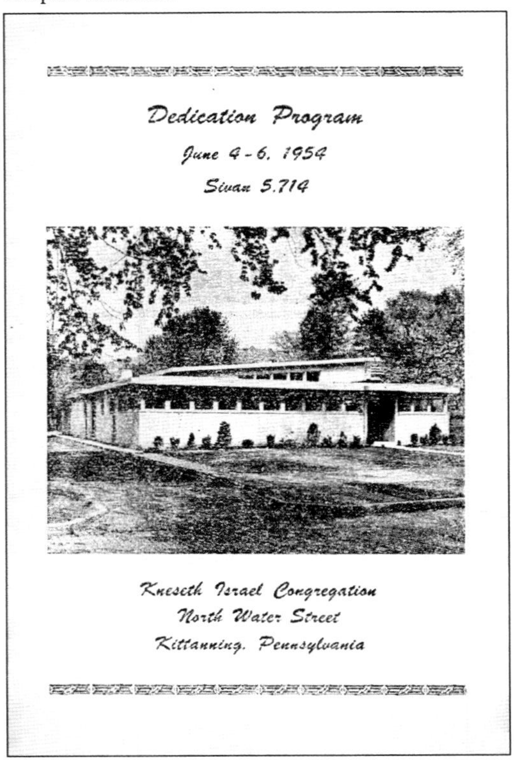

The cover of the program used for the dedication ceremony shows a likeness of the exterior of the synagogue, which fronts on the Allegheny River on North Water Street. The structure is now used as a community center by the Methodist congregation. (Courtesy of the Methodist Episcopal Church.)

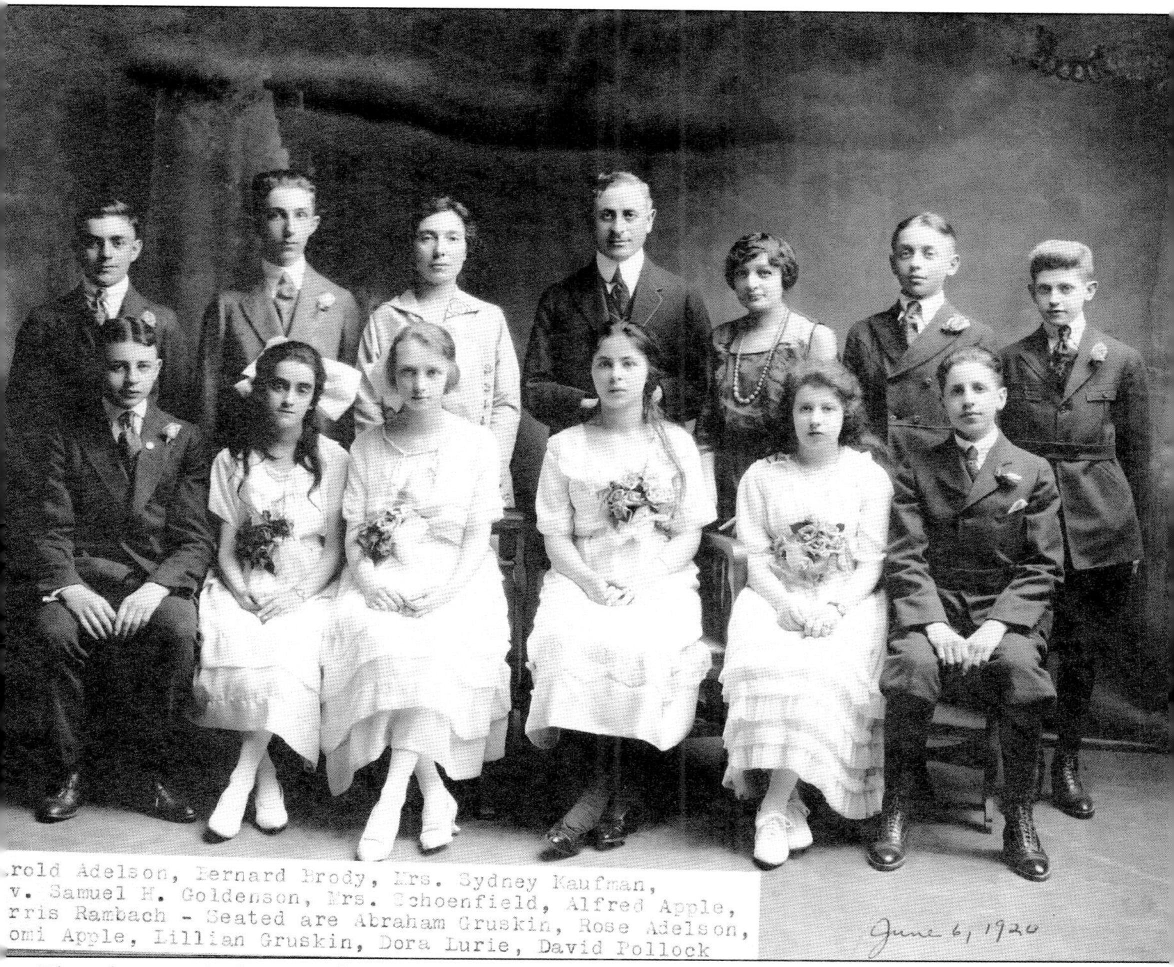

This photograph shows students of the Jewish faith in Kittanning as early as 1920. From left to right are (first row) Abraham Gruskin, Rose Adelson, Naomi Apple, Lillian Gruskin, Dora Lurie, and David Pollock; (second row) Harold Adelson, Bernard Brody, Mrs. Sydney Kaufman, Rev. Samuel H. Goldenson, Mrs. Schoenfield, Alfred Apple, and Morris Rambach.

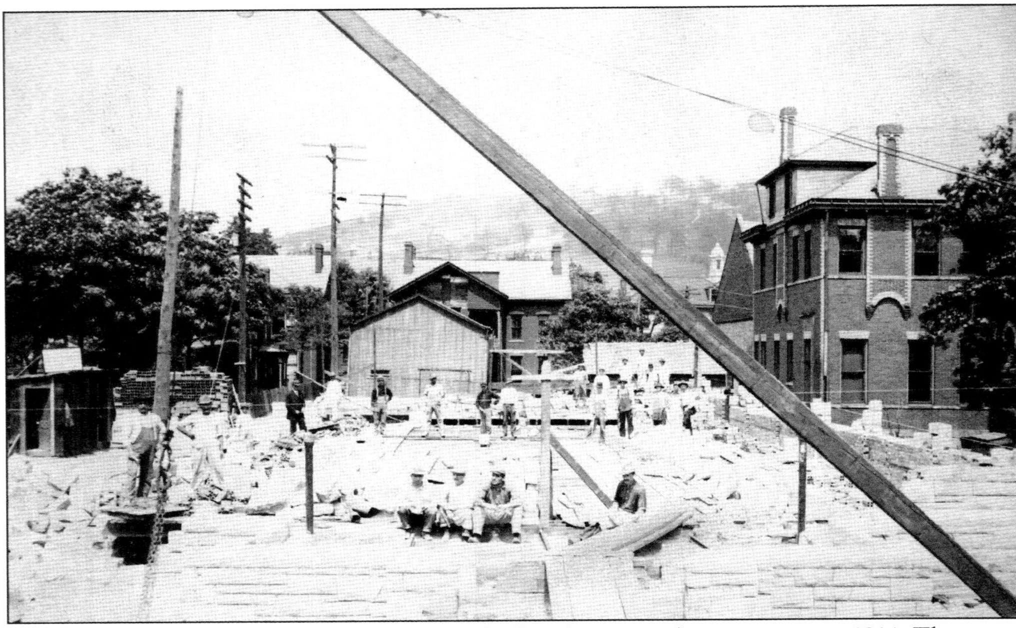

These photographs show St. Paul's Episcopal Church as a work in progress in 1914. This stone structure can still be found near the corner on Water Street. Workers can be seen sitting around the perimeter of the church's foundation in the photograph above. Below, a service is held for the laying of the cornerstone to the left of the worship leaders' platform.

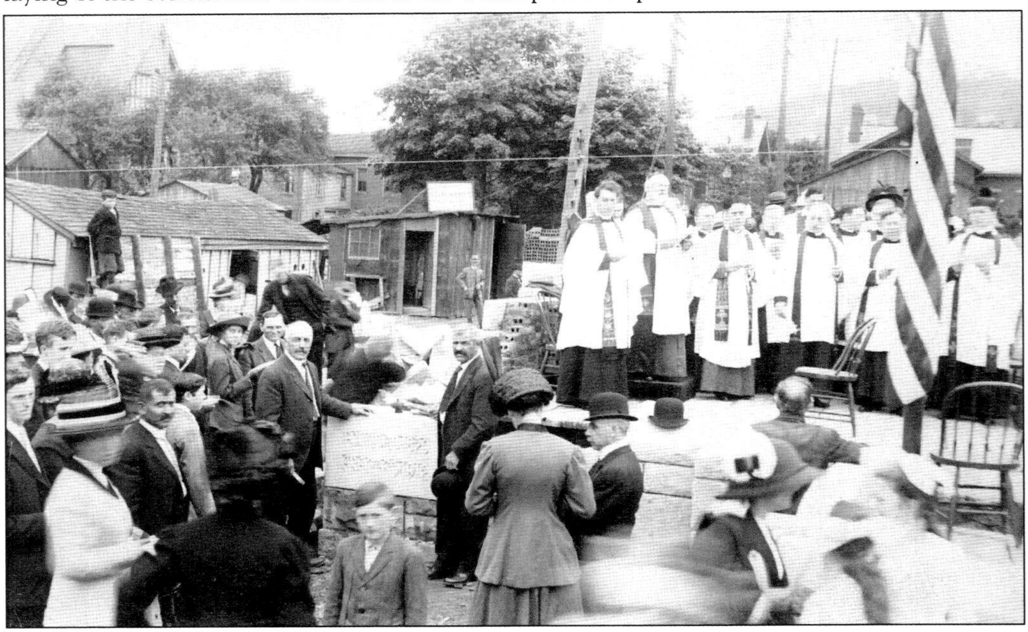

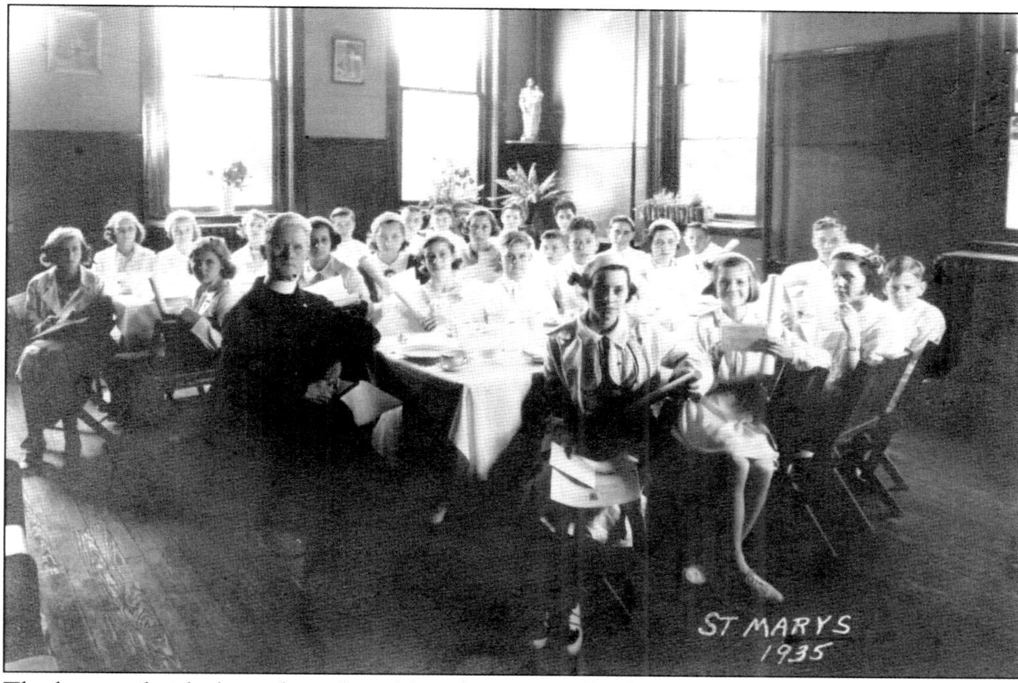

The boys and girls dressed in white (above) appear to be sharing a celebratory dinner with the church pastor of St. Mary's in 1935. The same pastor of St. Mary's appears with a similar age group of youth. In the 1935 photograph below, 25 boys and girls are gathered in this, suggesting a school group by their dress.

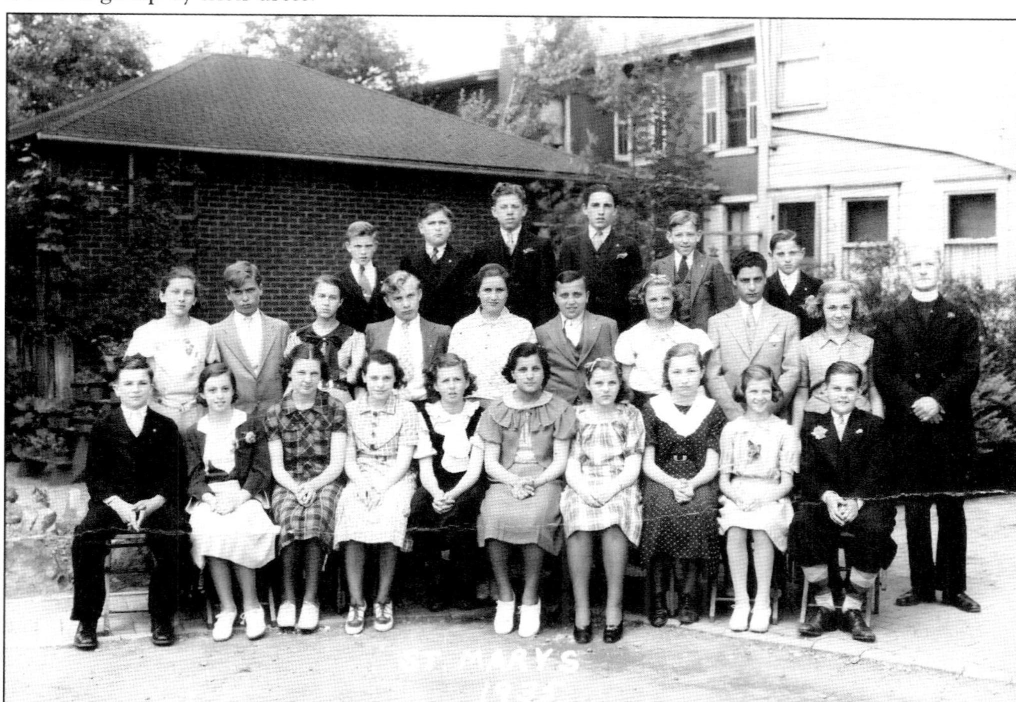

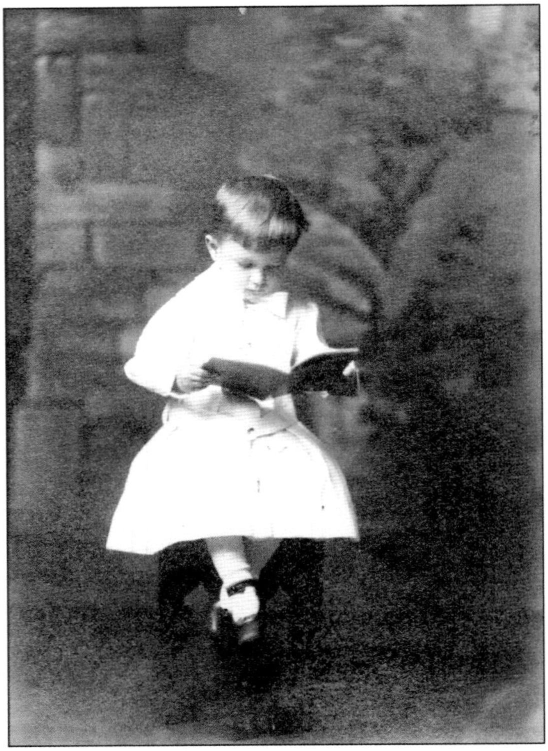

This precious photograph of a little child reading captures an idyllic concept of early childhood education. The child's identity is unknown; however, he typifies what many might assume a child's life to have been like in the previous century.

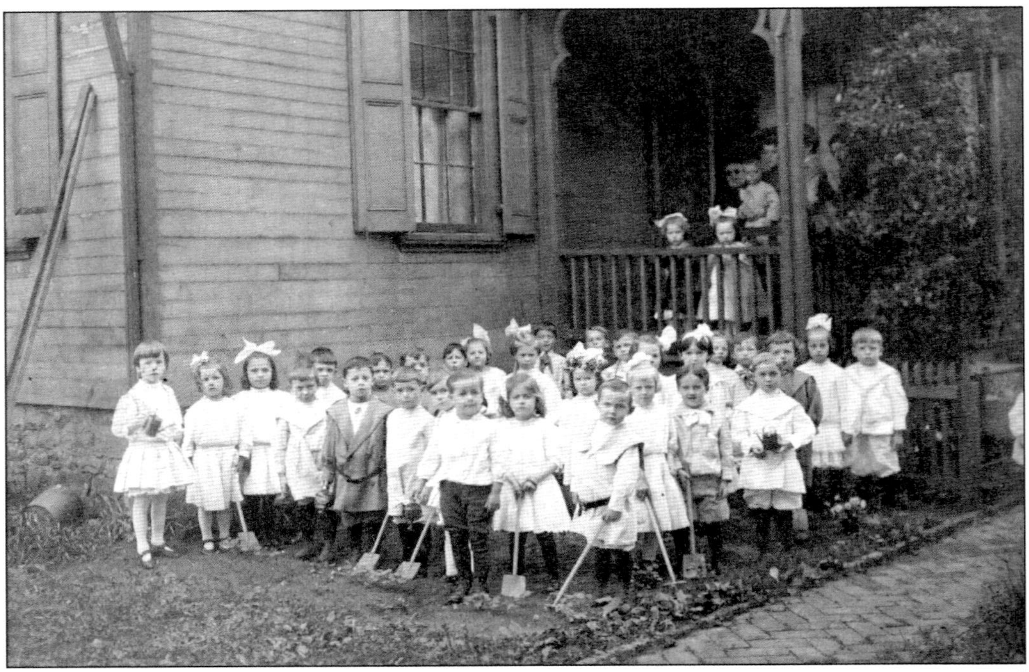

This is one of many school group photographs donated to the Armstrong County Historical Society. The names of these students, as well as date and place the photograph was taken, are unknown.

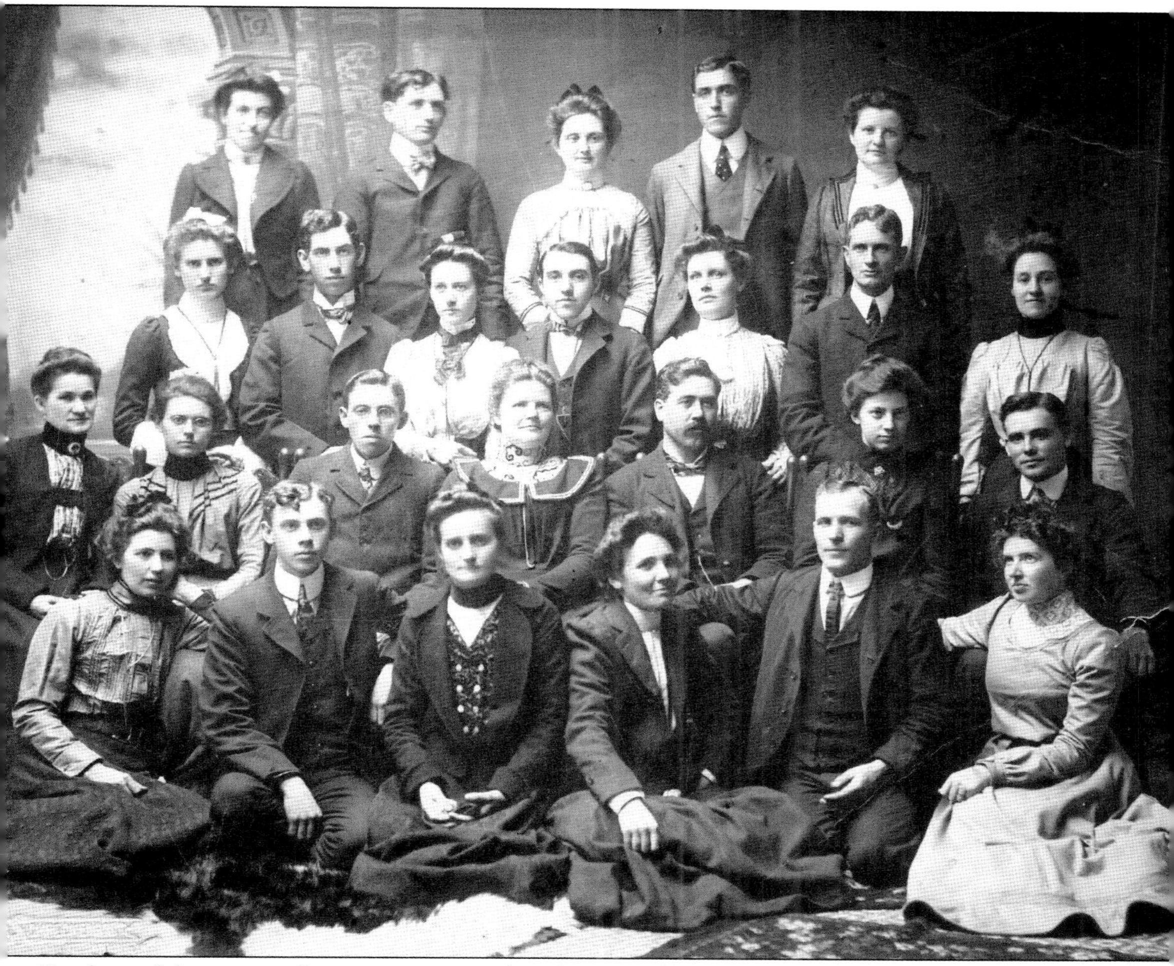

Teachers of Armstrong County are pictured at the annual institute, probably at the beginning of the 20th century. Those identified are Minnie Young, Mary Moore, Agnes McCain, Cora Wylie, Laura Patton, Rachel Moore, June Blose, Sadie Lamb, Margaret Campbell, Mr. Clark, Ralph Bowser, Frank Shubert, M. E. Thompson, Mr. Culp, Robert T. McCauley, Charles Riggle, Merle Minteer, and J. B. Rupert.

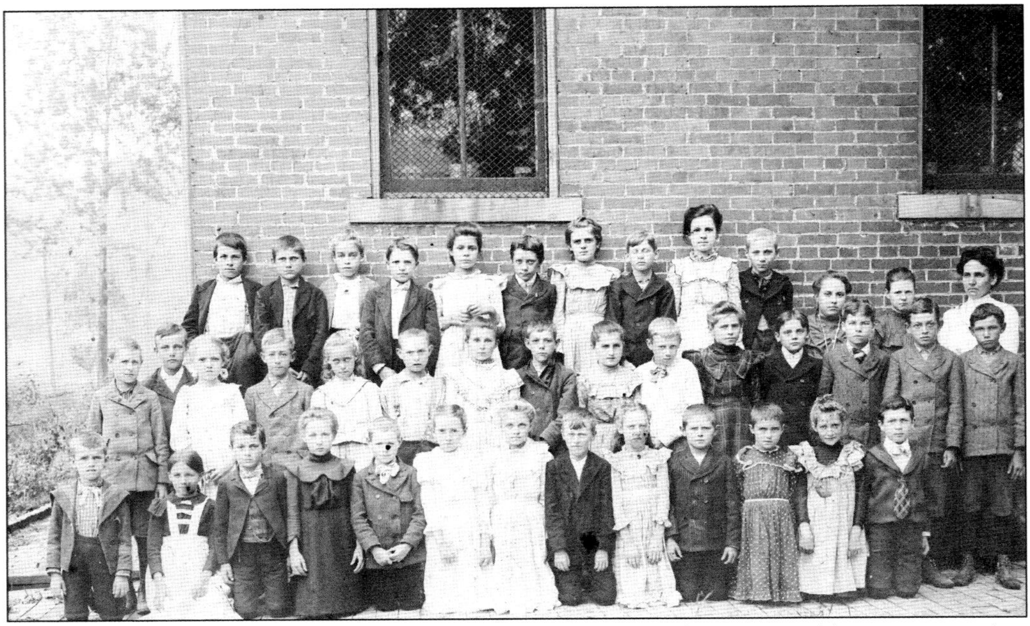

These boys and girls are believed to be elementary school students in Wickboro, an area that adjoined Kittanning on its northern border. On December 29, 1913, a majority of votes from residents of Kittanning and Wickboro decided in favor of the consolidation of the two in order to create a greater Kittanning population of 7,086. This merger enabled the newly formed borough to issue bonds for municipal and lighting plants. The total vote for the merger from both boroughs was 758 for and 89 against, with the staunchest opposition heard from the utility companies, who anticipated lost revenues from this union.

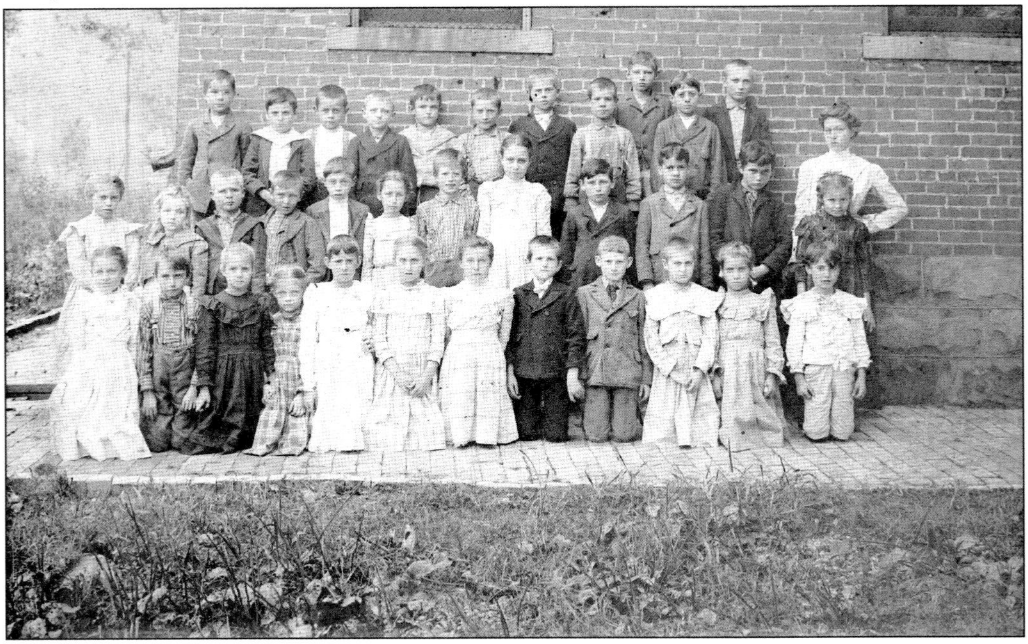

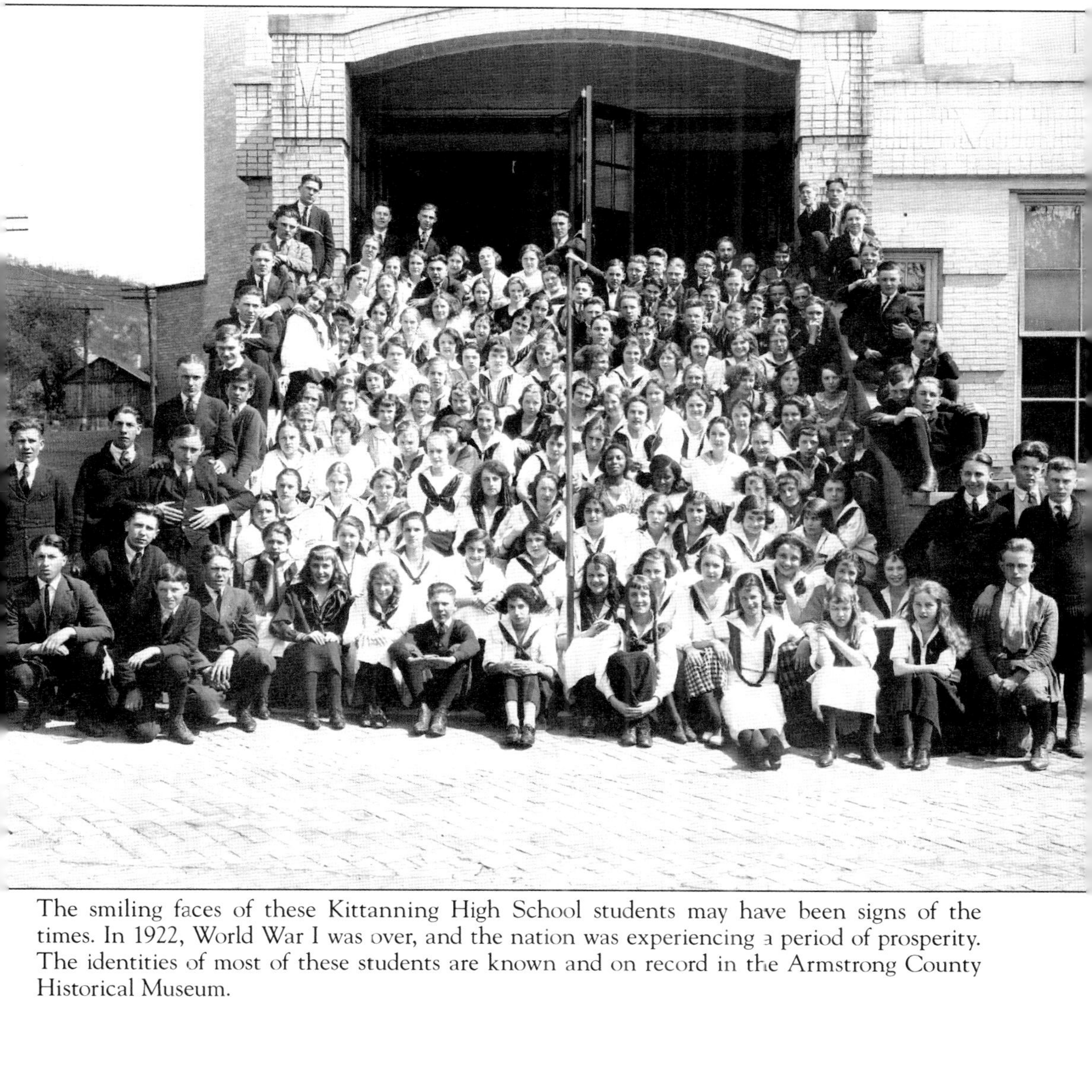

The smiling faces of these Kittanning High School students may have been signs of the times. In 1922, World War I was over, and the nation was experiencing a period of prosperity. The identities of most of these students are known and on record in the Armstrong County Historical Museum.

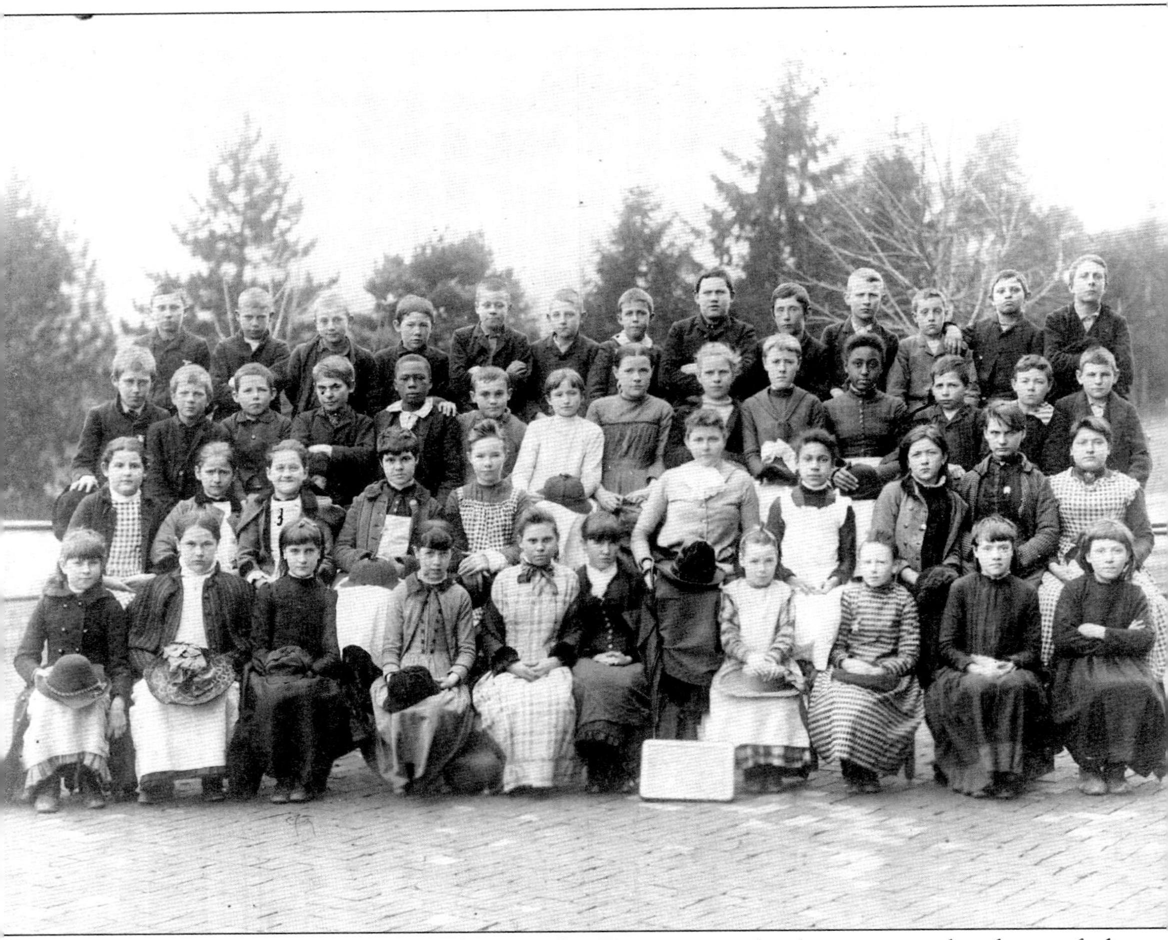

Mary Lindeman, a young student in the Kittanning school system at the dawn of the 20th century, can be found in the second row, third from the left. This was just the beginning of the education of a lifelong educator, who returned, after college at Indiana Normal School, to Kittanning to begin a career of teaching foreign languages at the secondary level.

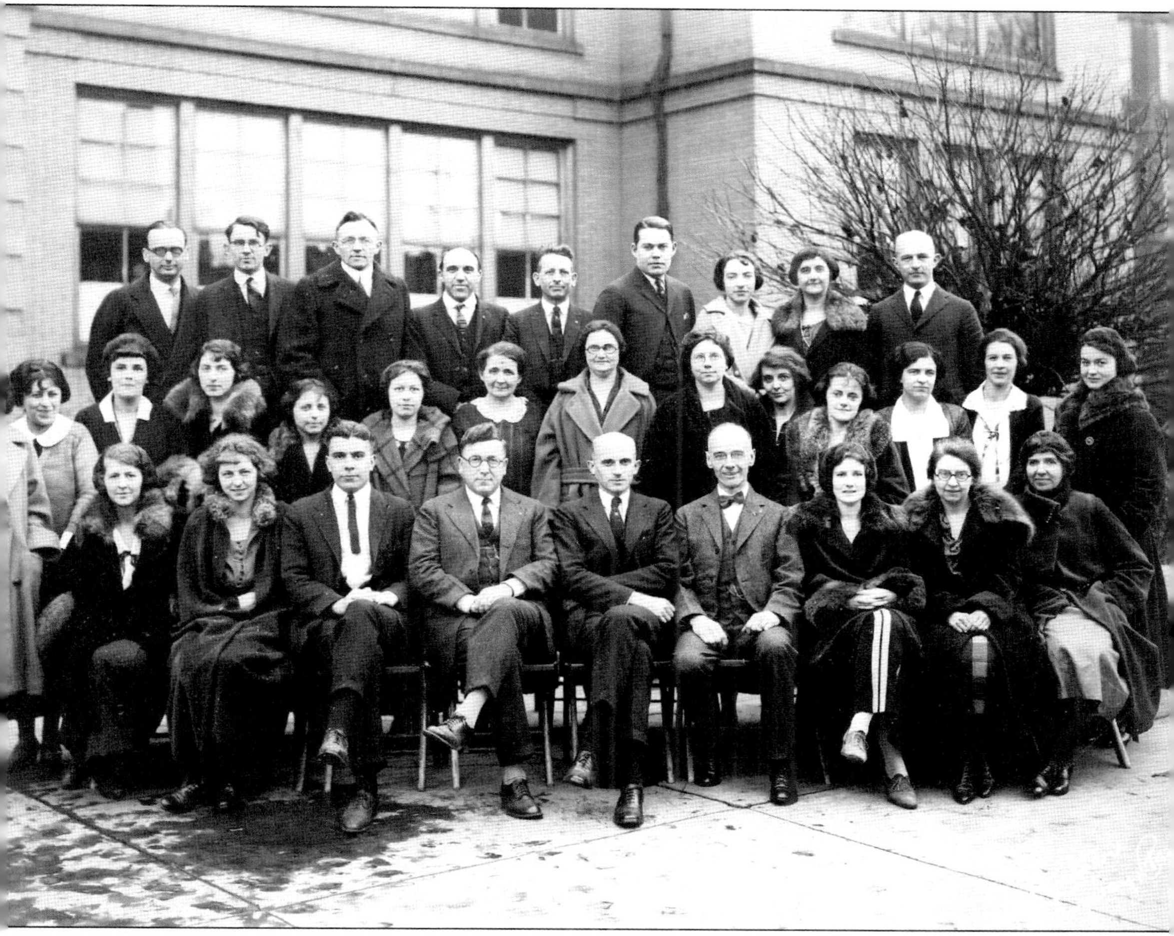

These area teachers pose for a picture while in attendance at the annual teachers' institute meeting, held in Kittanning. Now looking the part of a teacher, Lindeman is standing in the back row, second from the right. She taught German in the early years of her career, however, during World War I, her books were destroyed. This dedicated teacher responded by teaching foreign languages other than German, such as Latin.

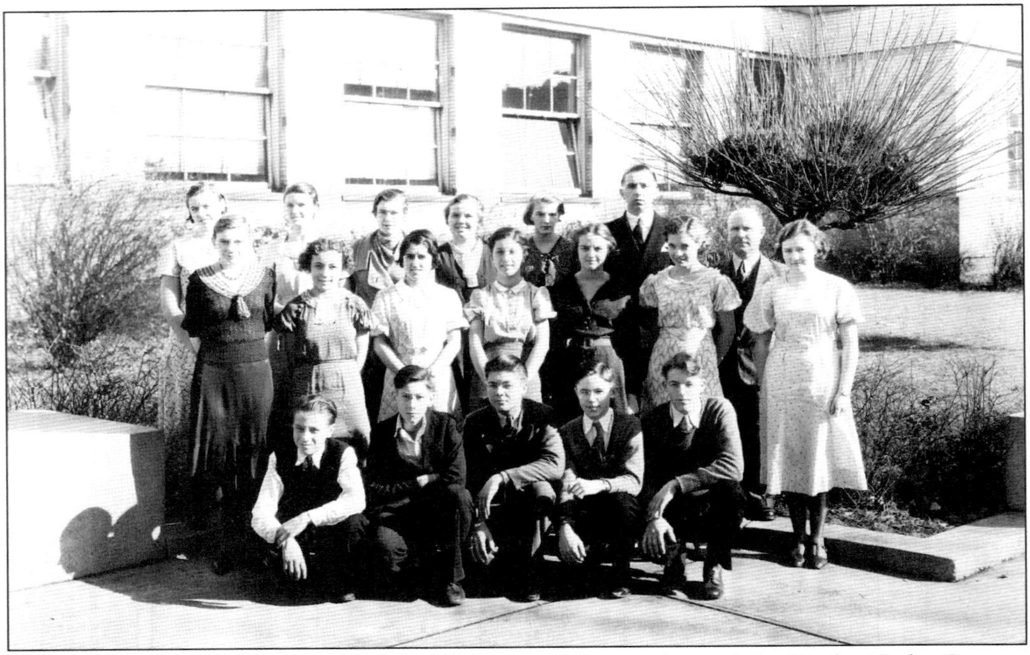

The life ambitions and career choices of these student members of the Epsilon Delta Science club may never be known; however, these look like enquiring minds that want to know.

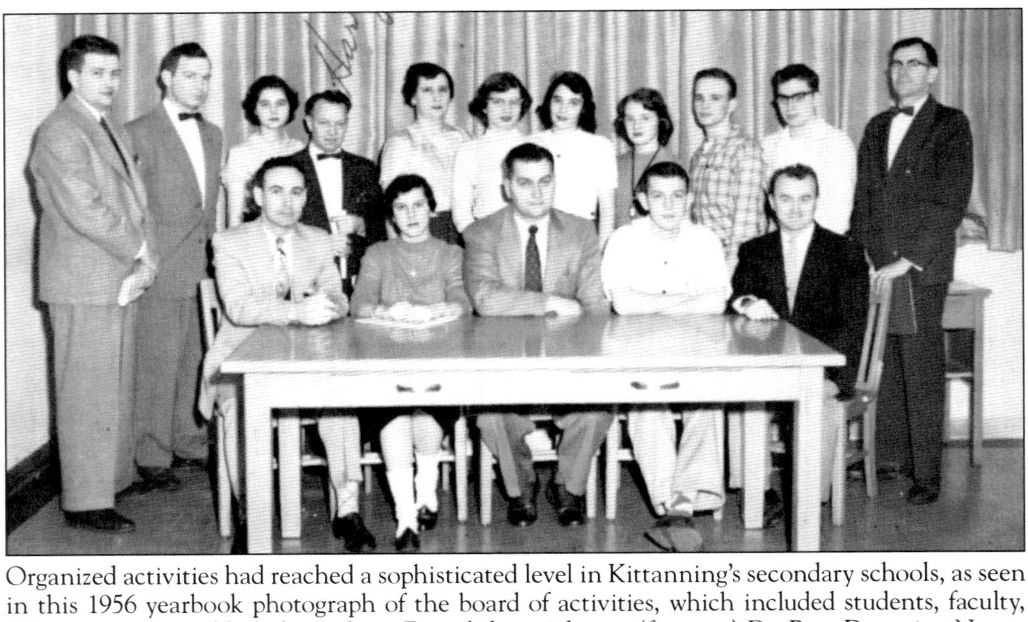

Organized activities had reached a sophisticated level in Kittanning's secondary schools, as seen in this 1956 yearbook photograph of the board of activities, which included students, faculty, administration, and board members. From left to right are (first row) Dr. Burt Dunmire, Nancy Tatsak, Paul Breon, Lee Montgomery, and Steve Kropniak; (second row) Spencer Pride, Ralph John, Melissa Fair, Harry Fink, Jean Painter, Martha Stitt, Carole Lindeman, Virginia Williams, Ed Todd, Larry Sparks, and Wade Hall.

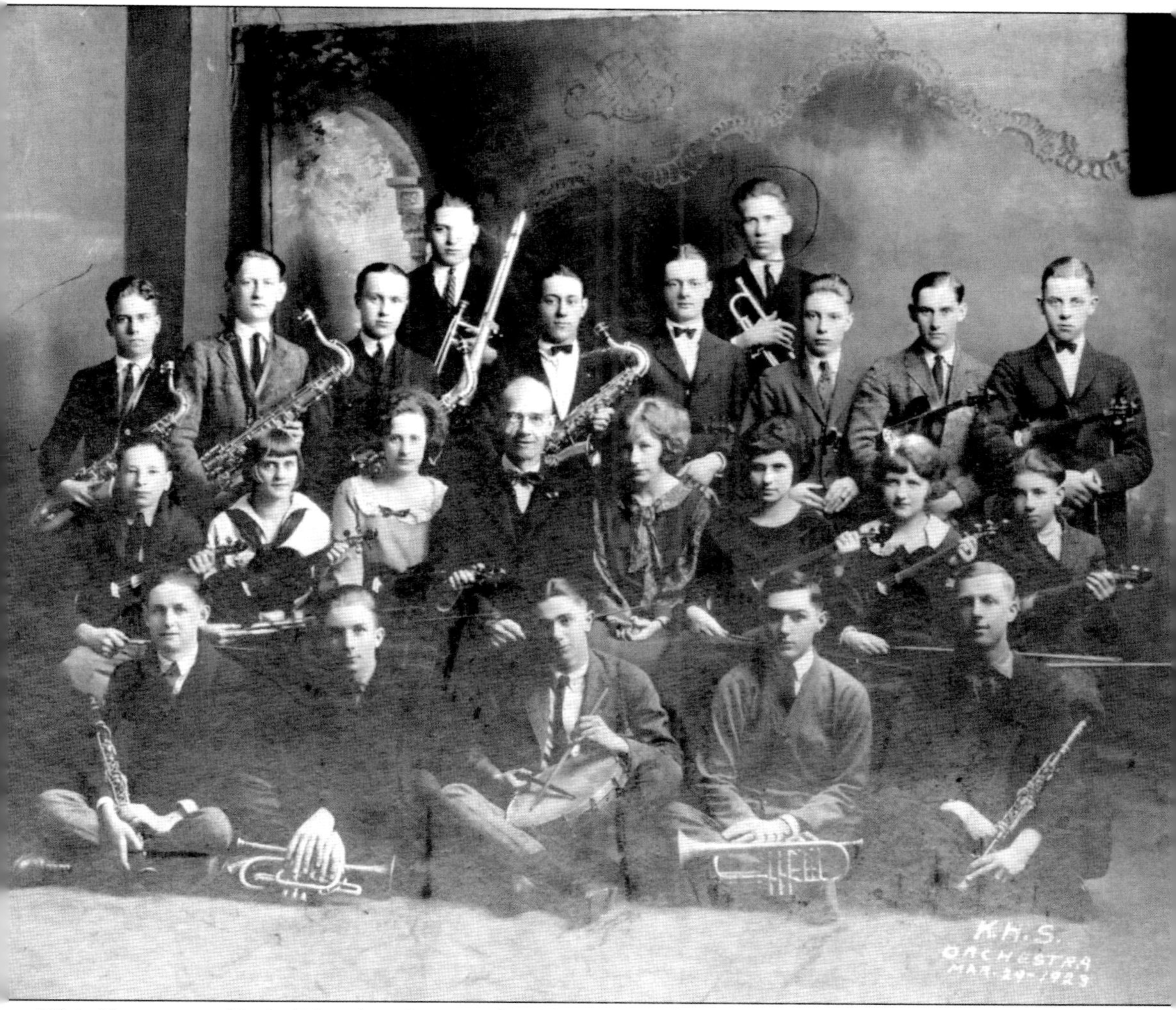

This Kittanning High School orchestra of 1923 was, in all likelihood, one of the last to play under the direction of J. Froehlich. Female students were permitted to play in Kittanning High School orchestras at that time, but the high school marching band was for boys only.

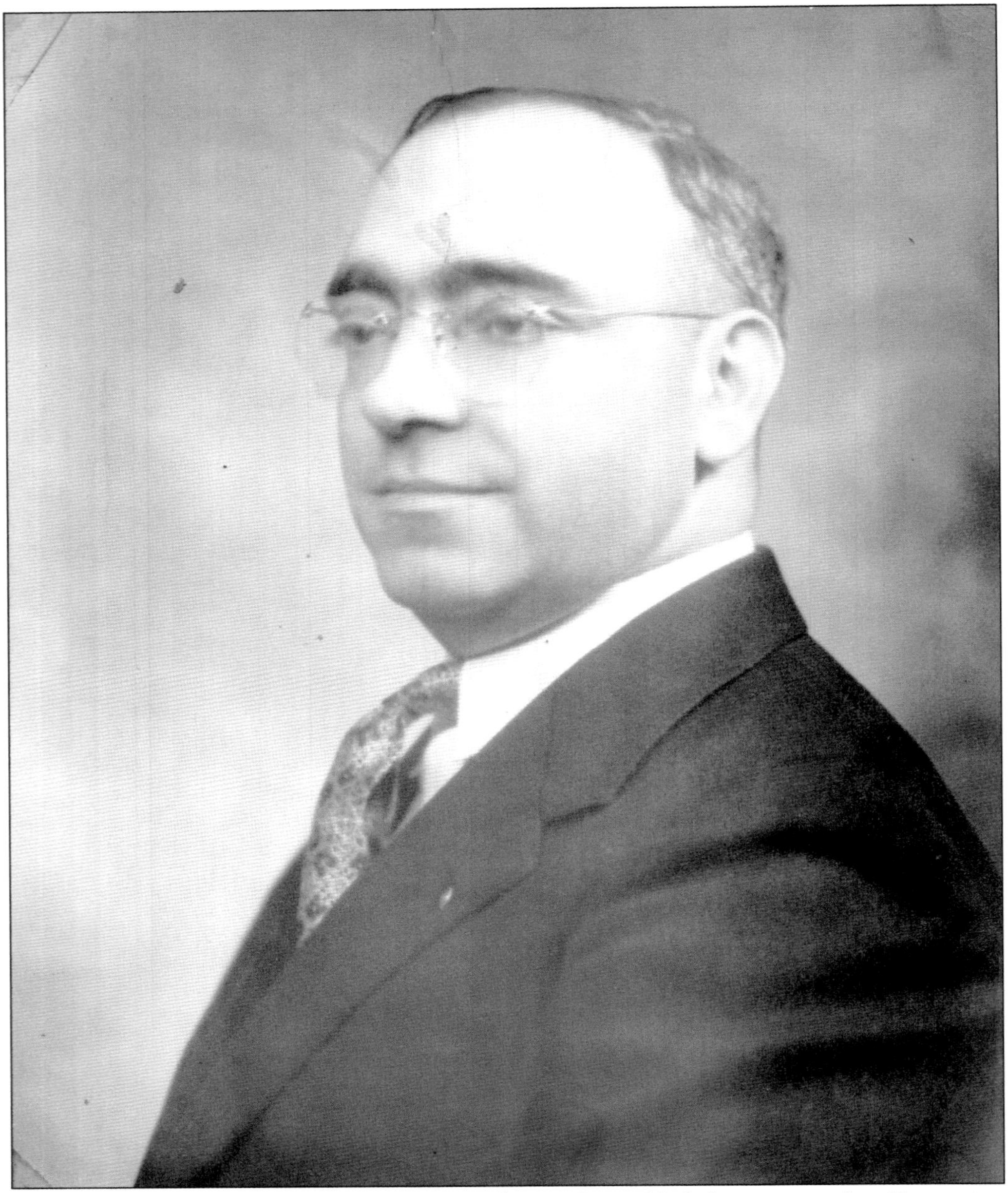

Known as the dean of school bands of Pennsylvania, James V. Colonna arrived in Kittanning in 1922. A young, talented music teacher and accomplished musician, Colonna's passion for this art began in Italy, where he began his studies at the age of five. Colonna was taught by another talented Colonna musician, his father. The elder Colonna, who was also a teacher, band director, and baritone soloist for John Phillip Sousa's band, immigrated to the United States in 1910, bringing his family with him, which included his teenage son.

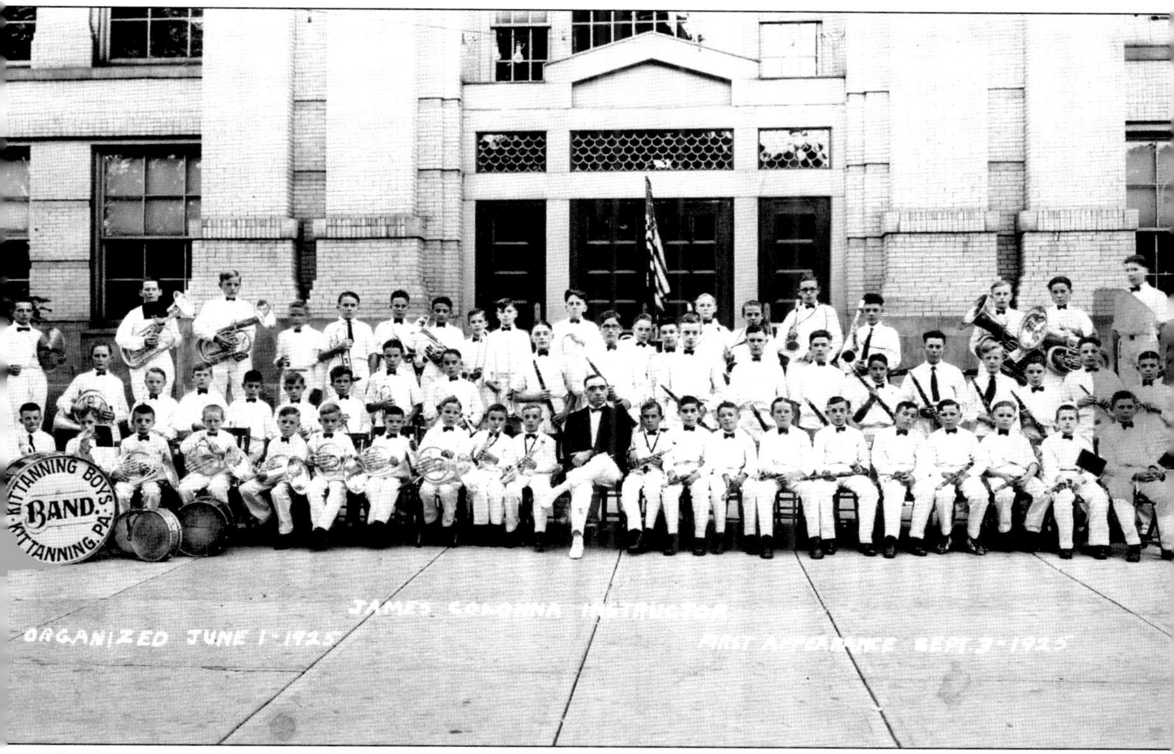

The Kittanning Boys' Band of 1925 was the first of many youth bands organized and directed by Colonna. This particular group, however, holds the distinction of being the first school band in western Pennsylvania. The band debuted in front of the school on September 3, 1925, after just three months of practice following their organization.

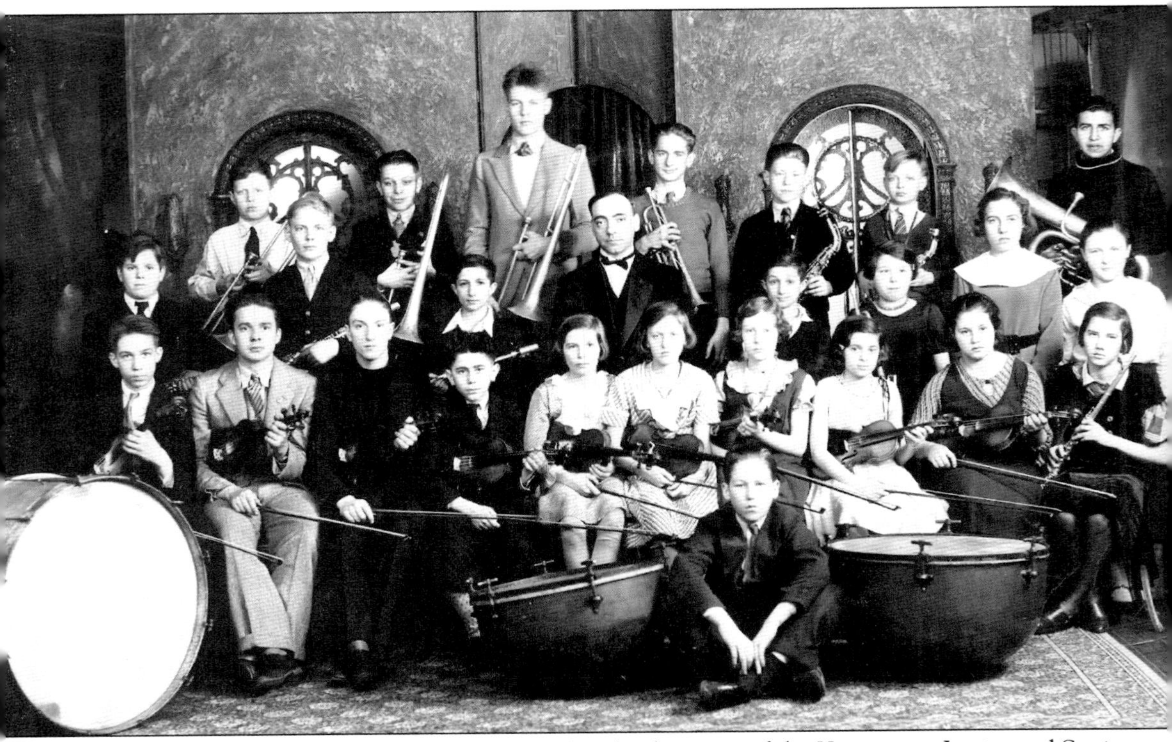

James V. Colonna was given the responsibility for direction of the Kittanning Junior and Senior High School orchestras just a year prior to the one when this picture was taken. The year 1933 was one of hardship for most Americans, as the effects of the Great Depression were evident throughout the country.

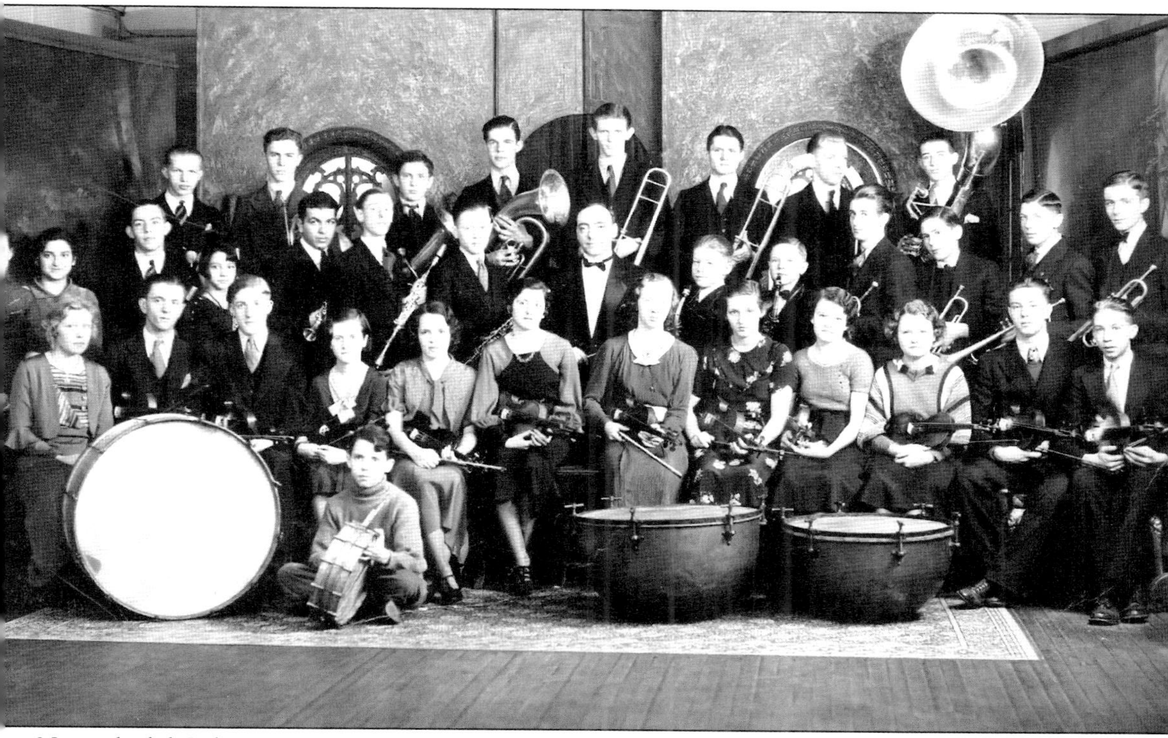

Not only did Colonna manage to keep this school orchestra equipped and operational at a time of extreme economic conditions, he also helped to manage and direct a Rural Valley band with his father and a Ford City school band with his sister Margaret.

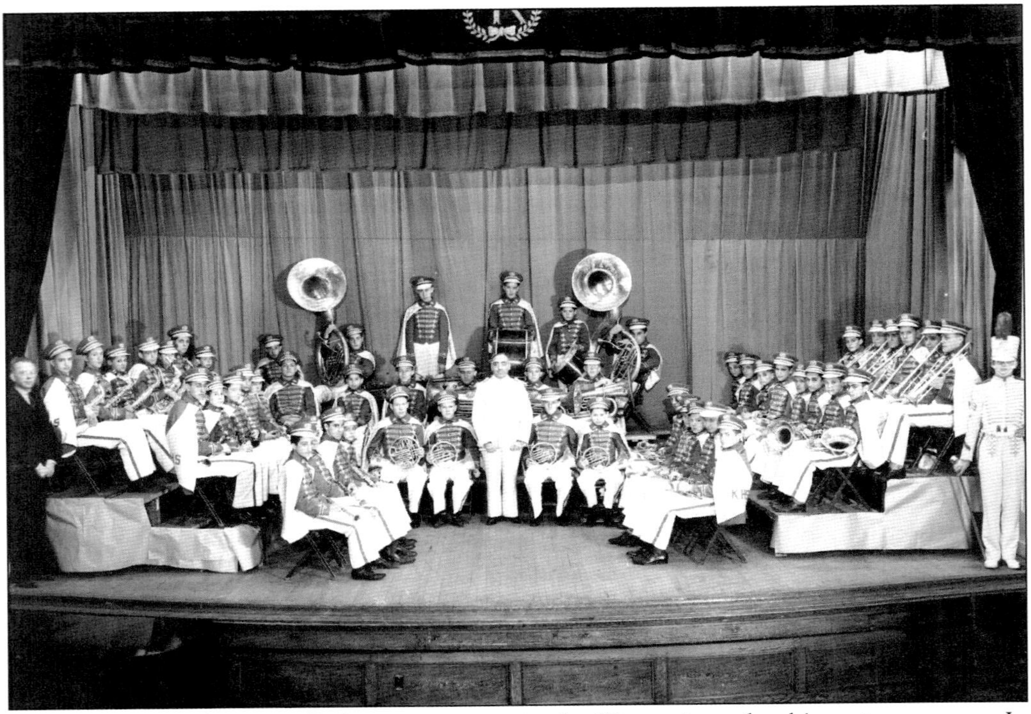

The all-boys' band eventually became extinct in the Kittanning schools' music programs. In 1955, while still under the direction of James V. Colonna, the Kittanning Boys' Band and the Kittanning Girls' Band combined to form bands in both the junior and senior high schools.

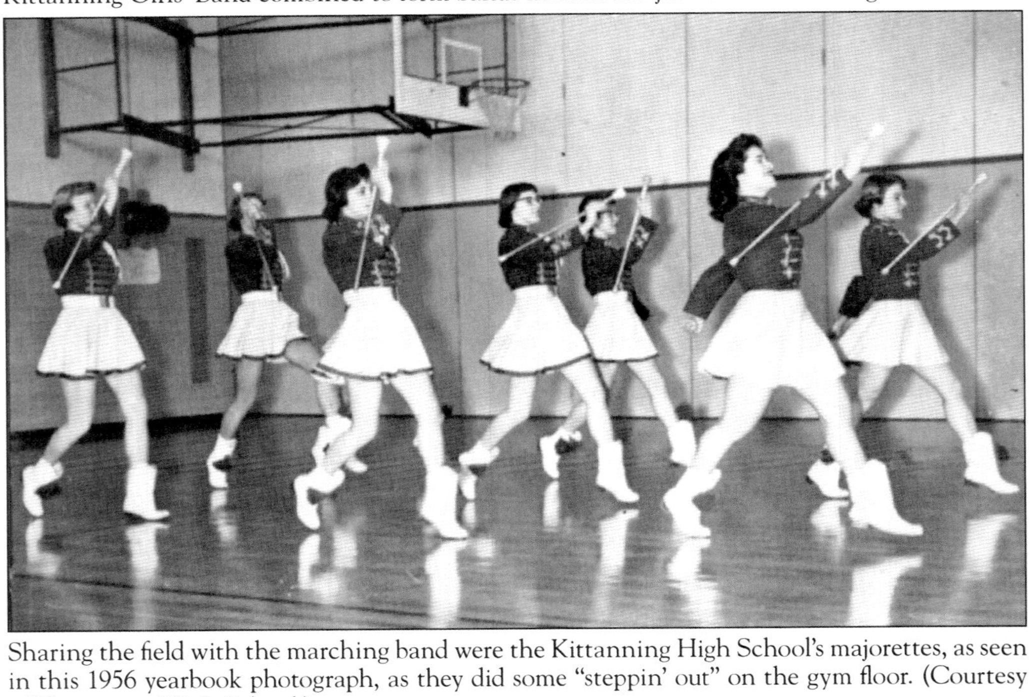

Sharing the field with the marching band were the Kittanning High School's majorettes, as seen in this 1956 yearbook photograph, as they did some "steppin' out" on the gym floor. (Courtesy of Kittanning High School.)

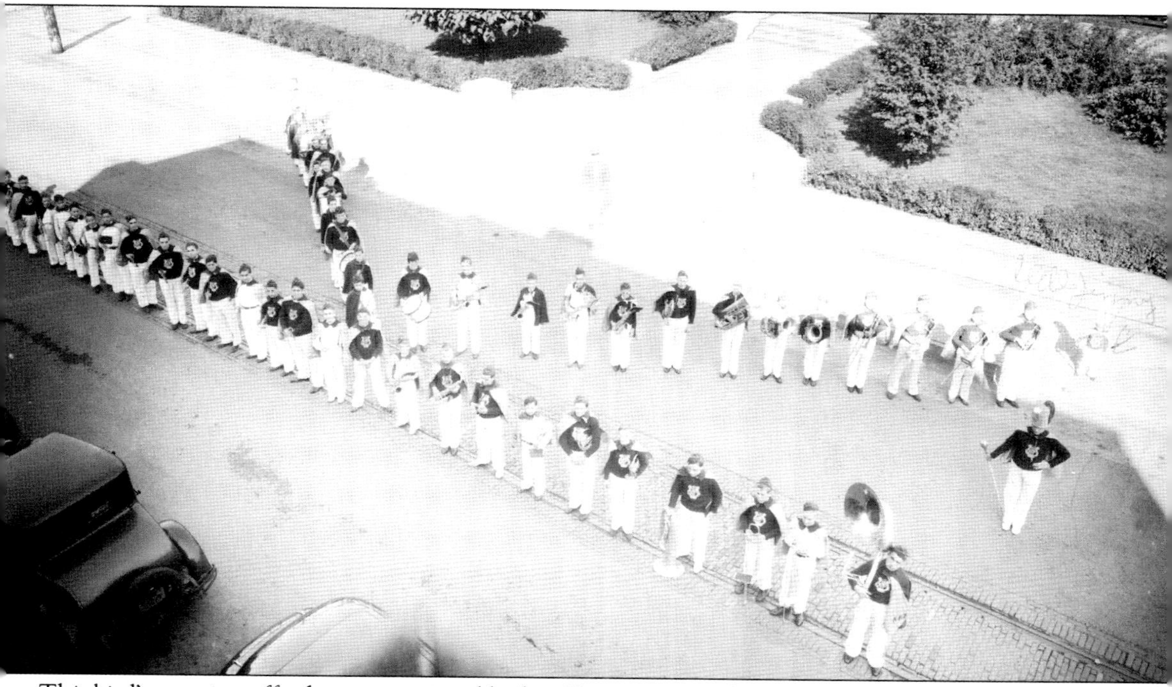

This bird's-eye view affords an exceptional look at Kittanning High School's marching band. The band's letter *k* was one example of Colonna's penchant for intricate movements and formations while playing intricate marches, many of which Colonna personally composed. Of particular note in this photograph is the presence of the band's youngest performer, the director's son Jimmy, who can be seen in the upper right of the formation. Colonna's wife, Jimmy's mother, Maria Mazza Colonna, designed and fabricated uniforms for her small son that replicated those of the high school players.

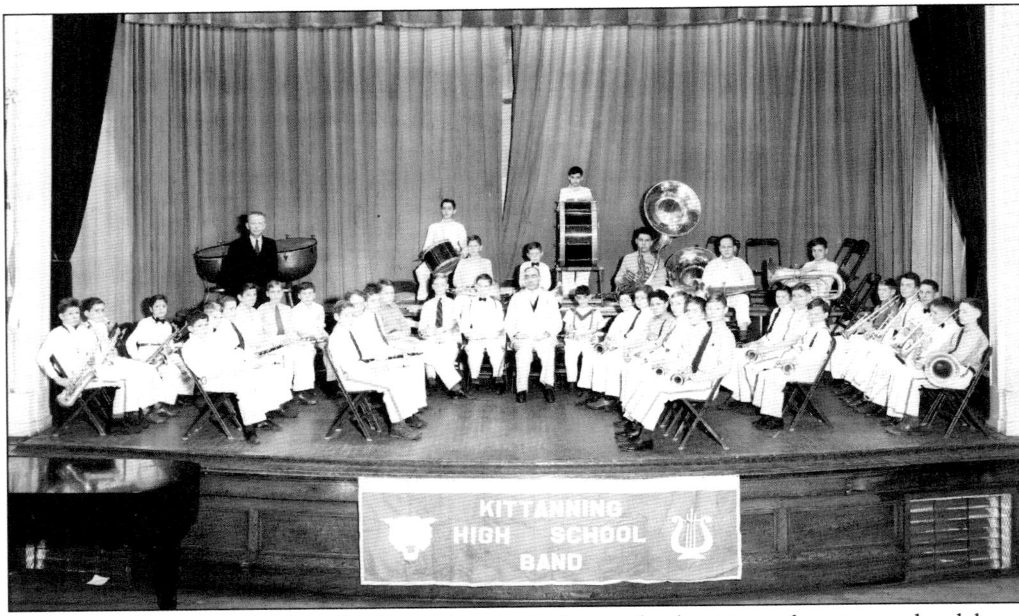

James V. Colonna helped to facilitate the formation and education of various school band programs in Armstrong County, including Freeport and Ford City. When contemporary Kittanning school bands play the Kittanning alma mater, they sound essentially like the band pictured here, as it was Colonna who wrote the music to accompany the alma mater's lyrics, written by Mildred Montgomery.

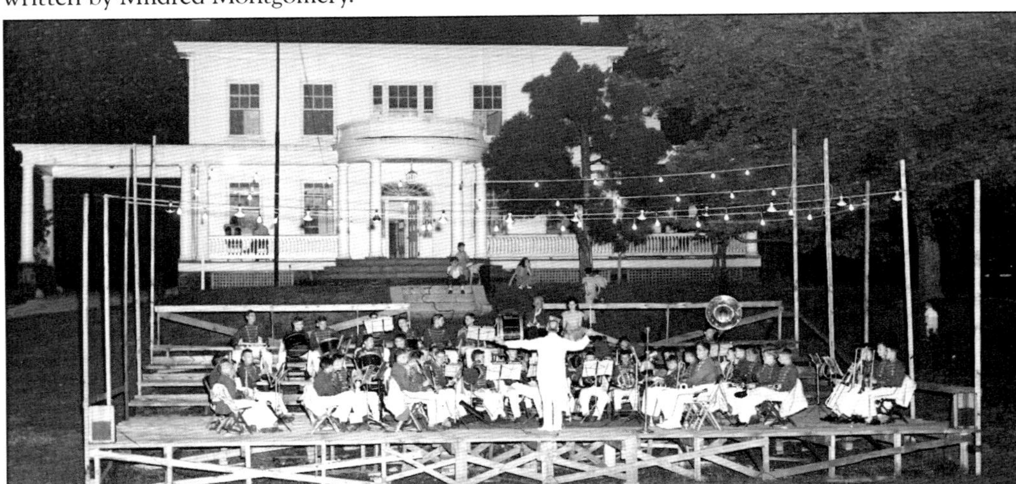

The McCain house provides the backdrop for the Kittanning school band seated on the bleachers in 1941. The house, located on the corner of McKean and Vine Streets, is now home to the Armstrong Historical Society Museum. However, at the time this photograph was taken, it was a school-owned building. Colonna was also known for motivating the band to play outside of the traditional school setting, especially as a farewell and welcome for soldiers serving abroad as they departed or returned to Kittanning by train. Distressed by the attack on America at Pearl Harbor, Colonnna composed "America Forever," a march that was published by Volkwein's Brothers Publishing Company and played by the United States Marine Band for their weekly national radio broadcasts.

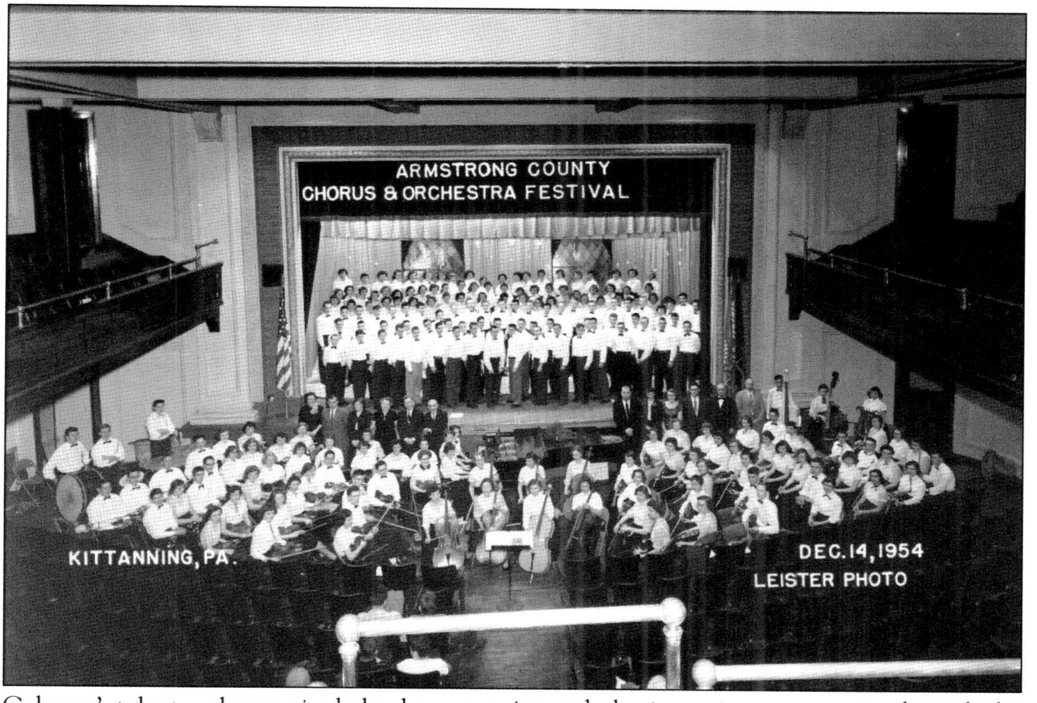

Colonna's talent and expertise helped to create interscholastic music opportunities through the many music festivals that he directed or took part in throughout Armstrong County.

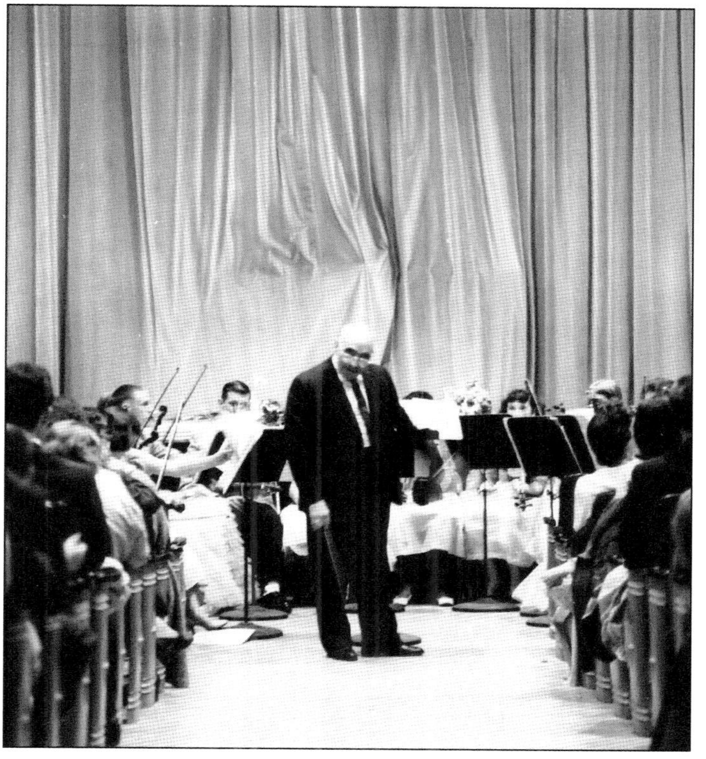

Beloved by his students and the community at large, Colonna is seen here in the latter part of his extremely productive career. He was successful in all his endeavors except for retirement. Colonna remained active by donating his time in order for the struggling school bands that he had nurtured to remain intact until another leader could be found. Colonna passed away in 1969, but he left a legacy of countless musicians, music educators, and bandleaders among his many students and especially his children Marianna Colonna, Enrico Colonna, James A. Colonna, and Jeannette Colonna Schmidt.

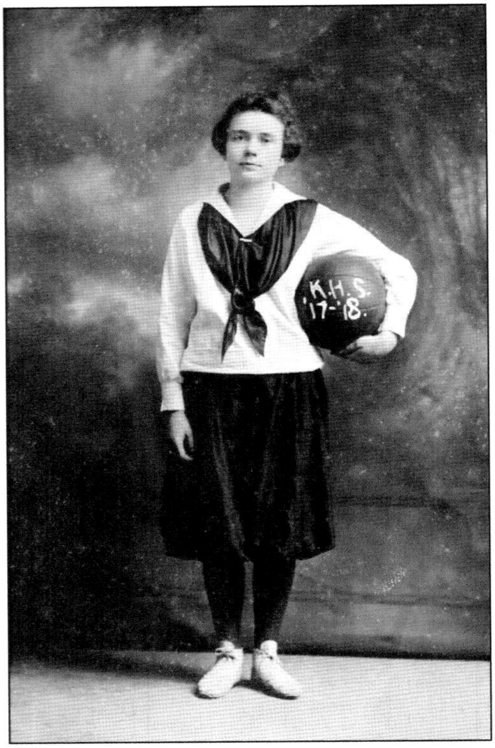

At a time when women were still unable to vote, this young athlete was able to benefit from Kittanning's progressive school program that offered organized sports for girls.

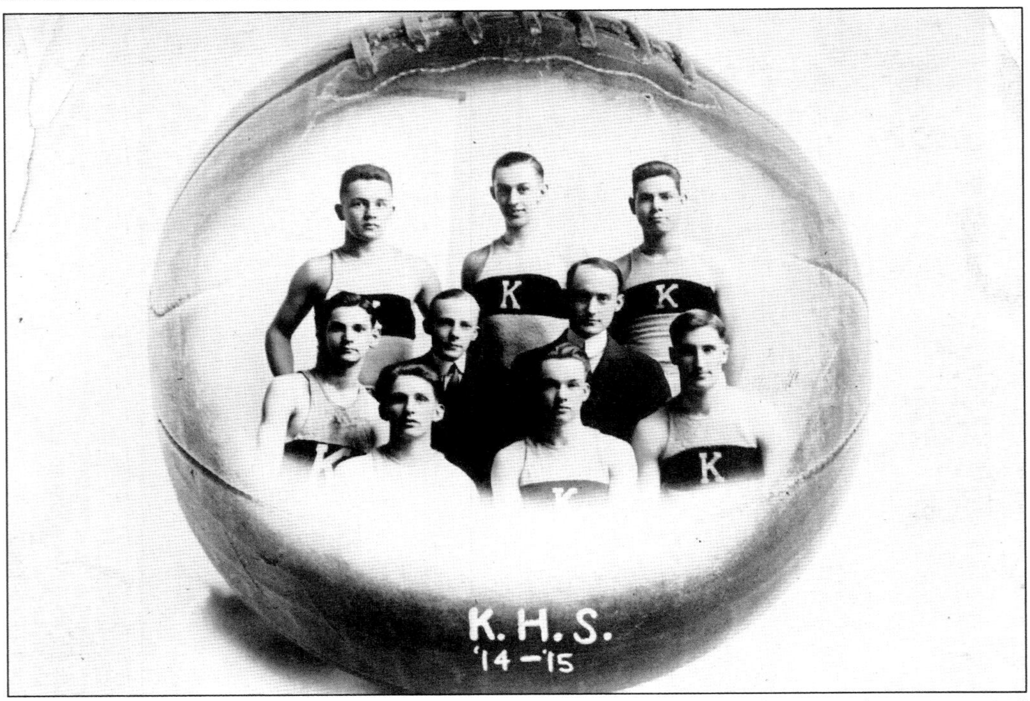

Using what would seem to be progressive photographic techniques for the time, these 1914–1915 Kittanning boys' basketball players and their coach are cleverly framed by their favorite sphere.

Looking very gentile and ladylike, these members of the 1917–1918 Kittanning High School girls' basketball team apparently hit the court in buttons (or at least high tops) and bows.

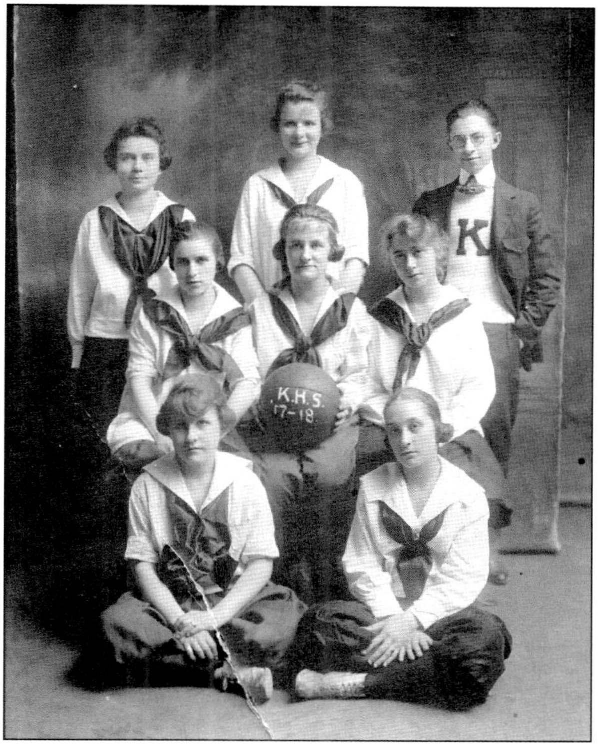

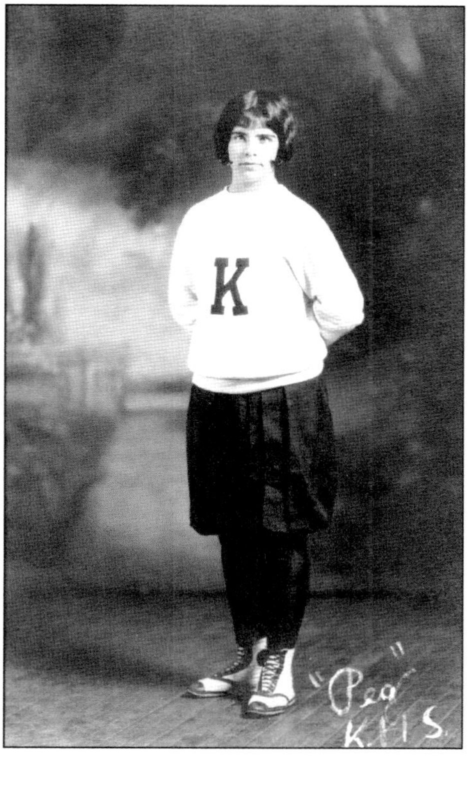

This lady athlete had a sense of syntax about her sporting self, as evidenced by the handwritten verse that accompanied this photograph. In the words of the athlete, "Nothing more / Nothing less / Just a friend from / KHS / 'Peg' Bowser, one of the hefty guards, better known as 'Nails.'"

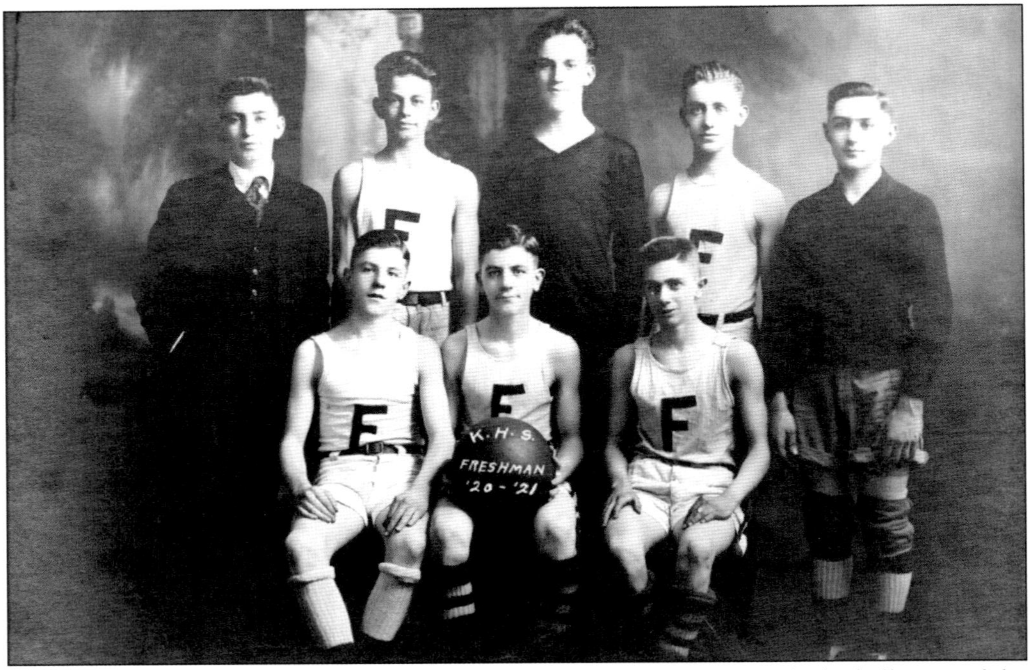

These young men represented Kittanning High School as the freshmen basketball team of the 1920–1921 school year. Until the 1955–1956 school year, there was no delineation of junior and senior high schools. Kittanning High School educated students, grades 7 through 12 in the two adjoining buildings known as the Central and High School buildings, located on the corner of North McKean and Arch Streets.

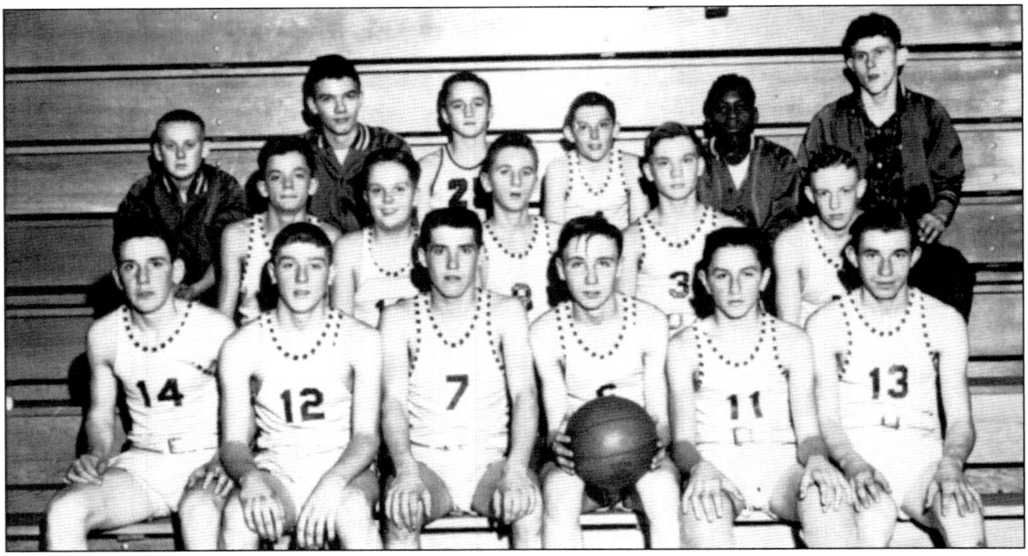

The first team to represent Kittanning Junior High School in the 1955–1956 school year is pictured here. From left to right are (first row) Paul Grafton, Ralph Wirick, Larry Skinner, Ted Round, Larry Gowetski, and Paul McDowell; (second row) Alan Shaffer, Dave Schrecengost, Paul Moore, William Heymers, and B. Heilman; (third row) Charles Hooks (manager), Harry Campbell, John Wheland, Amby Bauer, Perry Fancher, and Jim Anthony (manager).

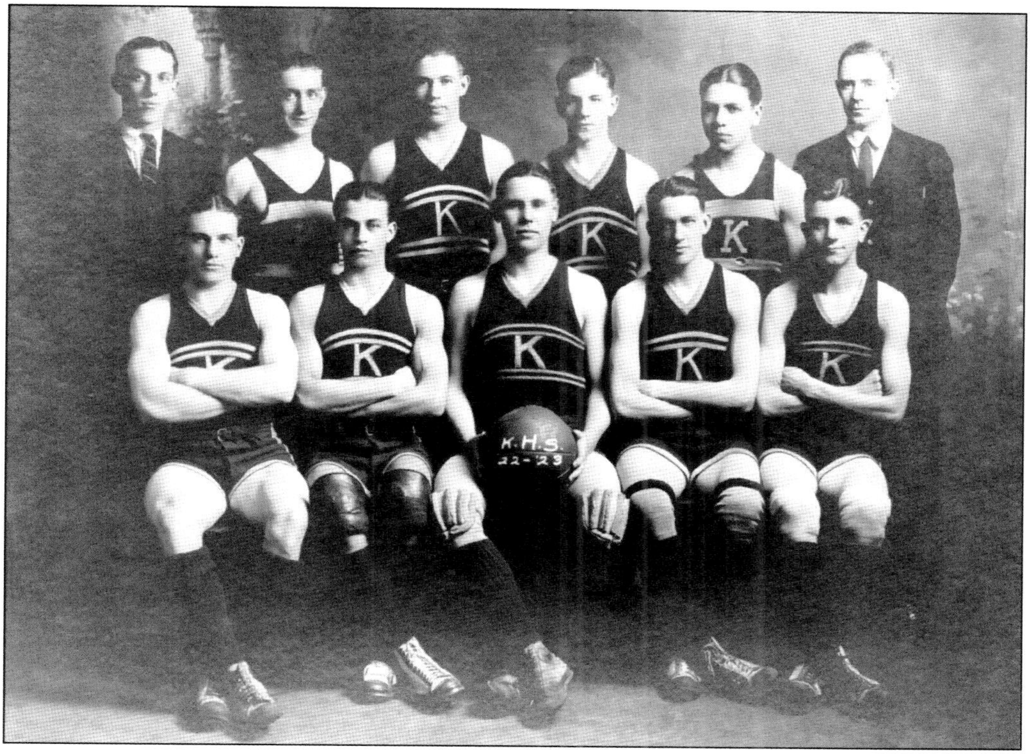

It is the same game but with different looks. The above traditional photograph depicts basketball, 1920s style, while the unique-looking collage art right showcases the 1955–1956 Kittanning High School team.

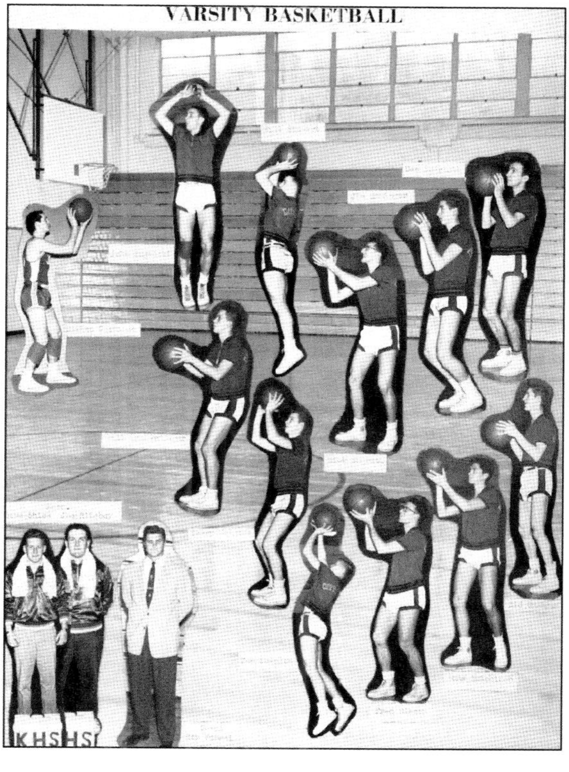

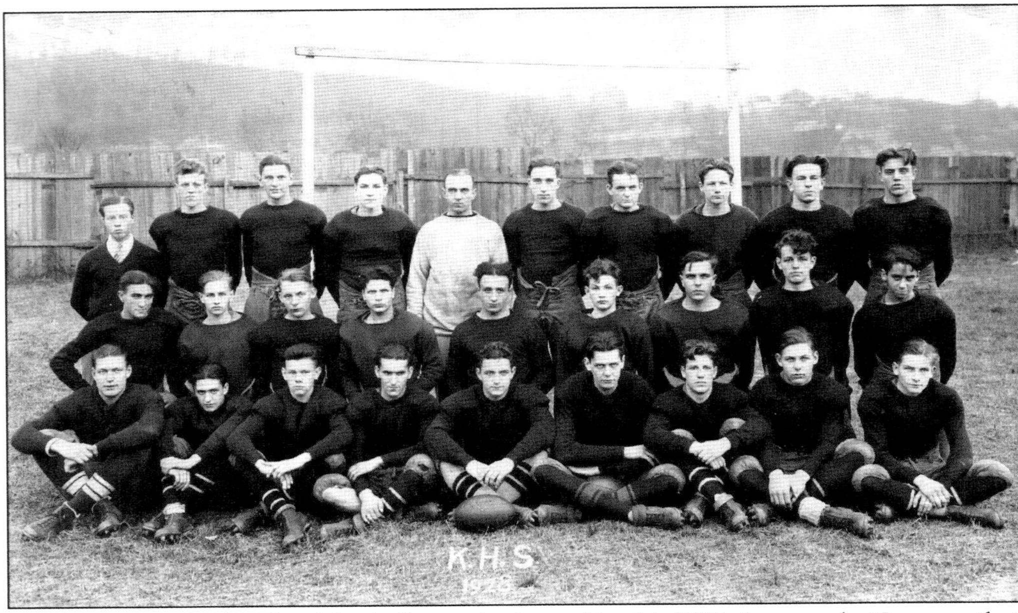

The Kittanning High School football team is pictured in this 1928 photograph. Nary a smile is seen on the faces of these young athletes, most likely to intimidate the opponent. Unbeknownst to these players and the rest of the community were the tough times that lay just a year ahead.

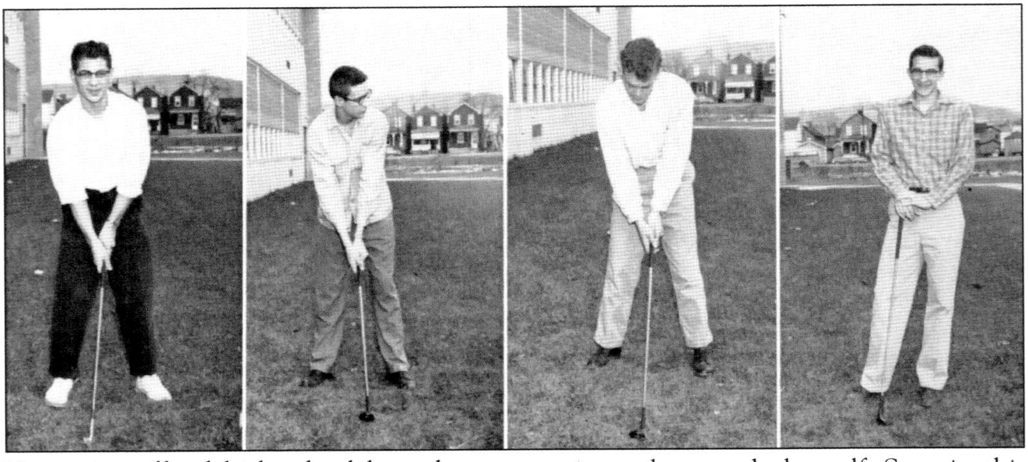

Kittanning offered high school boys the opportunity to learn and play golf. Seen in this photograph from the 1955–1956 school year are, from left to right, Dick Sagrati, Wayne Van Dine, Bill Ashe, and Paul Julius.

Three

FAMILIES AND FRIENDS

Kittanning's population grew much in the same way as many other western Pennsylvanian towns. Its first known inhabitants were Native Americans, most likely the Lenni-Lenape, a Delaware tribe. Western Europeans, primarily French, British, and Scotch-Irish immigrants, were the next group to populate the area after the 1756 battle of Kittanning.

The early to mid-19th century saw an influx of German and Irish families. The close of this century began what was a tremendous wave of immigration from such areas as Italy and eastern Europe, which continued at a consistent pace into the years of World War I.

Each ethnic group brought with them customs unique to their native lands. And while these practices may have fostered a sense of diversity, there were probably more values that were commonly shared among the different cultures than there were issues that set them apart.

The majority of men and women who made a deliberate decision to settle in Kittanning were undoubtedly seeking a better life for themselves and their families. Putting family first, many people sacrificed much in order for their offspring to survive and succeed in this new world.

Families and friends were often one and the same, as evidenced by photographs of extended families involved in social and civic groups. However, hundreds of photographs from numerous collections will never be able to tell their own personal stories, as their identities are not known.

With the help of Lindeman and Turner family members Dave Lindeman, Carole and Jerry Cable, and Esther Choncek, along with a well-identified photograph collection that was previously donated to the Armstrong Historical Society, five interconnected Kittanning families can be represented on the pages of this chapter.

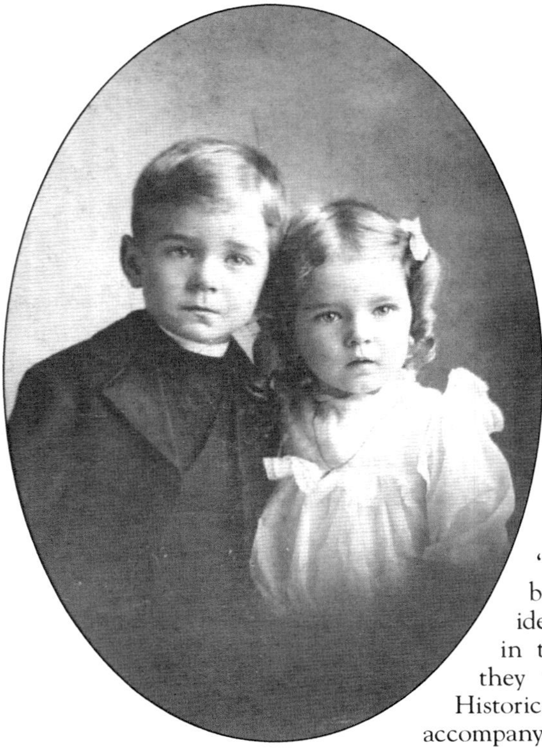

"Have you seen these children?" These beautiful children are not missing, but their identities are. Identity theft is not suspected in this case; however, what is known is that they were donated to the Armstrong County Historical Museum with no identifying marks or accompanying information.

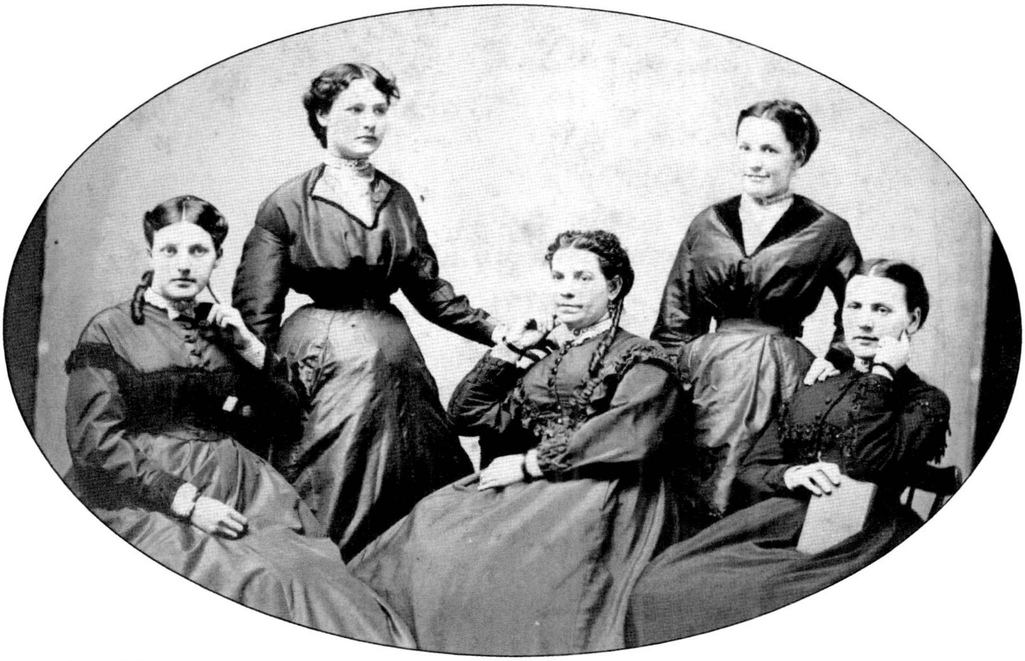

Even if nothing was known of the identities of these two groups of young women, it would not appear difficult to convince someone that they are two groups of sisters, which they are. Pictured above are the daughters of James and Sarah (Nulton) Johnson. Below from left to right are Grieb sisters Elizabeth, Mary, Eva, Carrie, and Anna.

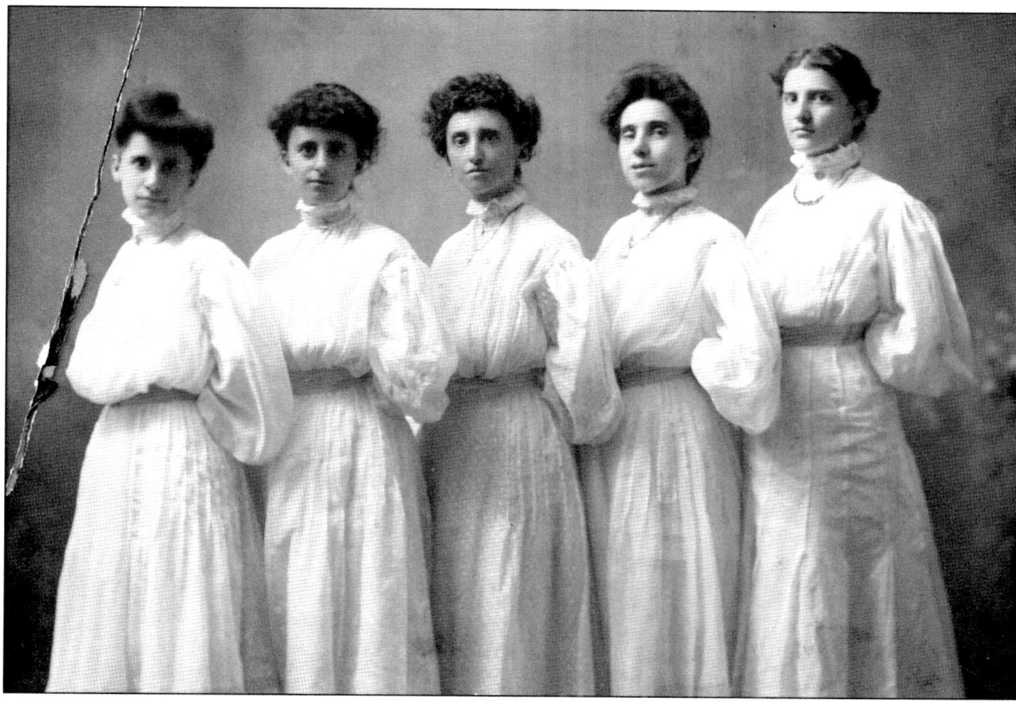

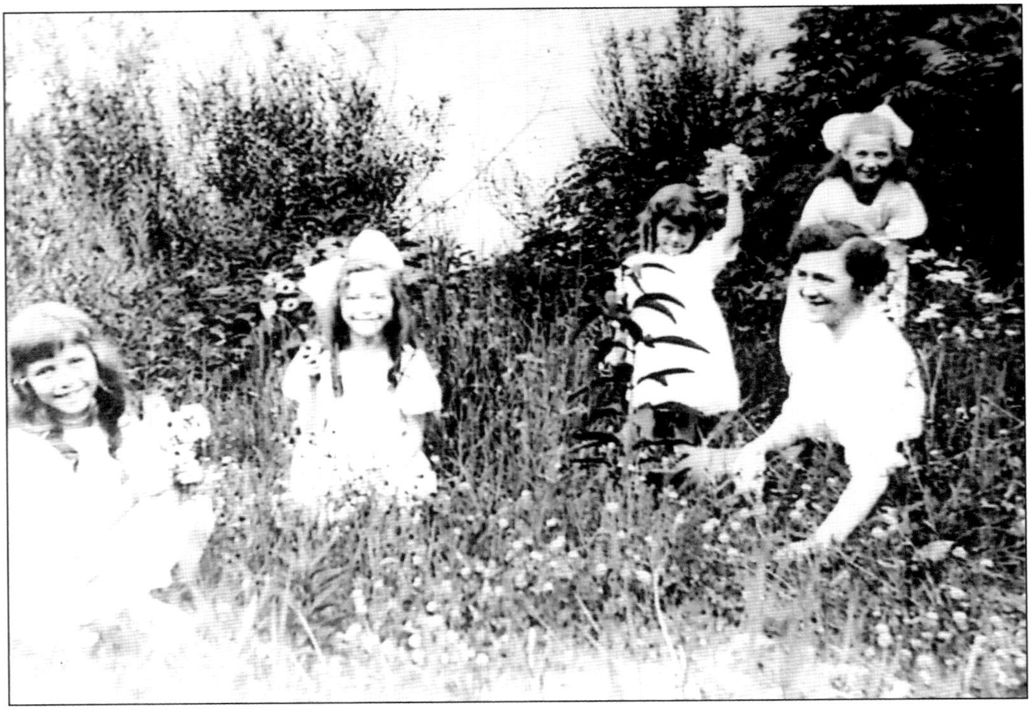

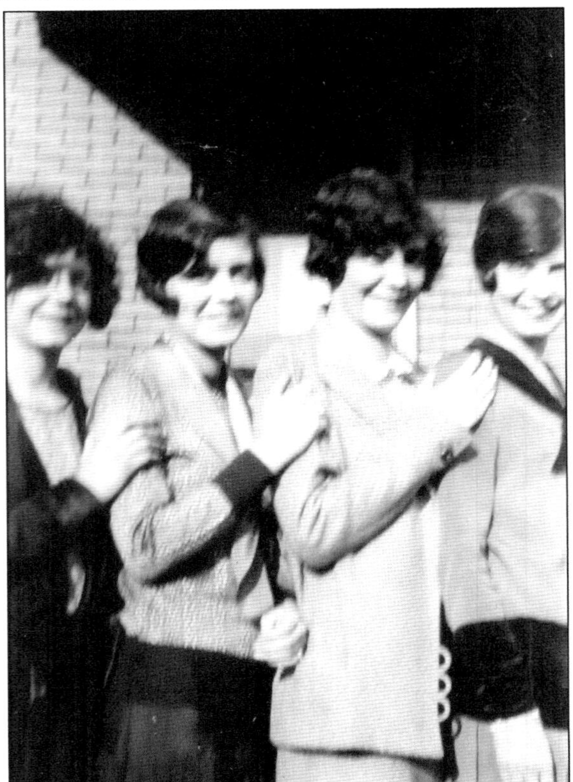

Seen above, looking fresh as daisies in this field of wildflowers along with their mother, Lulu, are the Turner girls. They are, from left to right, Sally, Lois, Audrey, and Velma. These same sisters, seen at left looking perfectly coiffed and sophisticated several years later, from left to right, are Sally, Audrey, Lois, and Velma. Brothers Howard and Tom and father, David, round out this particular family. Casual family interconnectedness keeps these sisters in relationship with one another even as they begin their own nuclear families. (Courtesy of the Dave Lindeman family.)

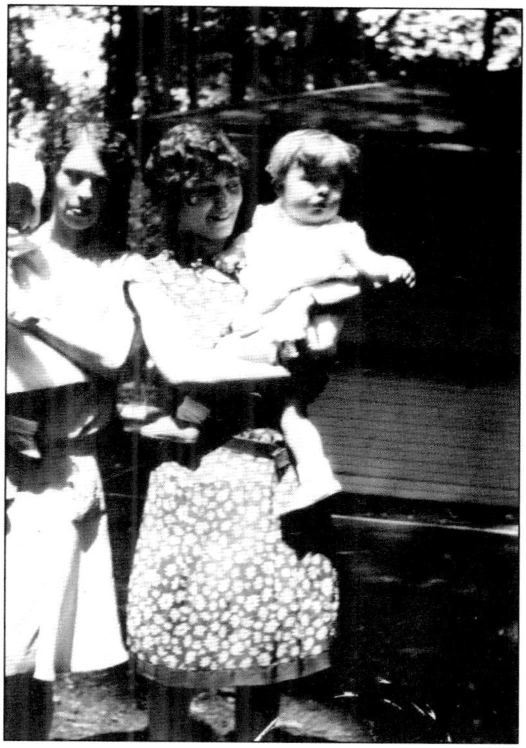

When a young man in a jalopy catches the interest of a pretty young girl, marriage can happen. In this particular case, John Lindeman married Lois Turner, seen here with their first child, son John. John and Lois would complete their family with a daughter and another son. John ran a successful business in Kittanning. The two were involved in their church and other community organizations for over 50 years of married life.

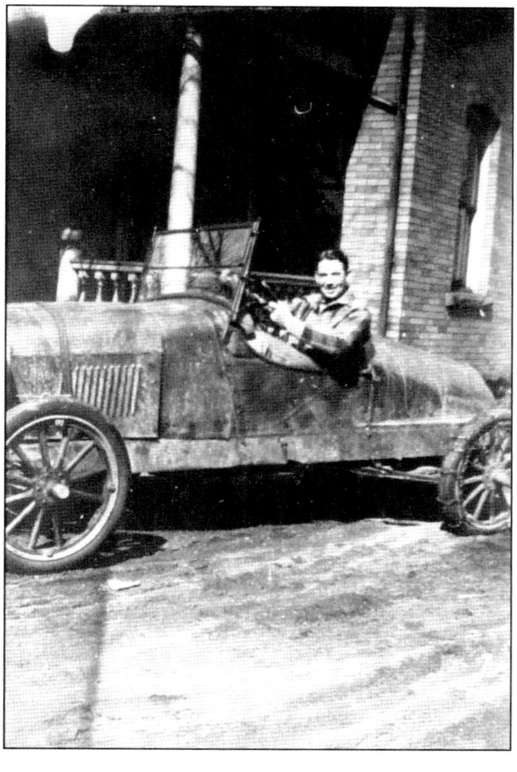

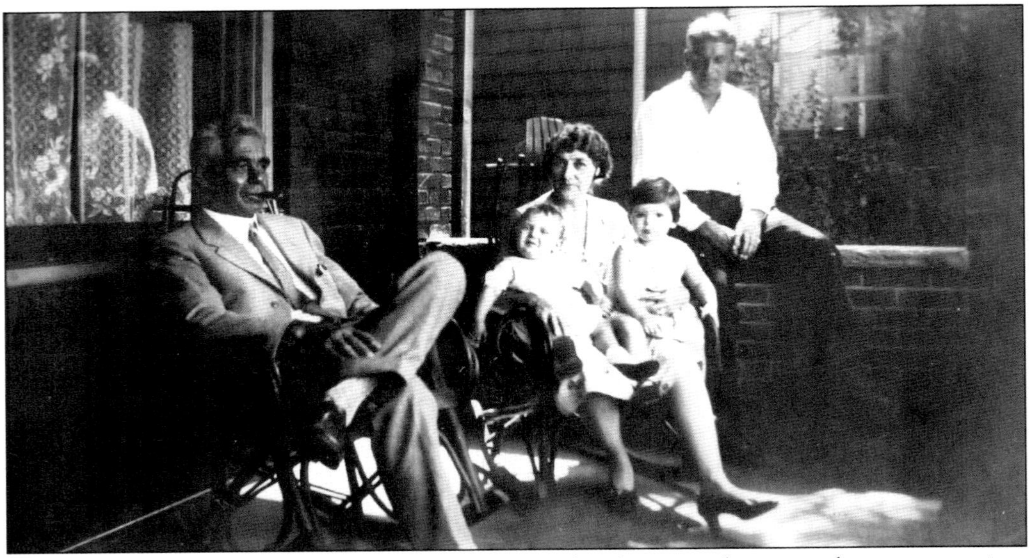

Three generations of Lindemans relax on the family's front porch, engaged in conversation. Fred Linderman, seated on the left, was a jeweler and a father of four. His wife is seated to the right, holding two of their grandchildren, while son John looks on from his seat on the right. A tight-knit family, like many others in Kittanning, the Lindemans enjoyed not only conversation but also sharing their vocal and instrumental talent. A unique New Year's celebration is now observed by generations of this family. It is now a Lindeman custom to sing the same songs and play the same games as those that were enjoyed at the first gathering in 1881. A special tradition is for family members to sign Annie Lindeman's autograph book, which is now over a century old.

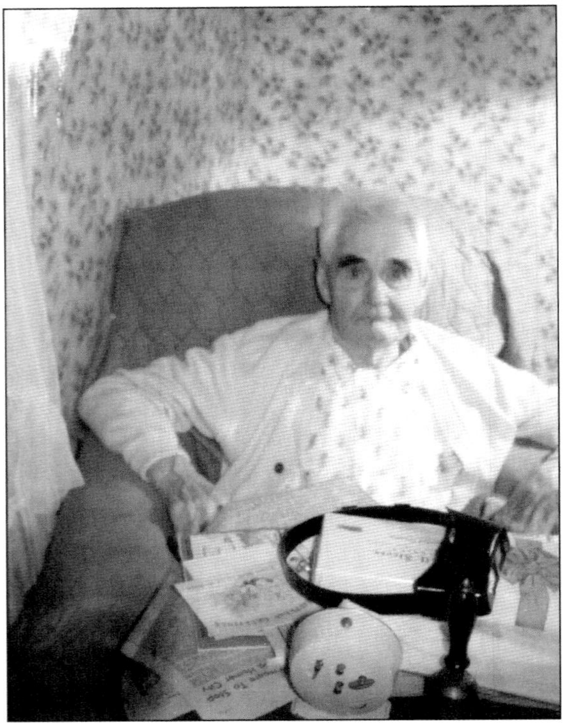

Fred Lindeman, pictured here, made his home with son John and his wife, Lois, in his later years. Just before his passing, Fred anxiously awaited the return of grandson Dave Lindeman from military service overseas. Dave recalls ascending the steps and hearing his grandfather call to him from his bedroom above. Dave went directly to see him, and after exiting the room following a brief conversation, Fred passed from this world. (Courtesy of the Dave Lindeman family.)

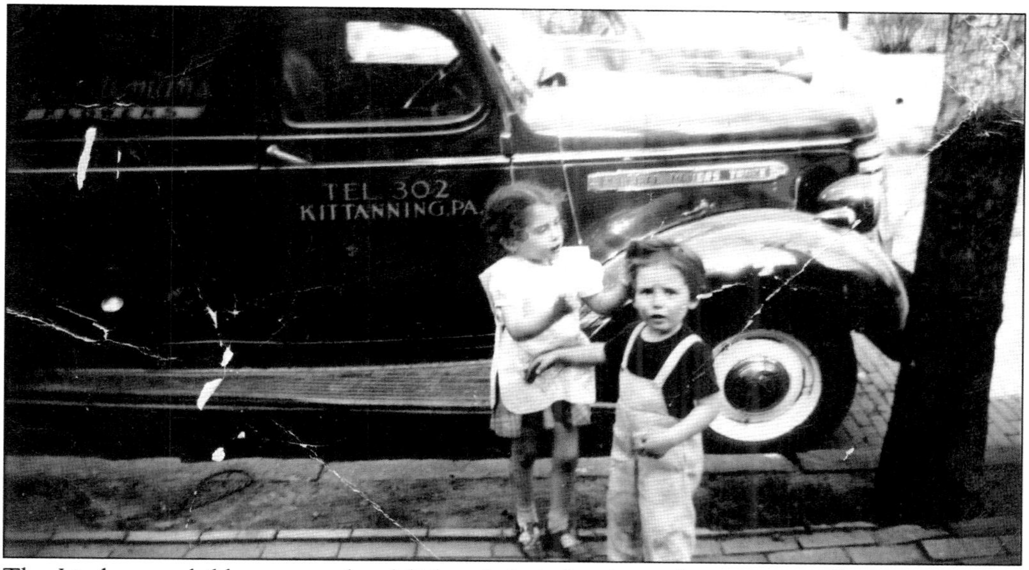

The Lindeman children were the delight of their family, and were especially loved by their grandfather, family patriarch Johann George Lindeman. Johann emigrated with his widowed father and four siblings in 1845 from Zwergen, a small village in northeast Germany, to America. By 1850, 19-year-old Johann was the only family member left alive. Without friends and family in this new country, his life was revived when he met Margaret Magdaline Oeh, also from Germany. The two married and made their home in Kittanning. The couple had 13 children, and 10 lived to adulthood. These photographs capture the images of five of their grandchildren. Carol Lindeman Cable and David Lindeman are pictured above, and below is their brother John Lindeman and cousins.

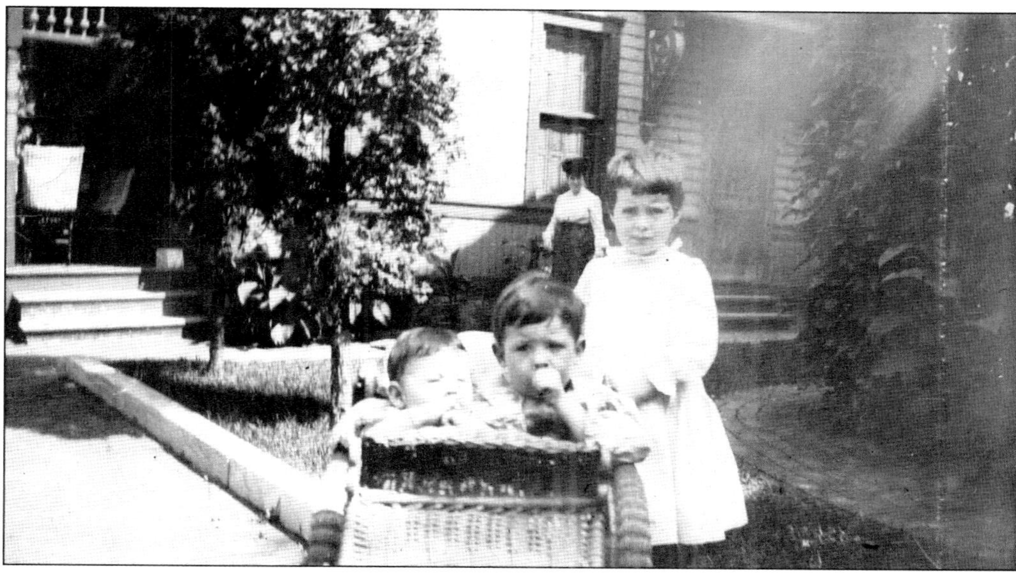

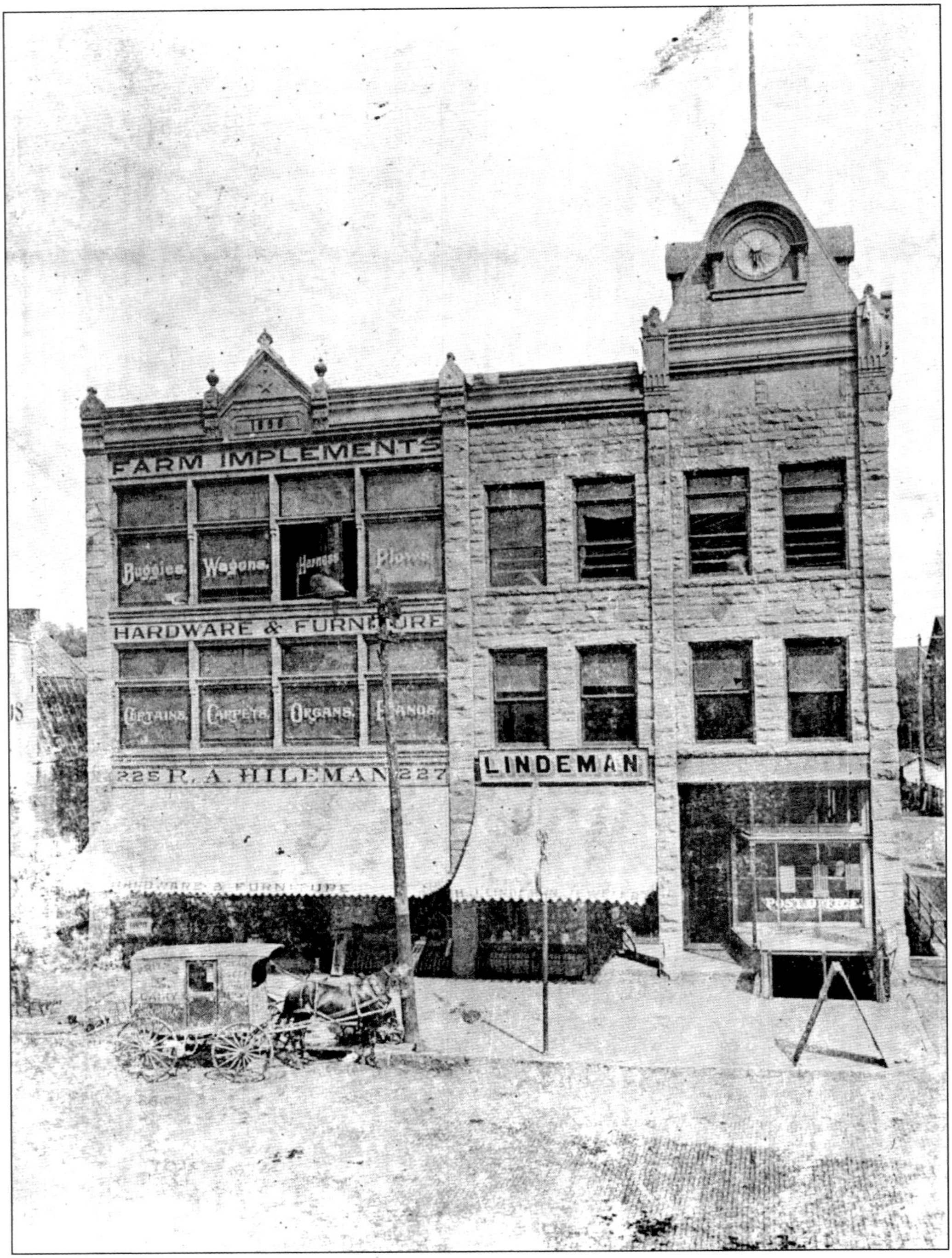

The Lindeman family made their livelihood in a variety of ways. Shown here is the Lindeman building located on McKean Street, where such family enterprises as their jewelry and floral businesses flourished. Not all of Johann George's children remain in the area but rather pursued medical, musical, and manufacturing vocations elsewhere.

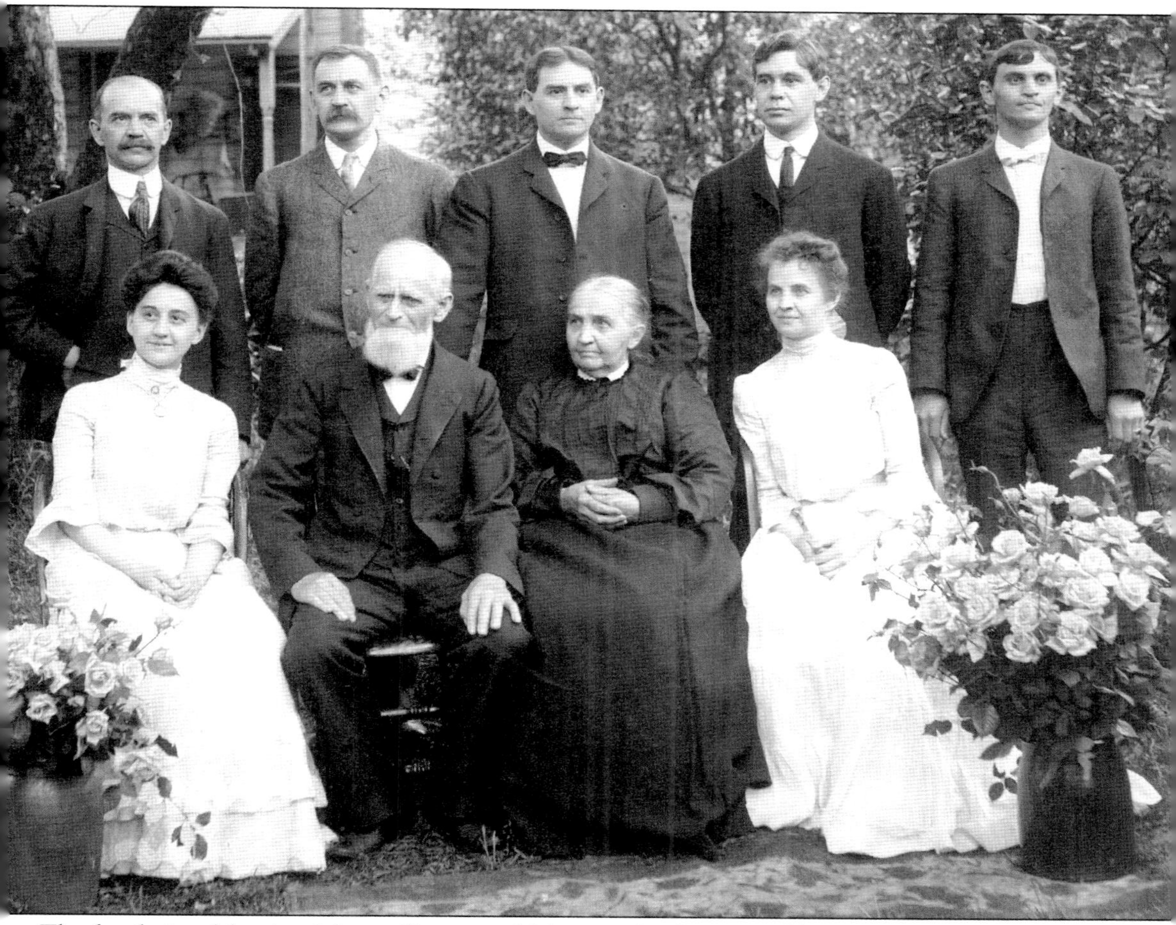

The family is celebrating Johann George and Margaret Lindeman's golden wedding anniversary in 1904. They are pictured here with 7 of their 13 children. From left to right are (first row) Mary Margaret, Johann George, Margaret, and Anne Magdaline; (second row) William, Heinrich Johann, Charles Edward, Frederick, and Walter. (Courtesy of the Dave Lindeman family.)

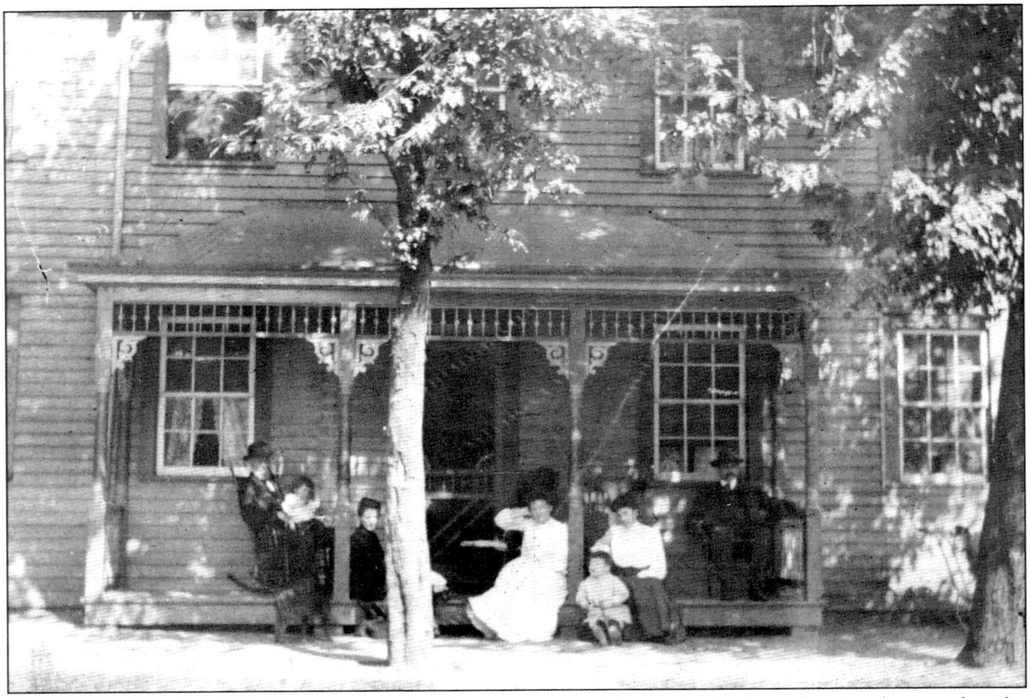

Porch sitting was a popular pastime for Kittanning residents, including the Lindeman family. Several members of this family are seen on the front porch of a well-shaded home.

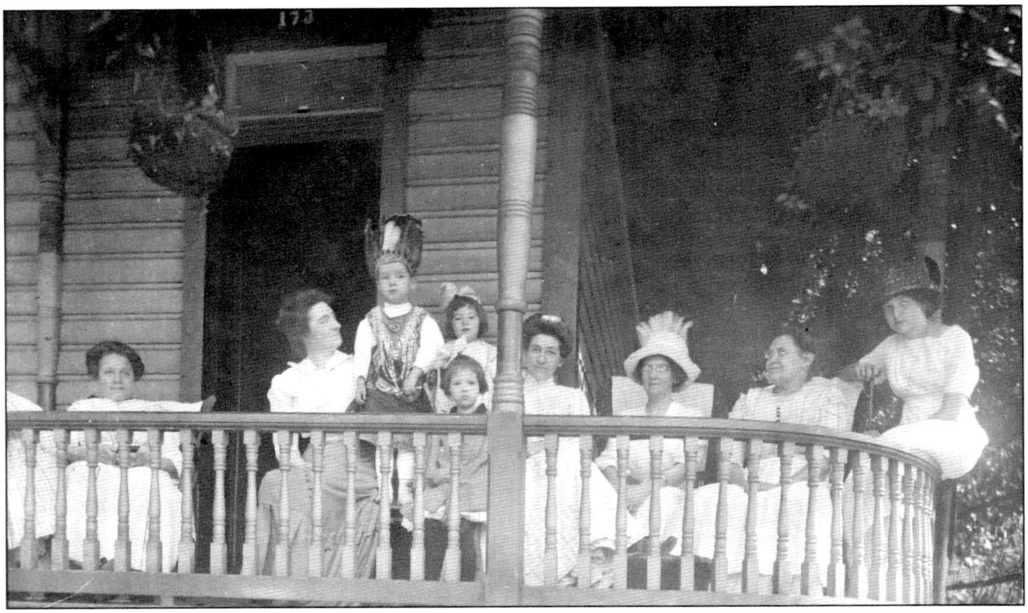

Kittanning seems to prove the correctness of the old adage that everyone loves a parade. Watching a parade from Bird Krow Foulis's father's porch, from left to right, are Mrs. Reynolds Crawford, Mrs. J. B. Kennerdell, her son James H. Kennerdell, Harriett Lindeman (front, wearing a coat), Anna Mae Lindeman (behind), Mrs. Fred Lindeman (mother of Harriett and Anna Mae), Mrs. Jones, Mrs. Foulis, and Eileen Jones.

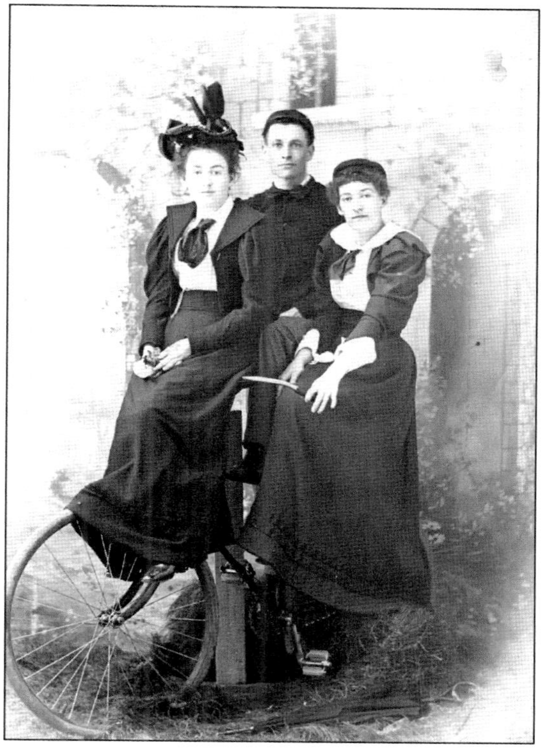

It was a bicycle not a jalopy that brought this Lindeman couple together. On this bicycle built for two or more are Alice Barr, J. Kennerdell, and Carrie Taylor. Taylor later became the wife of Fred Lindeman, pictured below.

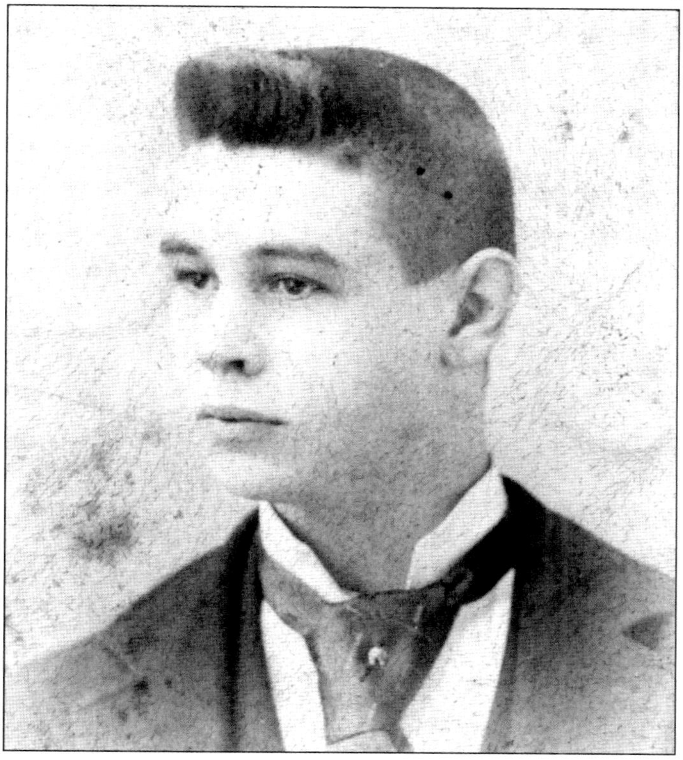

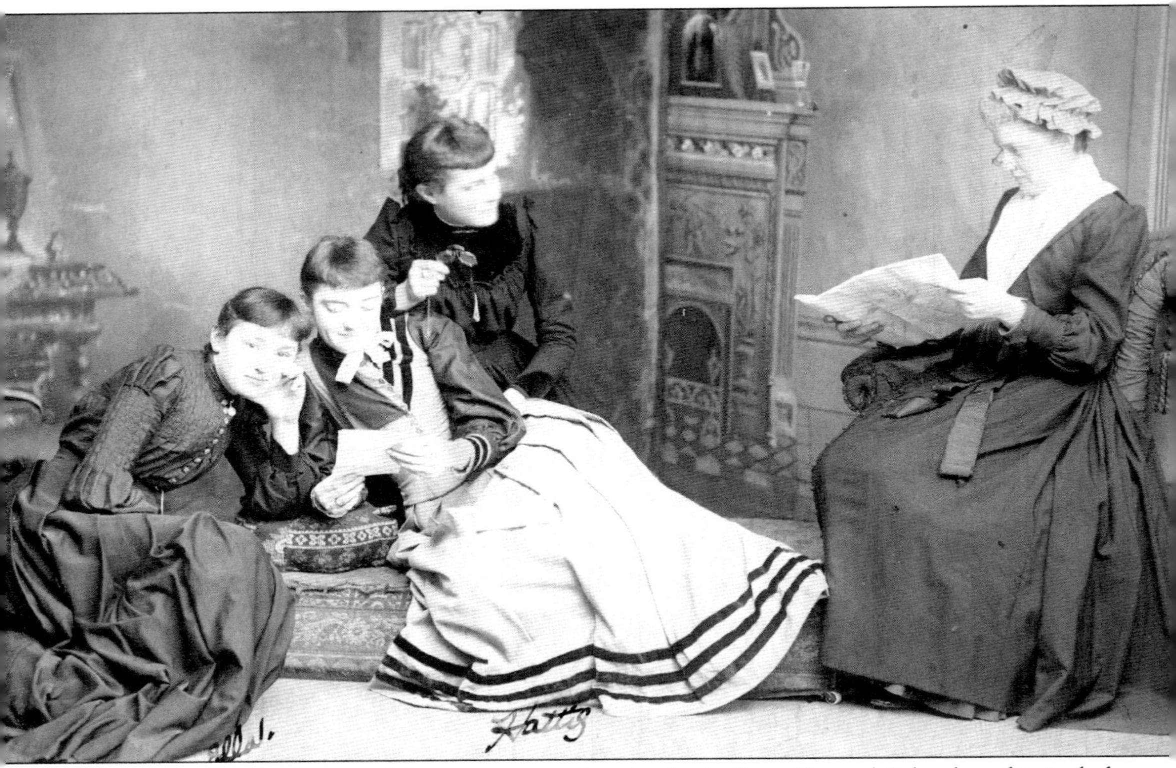

This portrait, reflective of the times, was taken in the Indiana Normal School, and it includes ladies of the Kennerdell, Henry, and Taylor family in repose. Normal schools, such as Indiana, later developed into what is known as Indiana University of Pennsylvania.

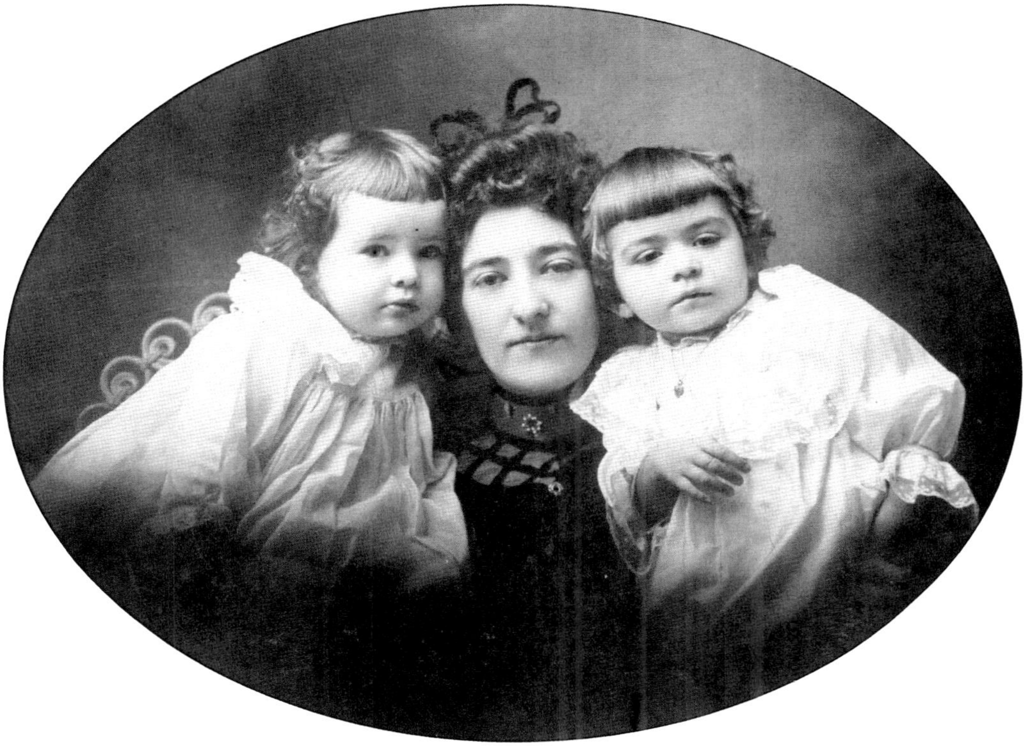

Family portraits often went beyond the nuclear family unit. Above, aunt Carrie Taylor's image is captured with two of her nieces in a holiday photograph. At right, the unidentified handsome gentleman is surrounded by attractive ladies.

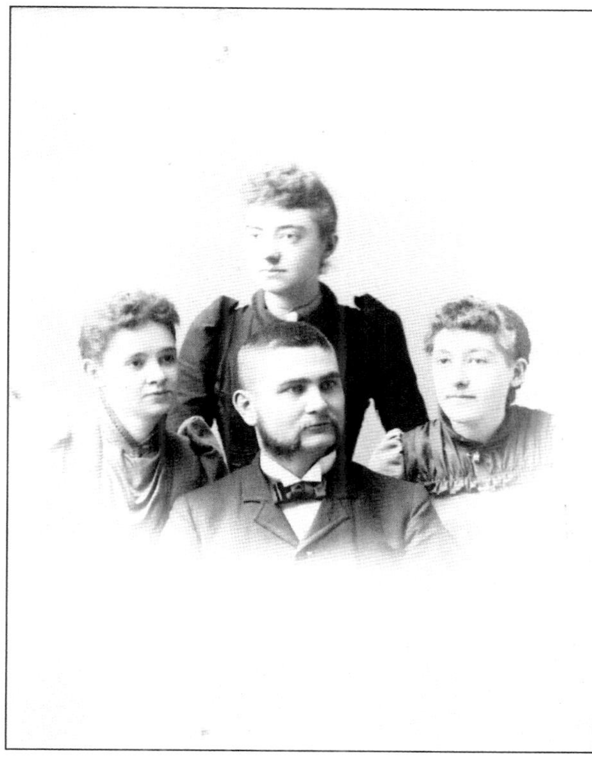

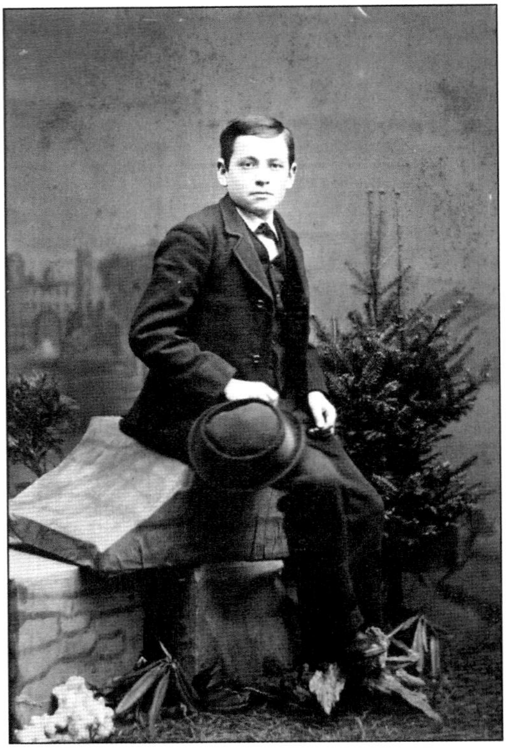

This picture captures J. B. Kennerdell in his Sunday best. Kennerdell, like many of his contemporaries, was not only active in the working world but also in social, fraternal, and civic groups. The Kennerdells were the proprietors of the Furnee and Kennerdell Stationery and Book Shop. Some of the other photographs in this book are examples of their professional photography services.

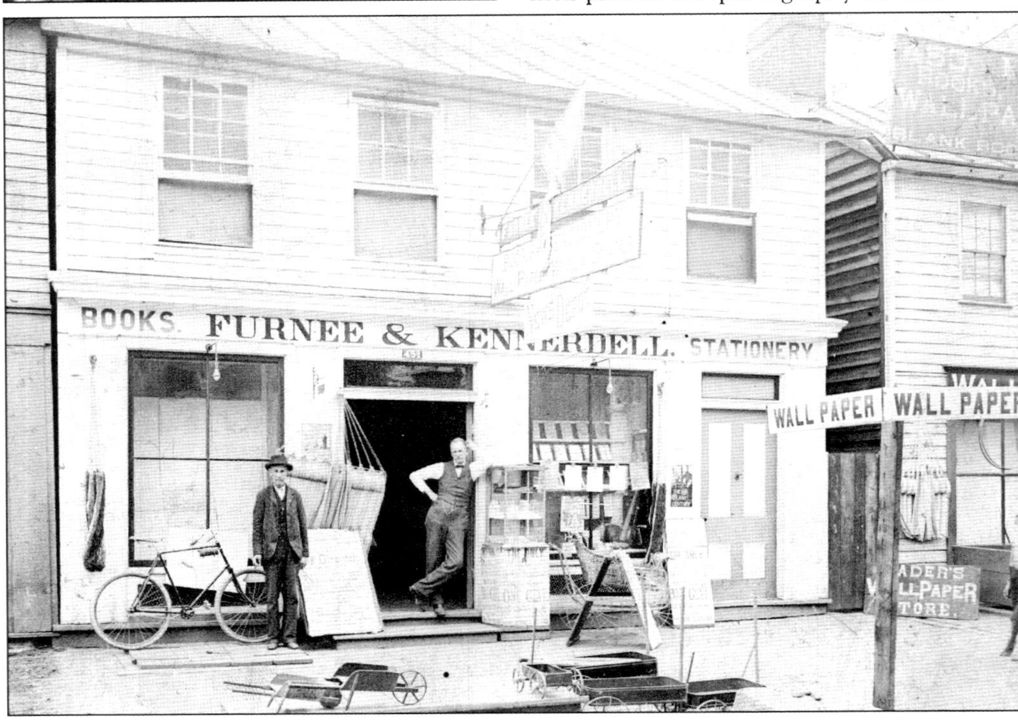

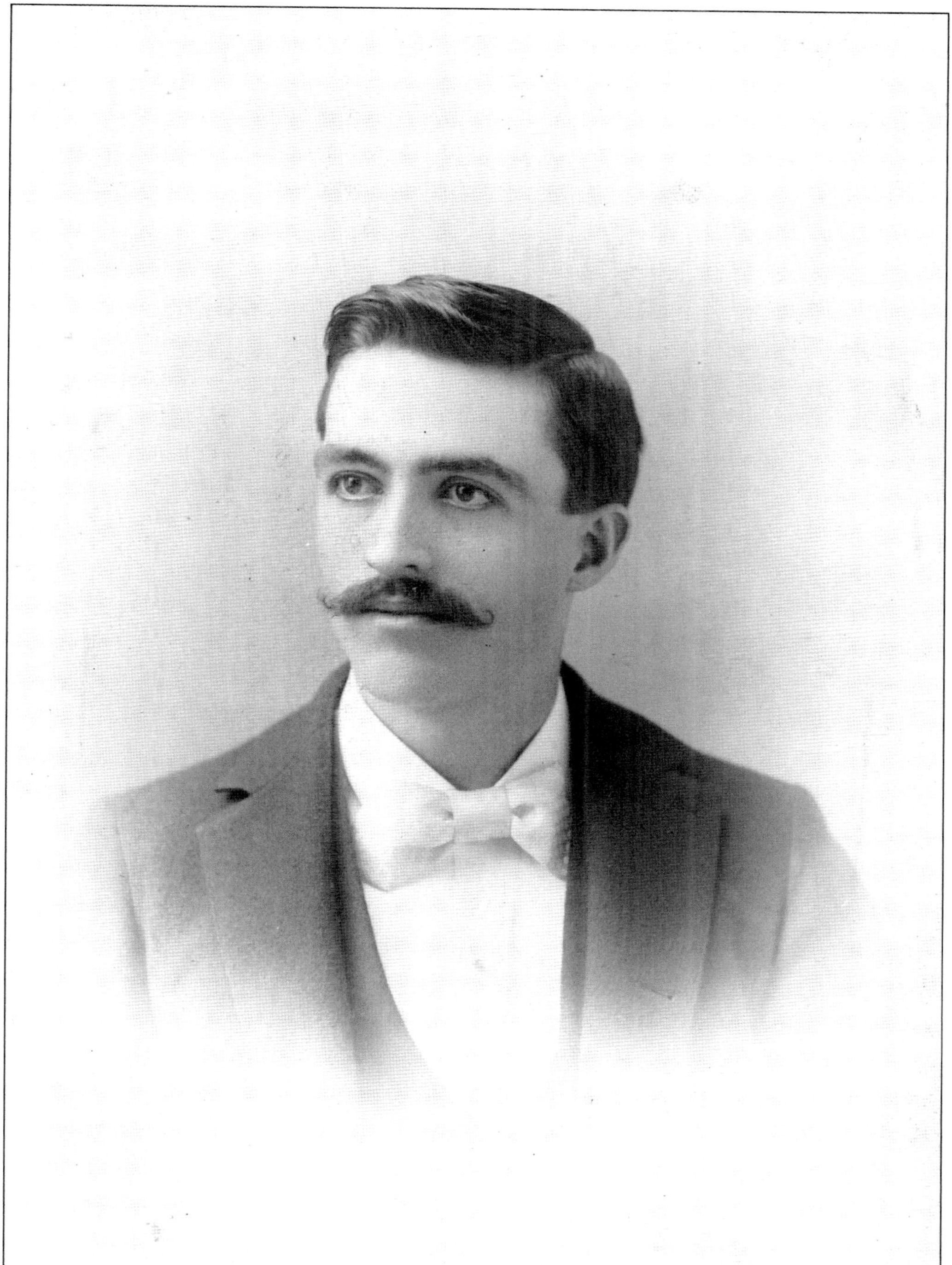

Alex H. Taylor, brother of Carrie Taylor Lindeman and the oldest child of Robert Nelson and Maggie Nelson, is seen here as a young man. He, like his family, remained active in various community organizations, including working as an instructor of the Cuba American drill team. He wed Mary Knoble in 1868.

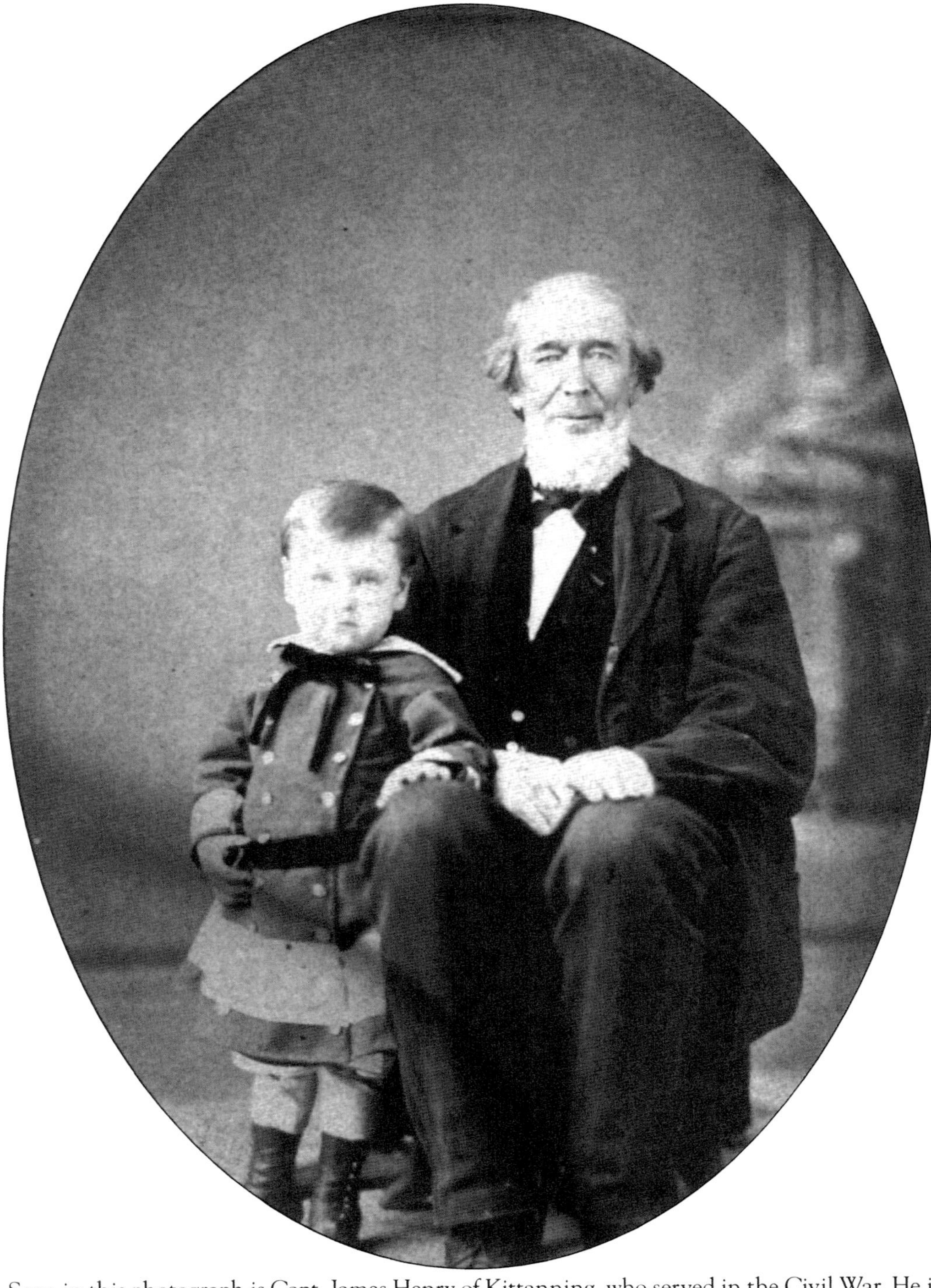

Seen in this photograph is Capt. James Henry of Kittanning, who served in the Civil War. He is seated here with one of his grandchildren. Because of Henry's participation in postwar reunions and celebrations, his family is believed to have added generations as his daughter Maggie is thought to have met her future husband at one such occasion.

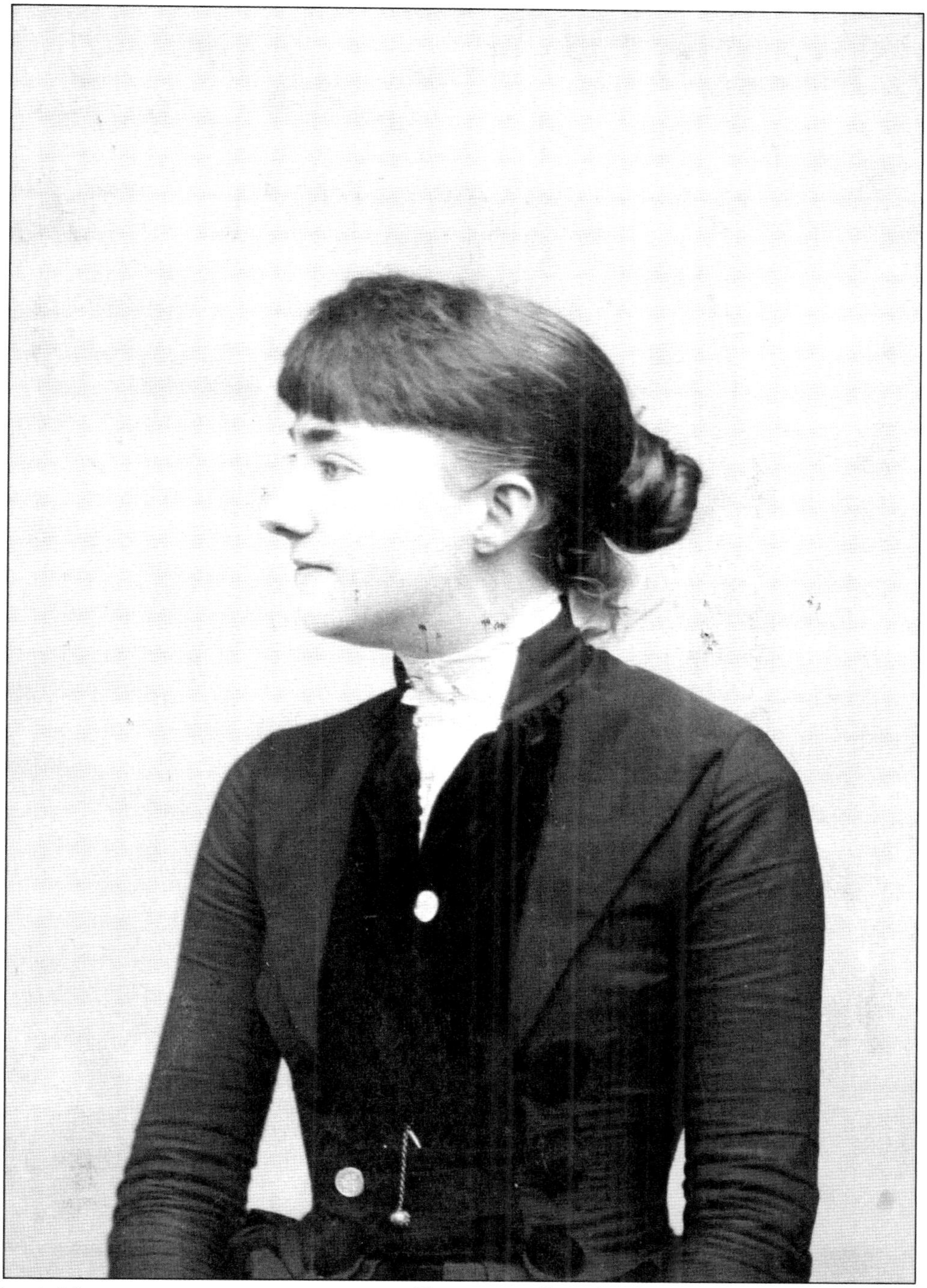

Maggie Henry as a young woman is pictured here in profile. The daughter of Capt. James Henry, she wed Robert Nelson Taylor, originally from the McKeesport area, who also served in the Civil War. The two wed and became the parents of Alex H. Tayor, Mary Alice Taylor (died at age 16), Harriett Taylor Kennerdell (wife of Jim Kennerdell), and Carrie Taylor Lindeman (wife of Fred Lindeman). The couple made their permanent home in Kittanning.

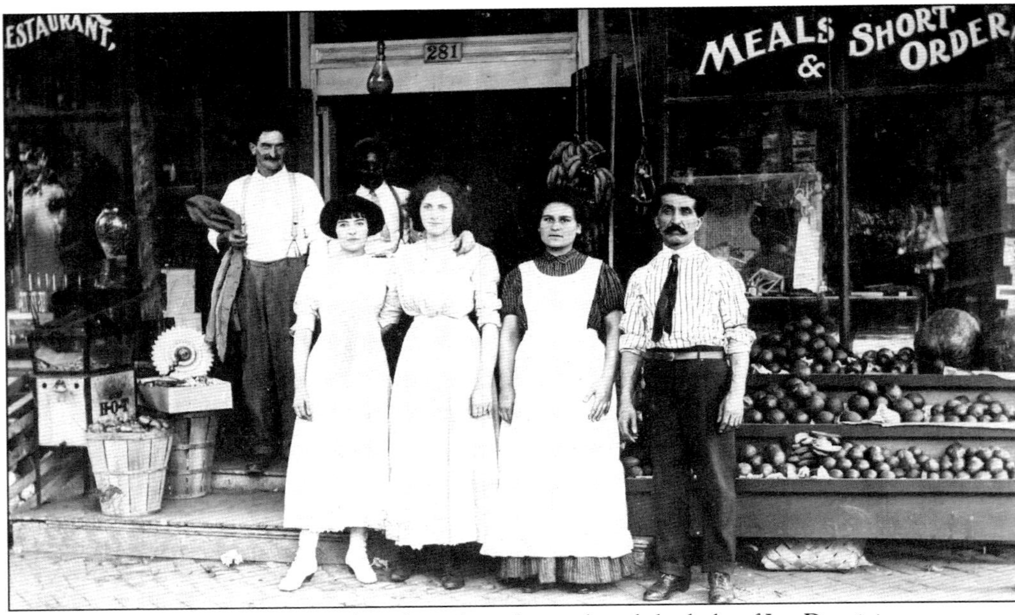

Little did the Scarletta family realize that when they enlisted the help of Joe Dentici, a young man from Italy, that they were signing on far more than an employee. Dentici not only fulfilled his obligation to help with the horses, but he also became a part of their grocery business and their family too. Dentici married their daughter and ultimately became manager of the Scarletta-Dentici family produce business, which still operates today. (Courtesy of the Dentici family.)

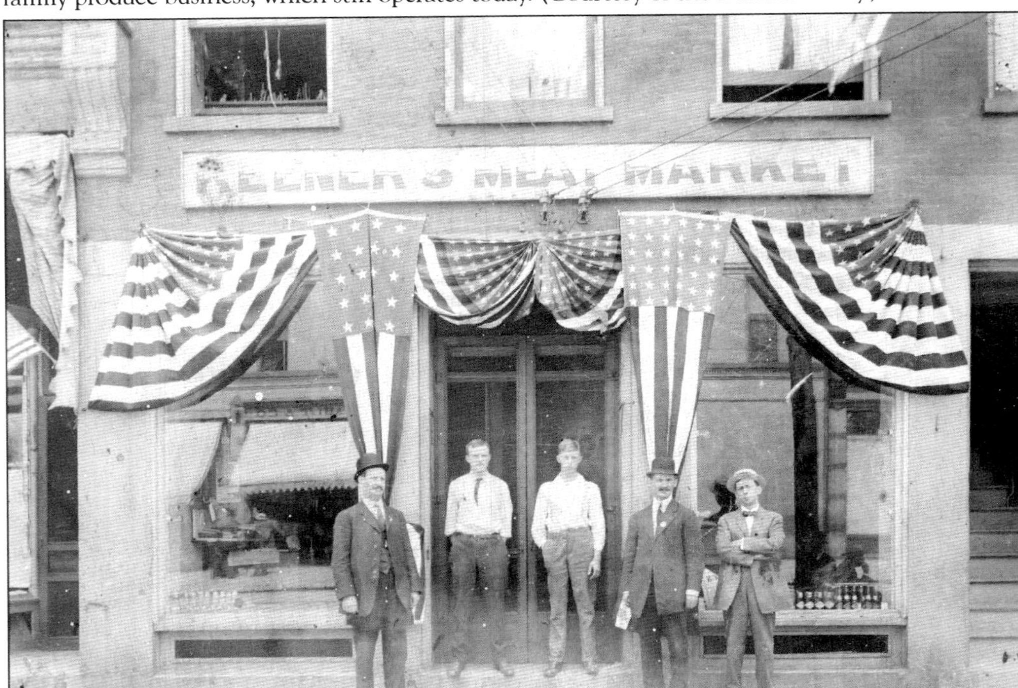

This business has been "all in the family," regardless of which family has owned it. Before Blaney's, it was Keener's Meat Market, located on Jefferson Street.

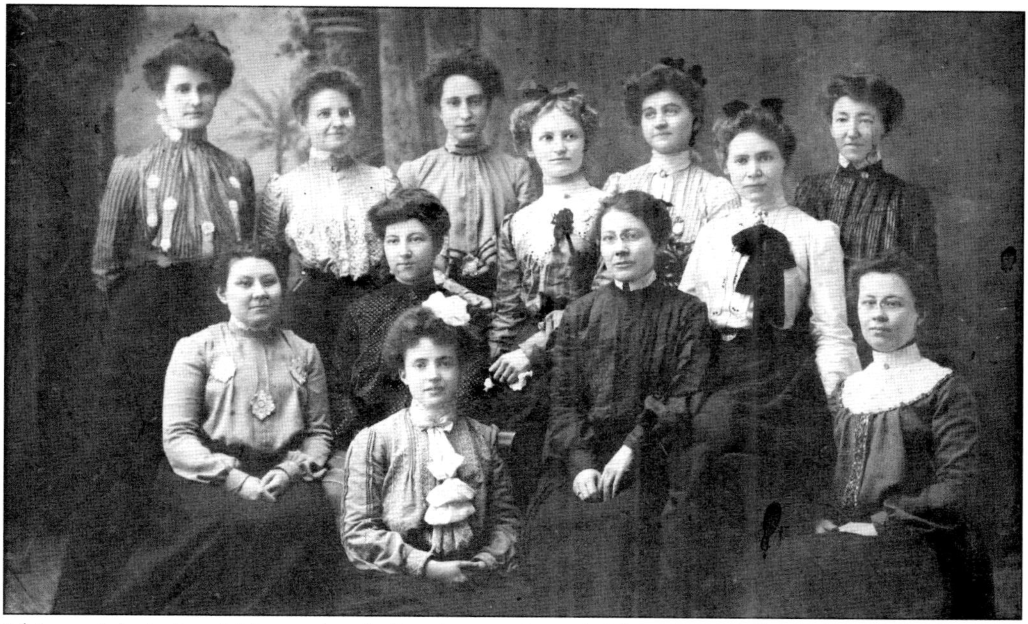

This social circle of Kittanning ladies is not identified by a particular name; however, it is believed that most lived in the first ward of town. Seen in this early 1900 photograph from left to right are (first row) Elwina Burge, Clara Lange Montgomery, Anna Burge Baum, Emma Burge, and Eliza Burge; (second row) Anna Leeger Gerheim, Anna Lindeman, Margaret Leeger, Zelma Hutchison Happi, Mary Lindeman, Dora Hutchison McCreit, and Bird Anderson.

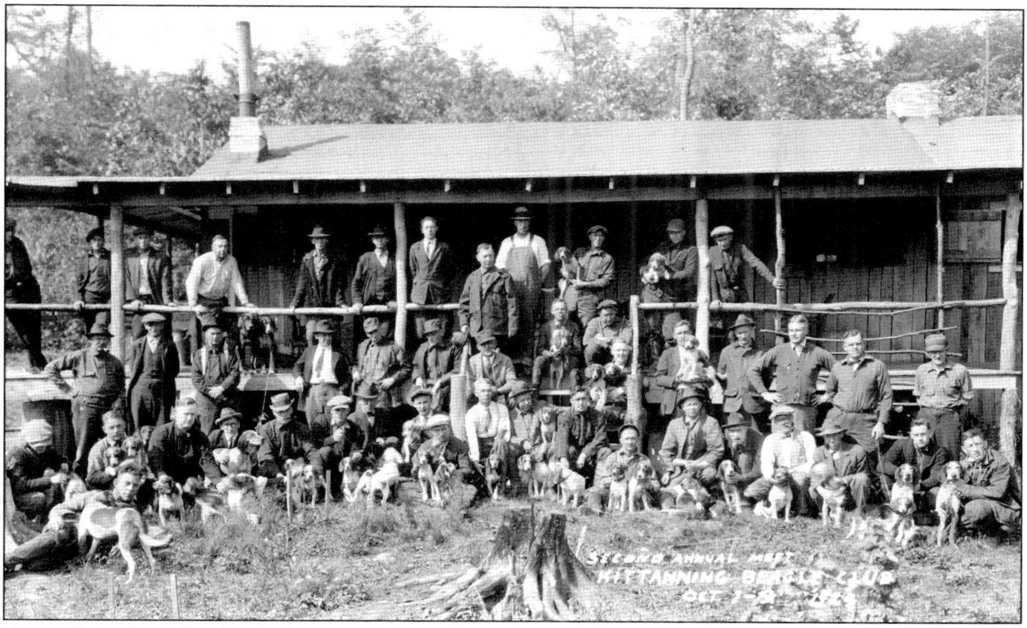

Even though individual identities are unknown, this group's purpose is easily seen. Close to 50 men and almost as many of "man's best friend" are pictured in this 1924 group photograph of the Kittanning Beagle Club. Kittanning is surrounded by an abundance of wildlife that could keep any sportsman or woman busy year-round, dog or no dog.

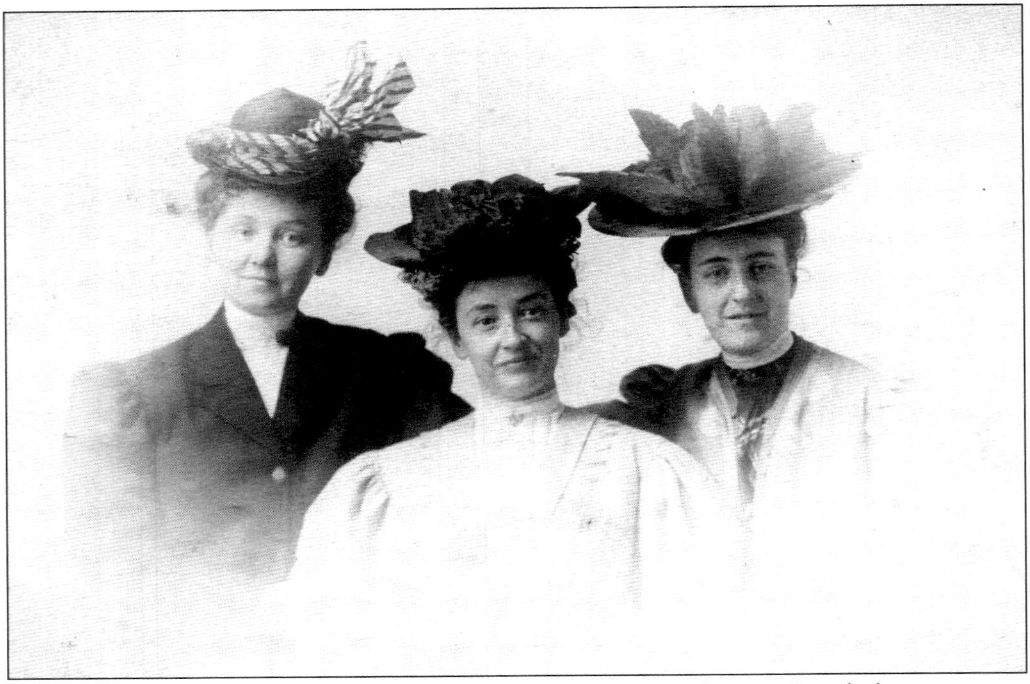

Such sayings as "birds of a feather stick together," or "a feather in their cap," might be appropriate for these photographs of ladies in their millinery. The popular use of feathers served as a catalyst for the formation of the Audubon Society in order to help preserve birds that were considered at risk because of the demand for their feathers in fashion.

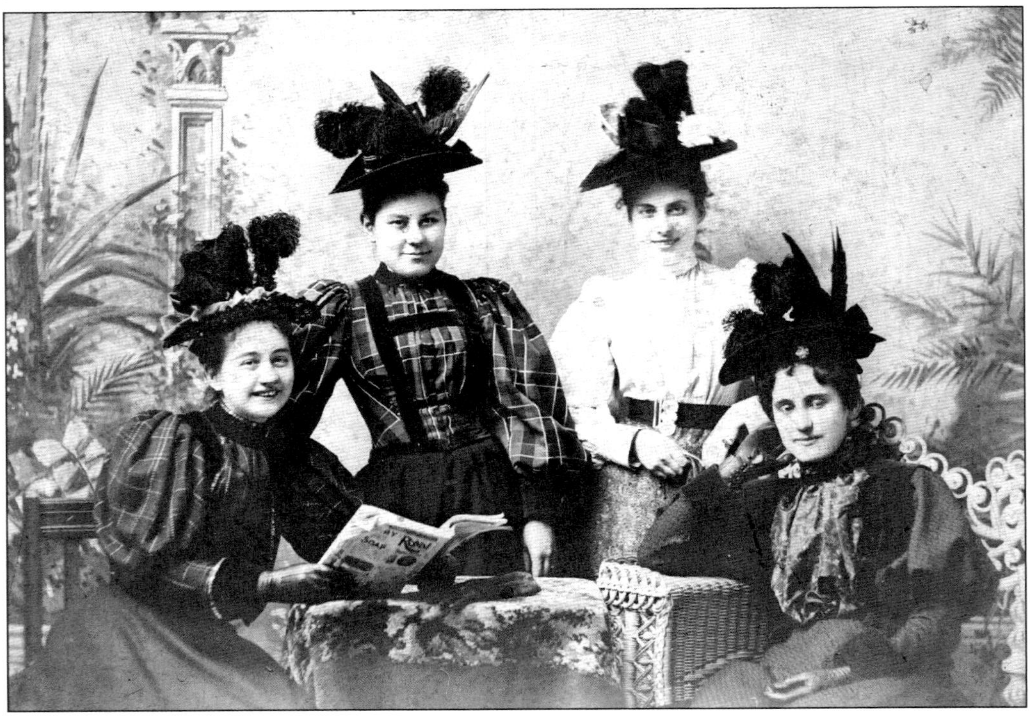

Hardly fine millinery, these two men, identified as Roy and Logan, nevertheless sport matching head wear in this amusing photograph. Kittanning is home to many fraternal, social, and church-related groups, all of which contribute to this town's family like atmosphere. Performances by amateur thespians like Roy and Logan were fairly common in the days of community-wide choral, music, and drama societies, however, most no longer exist.

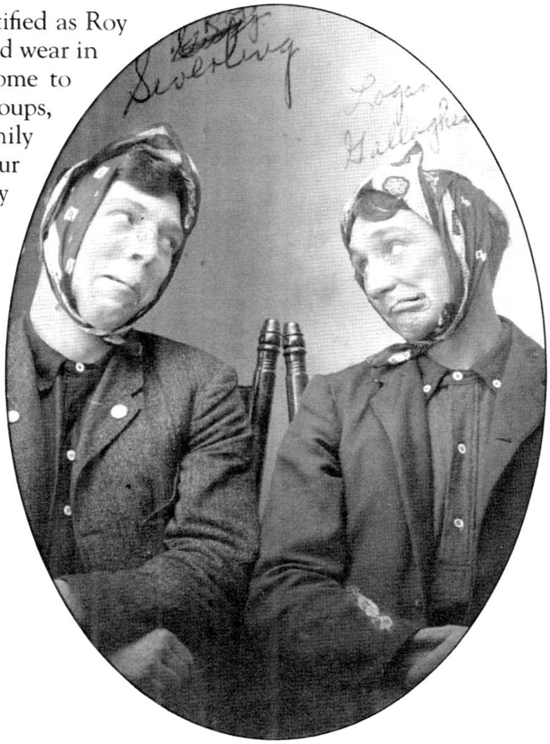

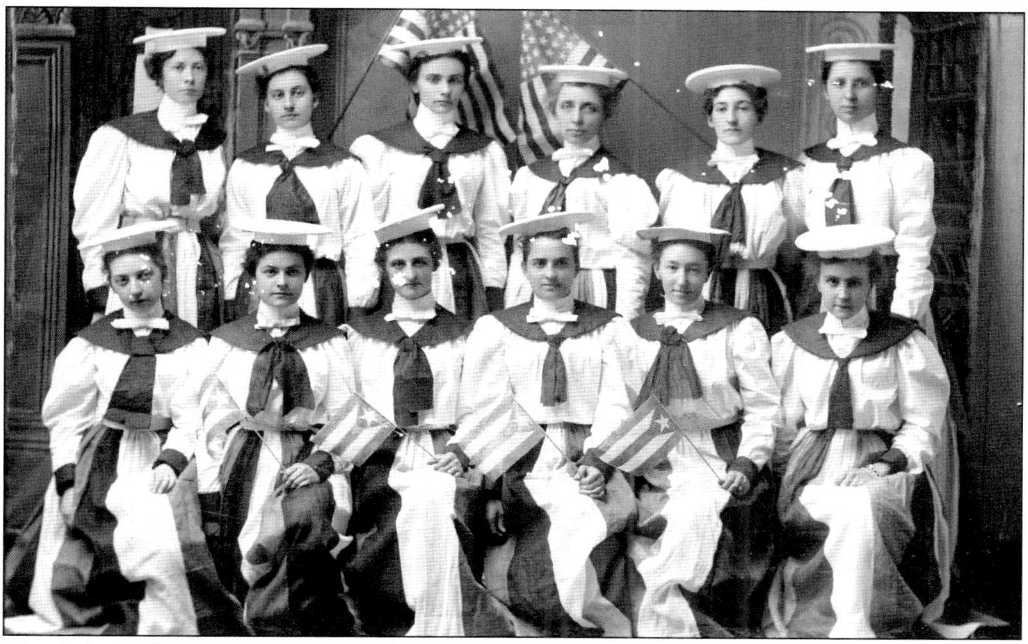

The Cuba and America Drill Team looks crisp in their matching garb in this late-19th-century photograph. It is believed to have been a performing group that emphasized synchronized, choreographed movement, but not much else is known about its specific origin or history. Alex H. Taylor is identified as the drill team's instructor and leader.

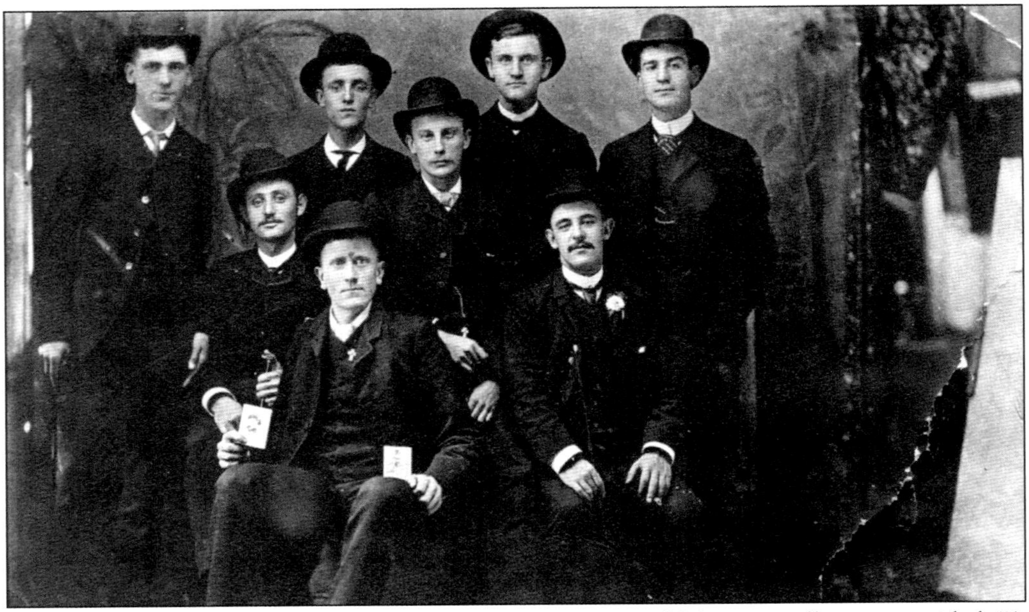

This photograph, a part of the Armstrong County Historical Museum collection, is titled, "A Popular Pastime of the 1880s—Having a group photograph made of hometown friends." In this particular case, the friends, from left to right, are (first row) Jacob R. Einstein, E. R. McMasters, and ? Wilson; (second row) James M. Stone, Basil Oswald, Henry Reichert, Dr. Alonzo P. N. Painter, and Walter Hays.

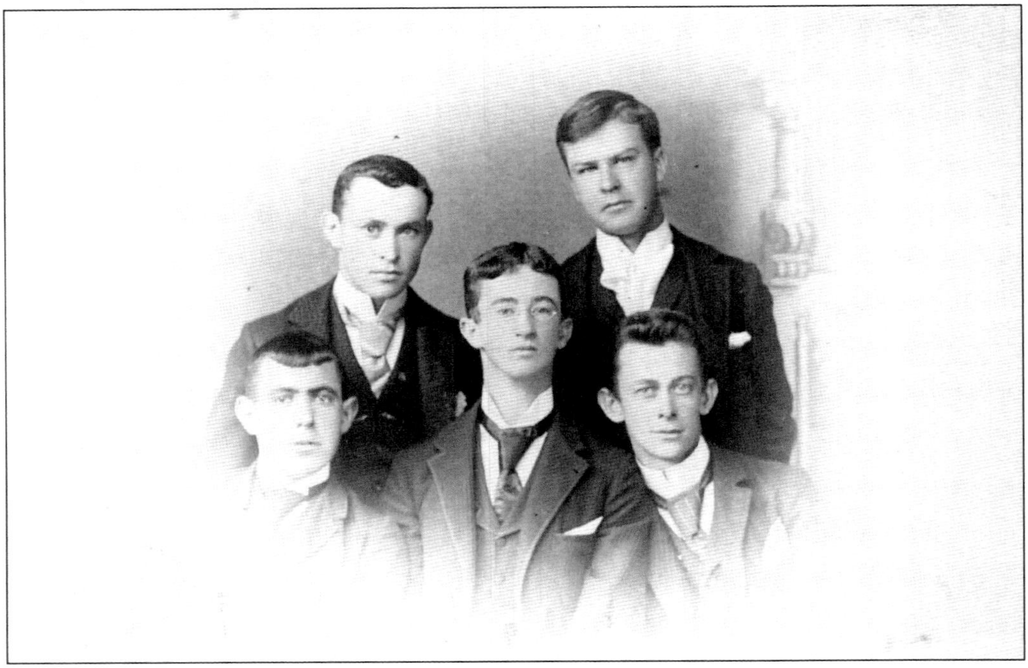

The popularity of group photographs apparently lasted at least until the next decade, as evidenced in this group of dashing young gentlemen, pictured in 1890. They are identified as Walter Jackson, Ross Sutton, Dave Blair, Will Hildebrand, and Hal White.

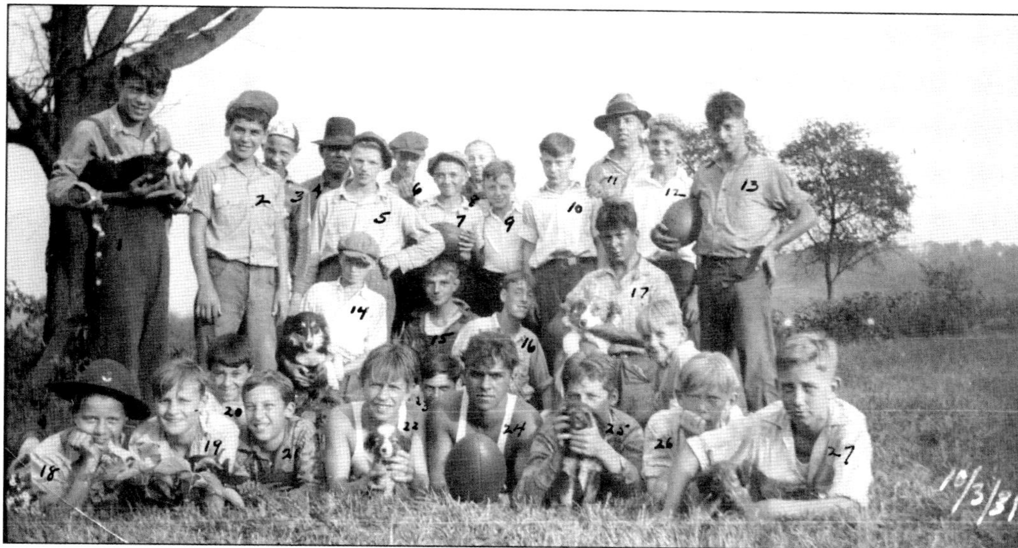

The boys pictured in this October 3, 1931, photograph are a reminder that there is no price tag on fun. From left to right are (first row) Donald Schrecengost, Bill Blaney, James Callas, Sam Hill, Walter Orr, Russell Beach, Joseph Angelo, Ogden Johnson, Vale Turney, and Everett Patton; (second row) Paul Hooks, John Blaney, Charles Stennett, Jack Mazzotta, and unidentified; (third row) David Cooke, Arthur McCullough, Gerald Schwartz, Jack Berline, Wayne Stover, Robert Rumbaugh, Joe Saloski, Austin Henry, Frances Stouffer, Harry Flenner, Mr. Matisko, Jones Hetrick, and Peter Mazzotta. (Courtesy of the Lundeman family.)

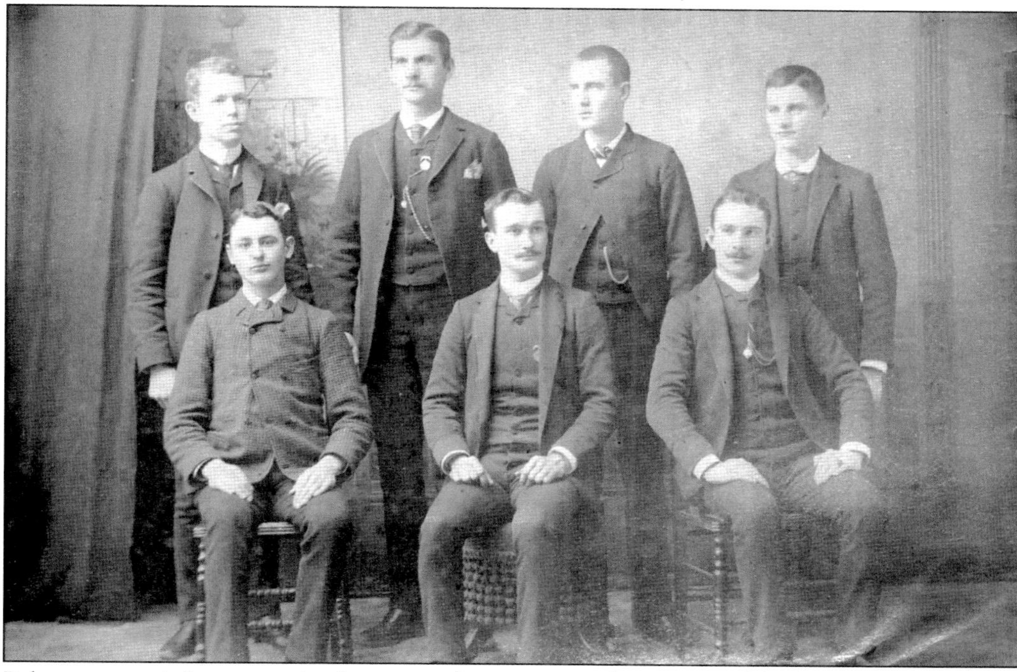

Polo was certainly not as simple to coordinate as a pickup game of football or baseball. But Kittanning did produce a polo team. Identified here are Bill Jessup, Joe McIlwain, Jim Kennerdell, Ed Hutchison, Bill Noble, and Jim Bush.

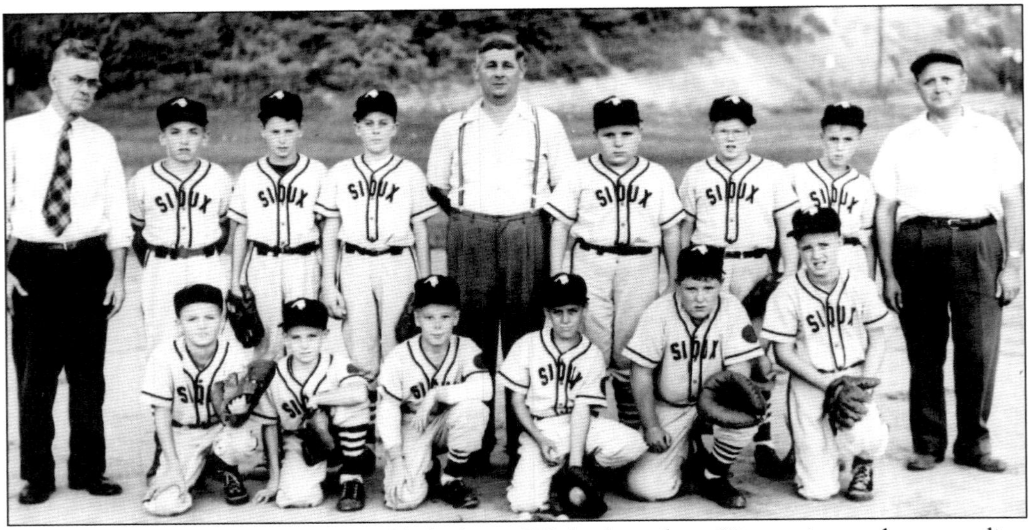

The Lenape Little League was established in 1950 for boys from Kittanning and surrounding areas. Pictured is the original Sioux team from the Wick City area. From left to right are (first row) Bob Hayes, Harry Beckwith Jr., Bill Hill, Bob Delp, Dale Slagle, and Jay Smith; (second row) George Starr, Jim Emminger, Hilton Williams, Bill Kammerdiener, Chuck Kammerdiener, Bo Yount, Ed Cravener, John Carley, and Harry Beckwith Sr. Harry Beckwith Jr. went on to follow in his father's footsteps and have a successful coaching career, with three students—Mitch Frerotte, Gus Frerotte, and Larry Shepard—going on to play in the National Football League. (Courtesy of Pete Harmon.)

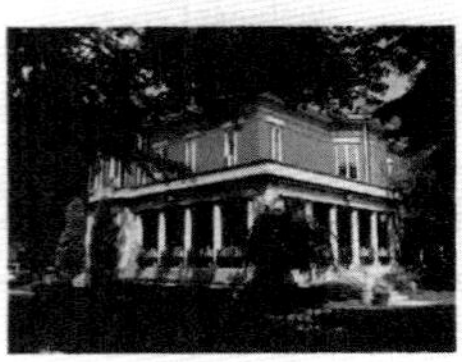

The Y began in 1869, when 16 young men gathered together to charter the organization, appointing officers, establishing committees, and approving bylaws. By 1870, however, participation greatly declined, and the group fell behind in its rent payments. With less than $10 in the bank and even fewer members, this small group took a big chance by hosting a public lecture series with such notable speakers as Samuel Langhorn Clemens (also known as Mark Twain) and political activist Frederick Douglas. Both Twain and Douglas were well received by the Kittanning public. The series netted an amazing $900, helping to put the floundering Y in the black again.

Four

Floods, Farms, and Folks at Work

Kittanning's close proximity to the Allegheny River has usually been a blessing to this town. Not only has the river provided life-sustaining water for consumption, it has also provided this commodity needed for so many other domestic and work-related practices. The Allegheny River, as a watery path to the rest of the world, has also enabled Kittanning to be engaged in commerce that would have otherwise been impractical or impossible.

Although man's attempts to harness this river for his own purposes have usually succeeded, there were such memorable events as the floods of 1913 and 1936 that reminded Kittanning's residents that the upper hand was not always theirs.

The rich soil of adjacent riverbeds provided Kittanning residents with edible crops throughout the years. While farming and other agriculture-related businesses have been the mainstay for many in rural Armstrong County, due to the size of town properties, among other factors, farming as a primary source of income was really not feasible in this county seat. This did not, however, prohibit other business ventures that utilized the abundant natural resources germane to this area to prosper in Kittanning such as clay mining and brick making.

Kittanning's role as the home for county government allowed businesses that provided goods and services for travelers and county residents come to town to prosper because of the steady stream of clientele. Family-operated small businesses were at the heart of Kittanning's work-a-day world.

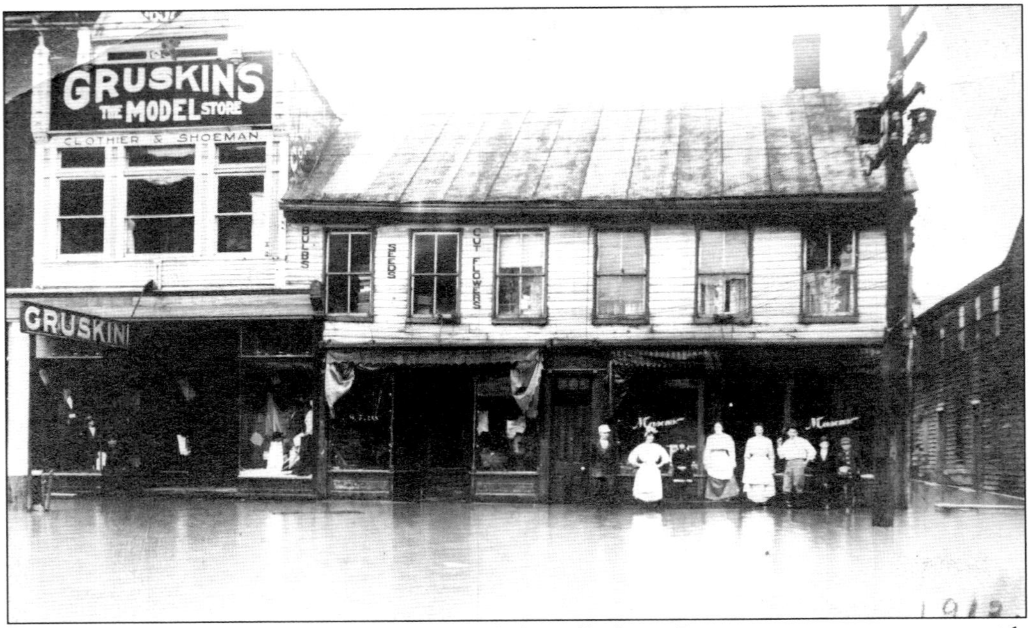

Although high water and minor flooding of the Allegheny River was not uncommon with cyclical weather changes, such as a spring ice melt, some floods remain unforgettable. Since its incorporation in 1800, Kittanning's floods of particular note were in 1832, 1835, 1837, 1865, 1875, 1913, 1936, and 1959. Seen in these photographs, the flood of March 27, 1913, wreaked much havoc in this county seat.

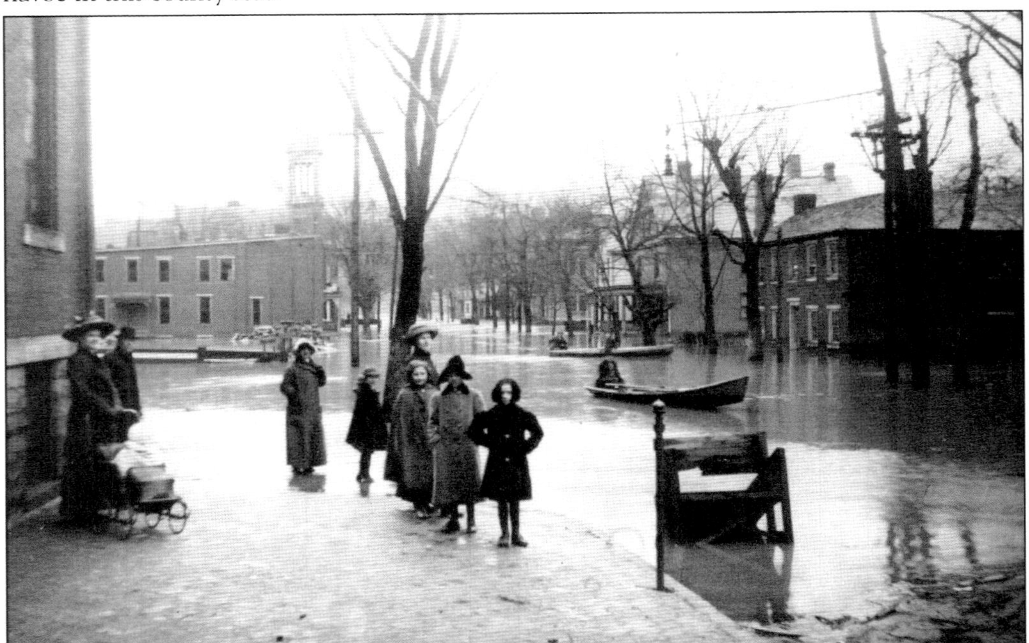

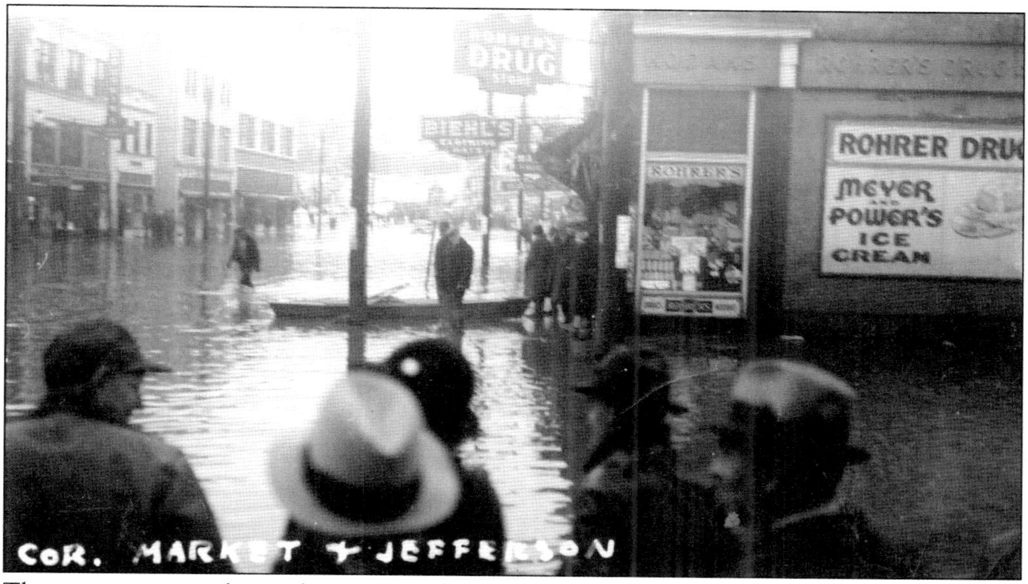

These street scenes depict the severity of the flood of March 1936. Although water levels were damaging to much of the downtown area, as evidenced by these photographs, Kittanning amazingly fared better than points south on the Allegheny River, including Pittsburgh. These photographs, attributed to the photography of Roger Stone, illustrate conditions at Market and Jefferson Street, above, and Vine and McKean Streets, below. As a result of this disaster, two flood-control dams were constructed in Armstrong County at Crooked and Mahoning Creeks.

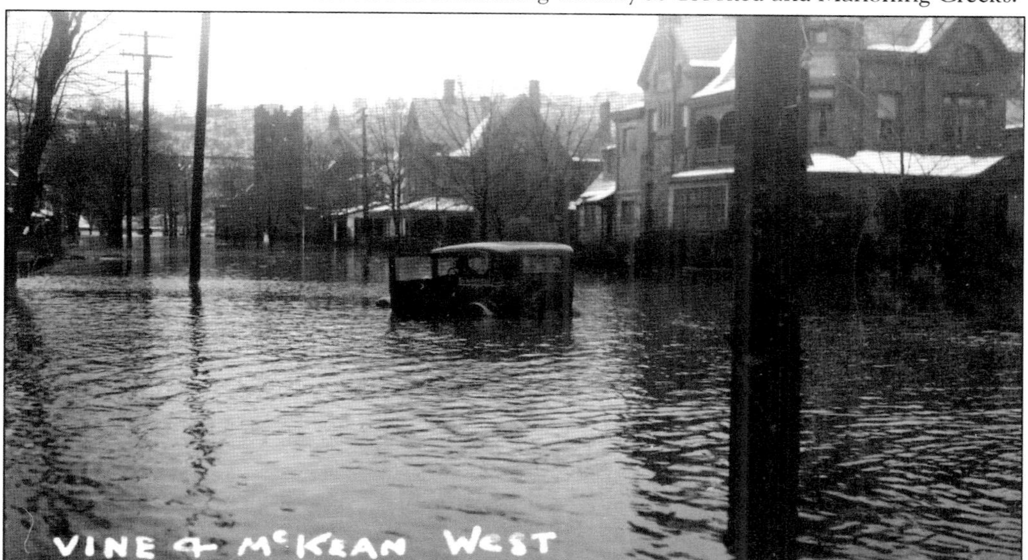

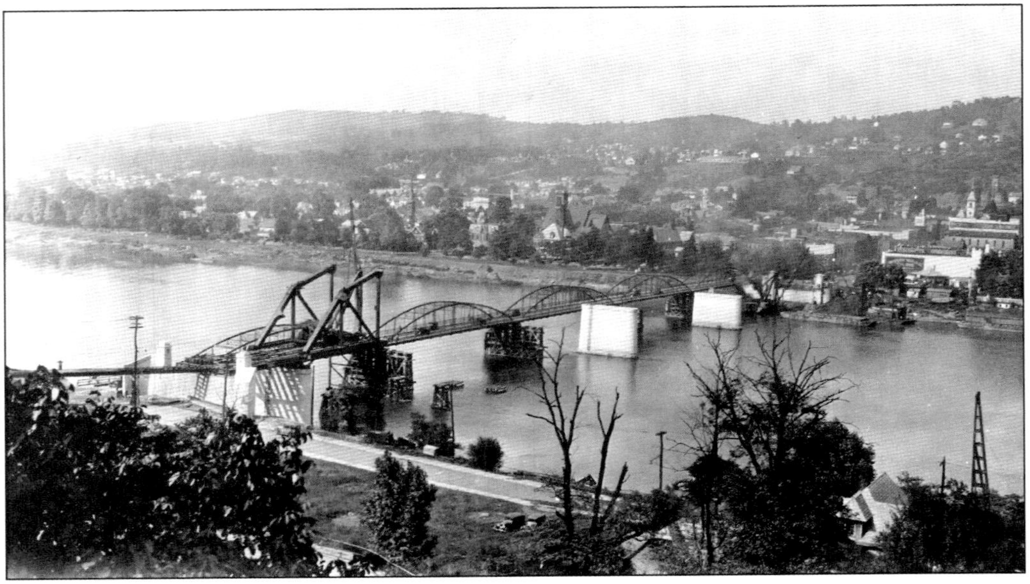

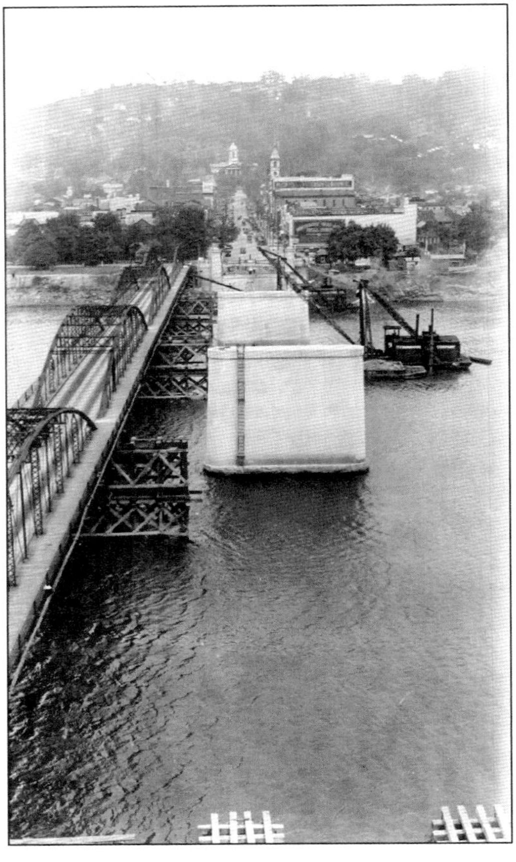

Known today as the Citizens Bridge, the span that connects West Kittanning and points beyond to Market Street and the borough was constructed in 1931. The entire process went smoothly and provided the community with a connection that has proven reliable since then.

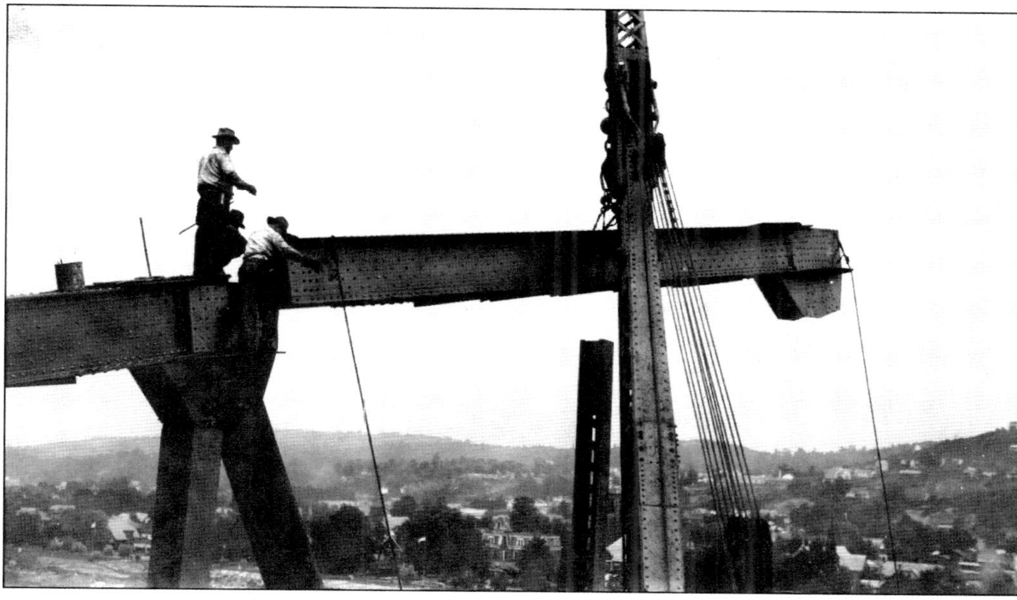

As seen in these construction close-ups, this was a bridge made of steel rather than the iron used for its predecessor. Records indicate that work proceeded ahead of schedule from start to finish, a bonus for area travelers.

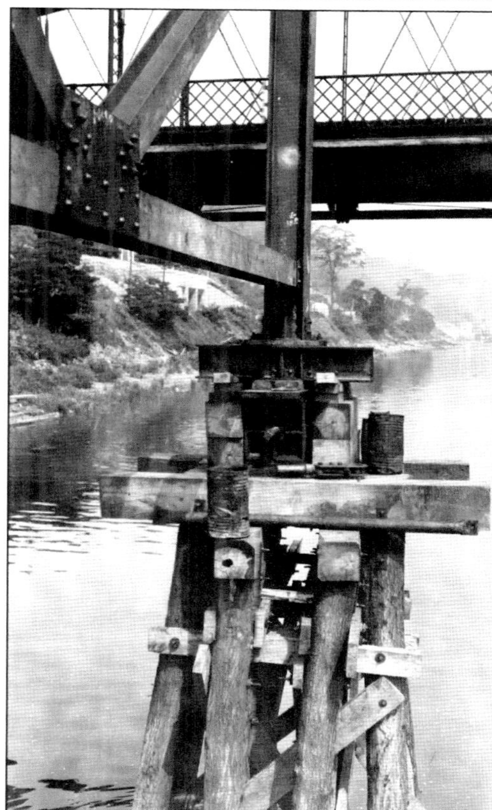

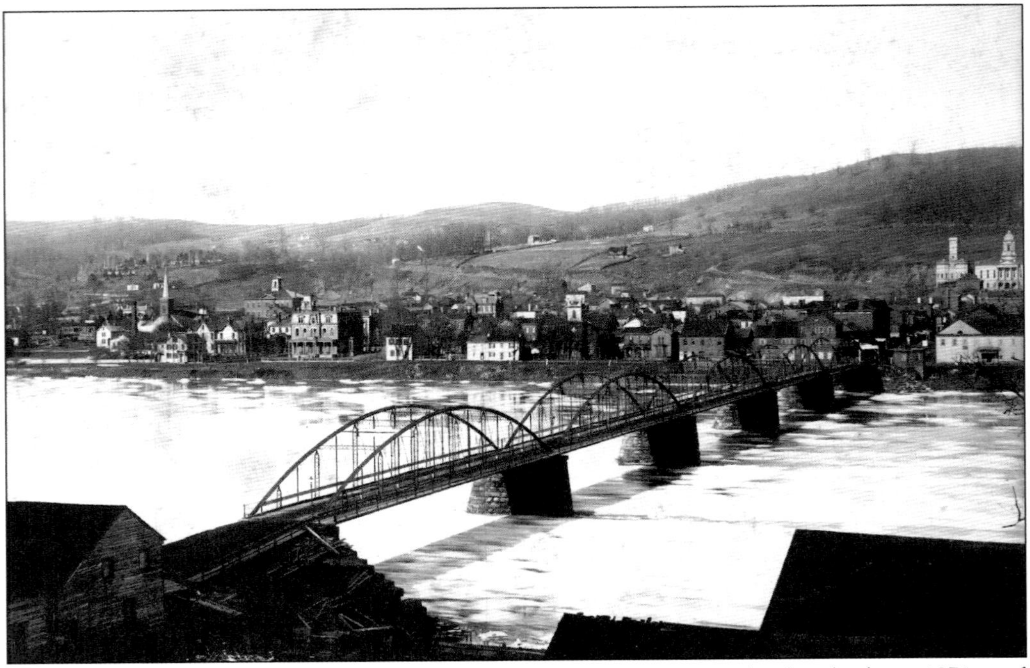

These photographs provide a study in contrasts of the Kittanning bridge, built in 1874, and the nearly-complete Citizens Bridge of 1931. Because of the engineering plan, which essentially coordinated parallel destruction of the older, stone-pillared bridge with the construction of the new, steel superstructure, traffic was only truly halted for a day.

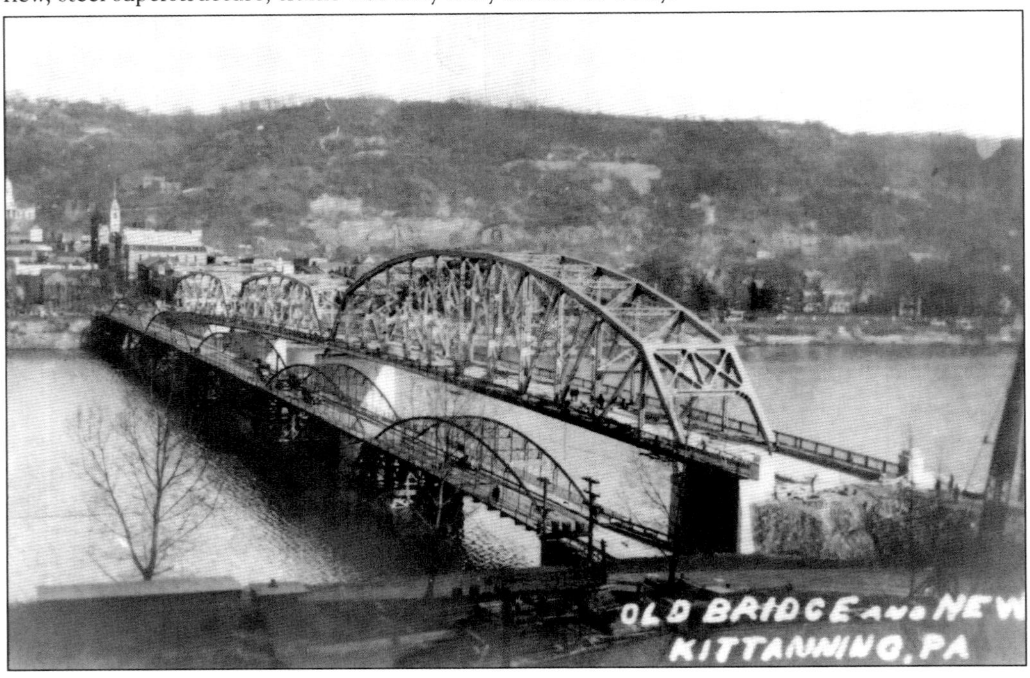

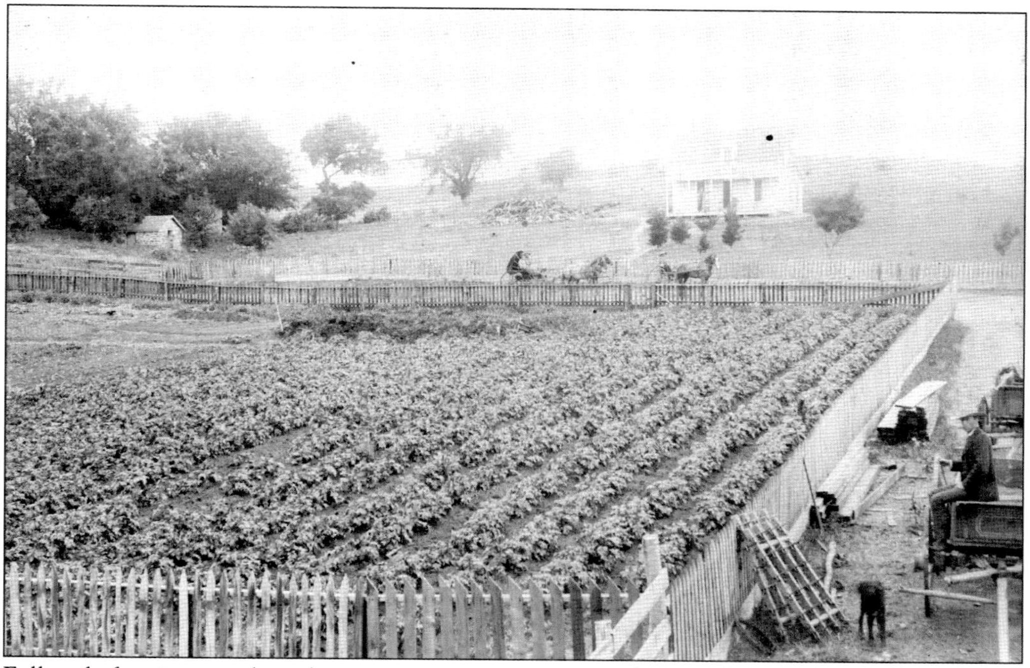

Full-scale farming may have been a common way to earn a living in Armstrong County but not in the borough of Kittanning, where vegetables grown in a garden this size would be considered a bumper crop.

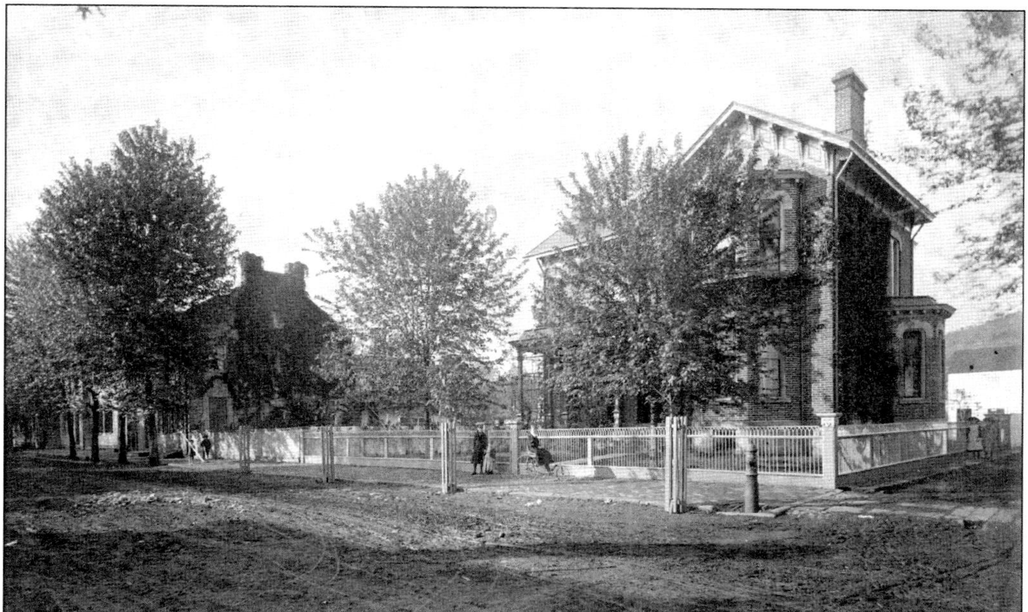

This grand house located on the corner of North Jefferson and Arch Streets was not a typical borough bungalow, but it does illustrate the close proximity of neighbors and limited lot size. No longer a single, private residence, this house has been home to tenants such as the public library and professional offices.

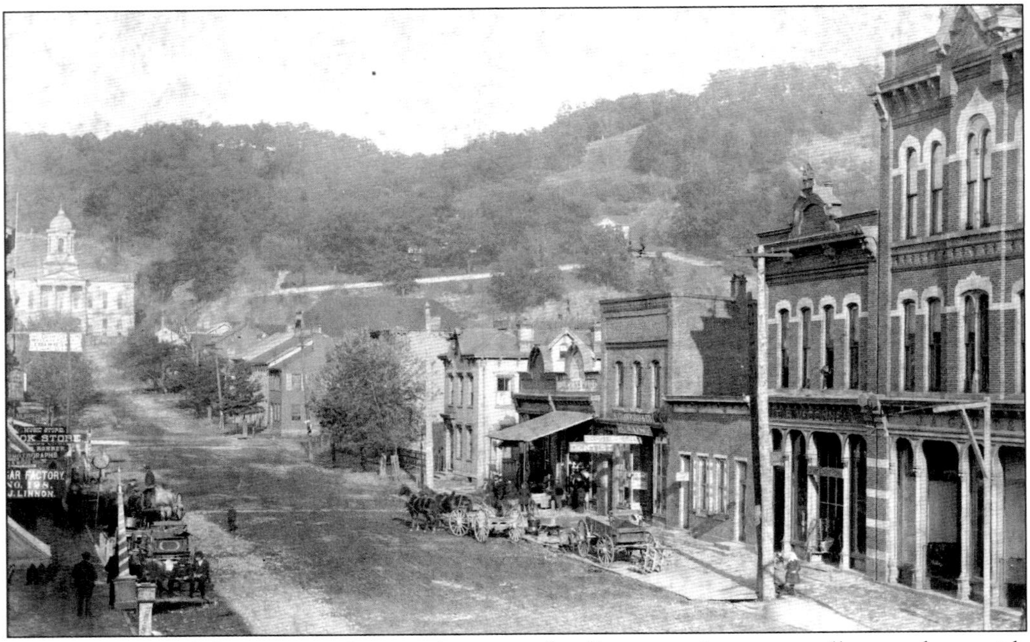

This is a view of downtown of many days gone by. Street paving eventually was done with mostly bricks, however, dirt and mud remained an annoyance and health issue even into the 20th century.

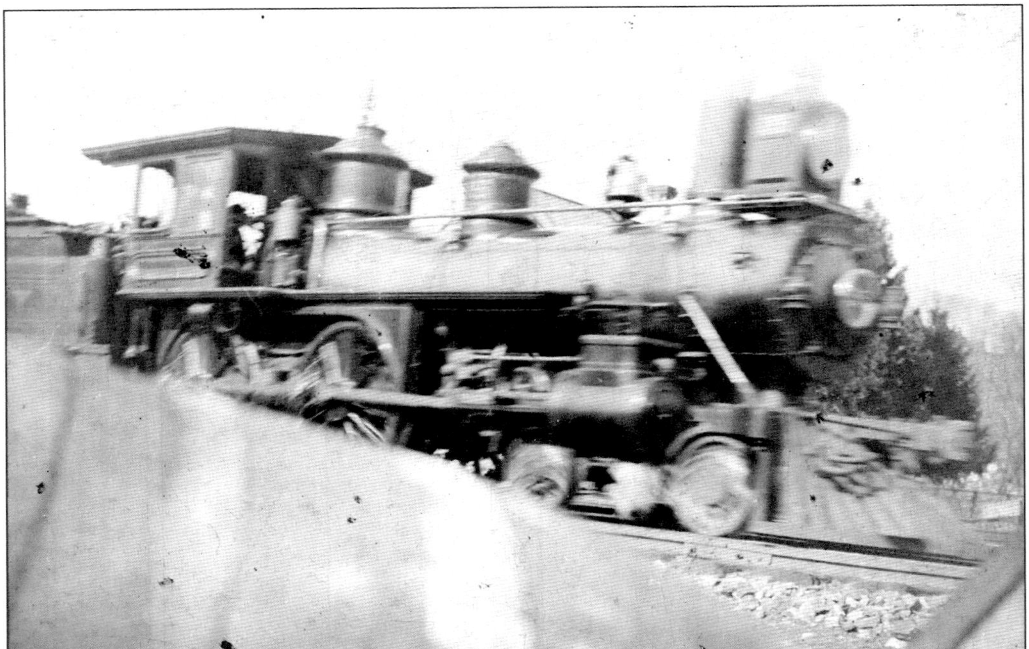

The steam engine came to town in 1856, 100 years after the battle of Kittanning. The Allegheny Valley Railroad added its rails to these trails, as seen in this 1893 photograph of an engine.

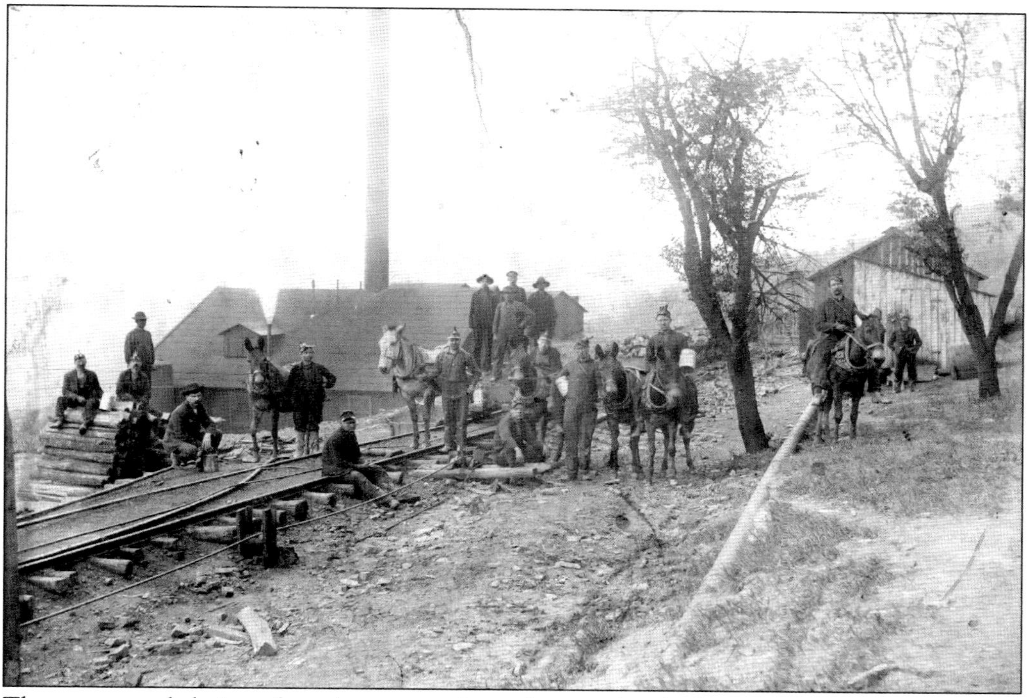

These men and their mules take a pause from their work, which was converting Kit-han-ne's trails to Kittanning's rails.

Red, White and Blue

J. E. REICHERT, City Drug Store,
E. H. WRIGHT, Dentist.
TYSON HEILMAN, Real Estate,
H. A. ARNOLD, Insurance Agent,
JOHN MARSHALL & CO., Foundry,
CLAY MANUFACTURING CO.
JOHN RHODES, Cabinetmaker,
J. L. CLARK, Plumber,
A. L. GEORGE, Restaurant-Bakery
L. E. BIEHL, Clothier,

Represented by E. S. Hutchison, J. M. Stone, Frank Weylman, Joseph Volk, A. H. Taylor, J. M. Shankle, James Snyder, Frank Neubert, J. B. McClelland, J. B. Kennedell, Harry Hague, H. K. Mohr, H. E. Moesta, Bert Luker, W. F. Knoble, J. D. Knoble, A. L. George, R. A. Crum, J. O. Crum and J. A. Fox, comprising Hose Company, No. 2.

1 Kittanning, the gem of the valley,
Its merchants are honest and true,
Its tradesmen are prosperous and happy,
To their success we give you the cue.
They are men of all trades and professions,
Their names are not unknown or new;
They succeed in their chosen vocations,
They are men of the red, white and blue.

CHORUS.

Three cheers for the red, white and blue,
Three cheers for the red, white and blue;
Our merchants and mechanics forever,
Three cheers for the red, white and blue.

2 Go to Reichert when pain racks your body,
When pain racks your teeth go to Wright;
There is no sense in growling or cussing,
And it don't cure your teeth to get tight.
But Reichert has medicine to cure you,
And Wright's work is firm, and it's true;
See them both at the top of fame's ladder,
Wright, Reichert and the red, white and blue.

CHORUS.

Much time, effort, and sometimes corny humor went into the readings and songs that were crafted for this late 19th century community celebration. Many people and businesses were parodied in original works such as this, which were published for the occasion.

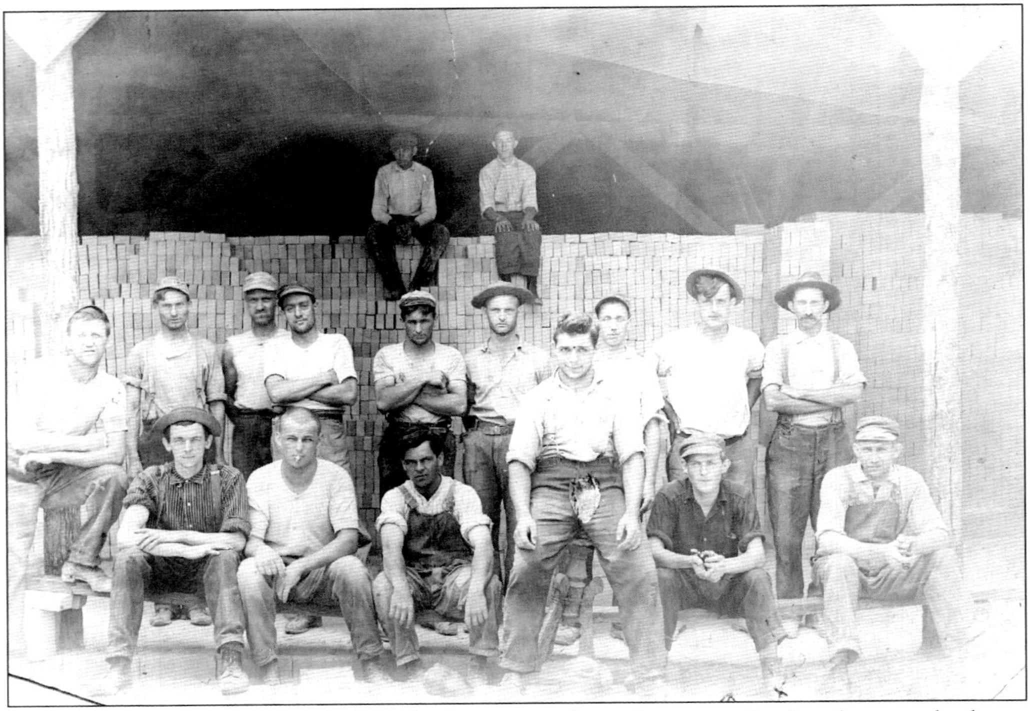

Kittanning brick making provided jobs for men such as these seen in the photograph above. Although the photograph below does not depict what one may think of as bricks, they actually are. Firebricks were and are a product that Kittanning brick makers have become known for in many areas of industry. Despite their size and shape, these refractory bricks are critical to the steel-making process. (Below, courtesy of Richard Laube and family.)

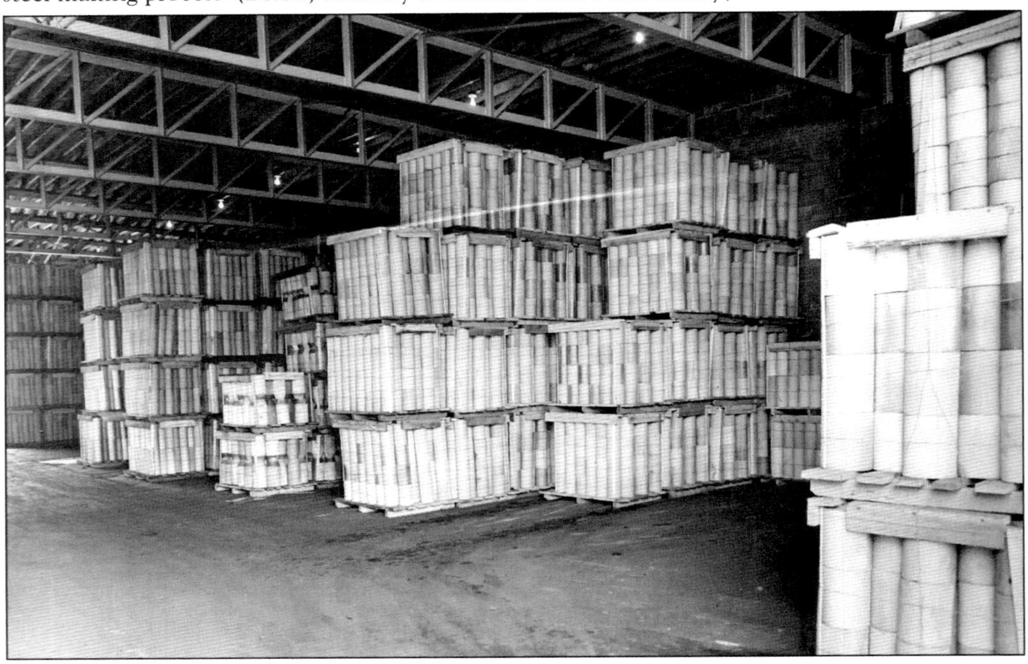

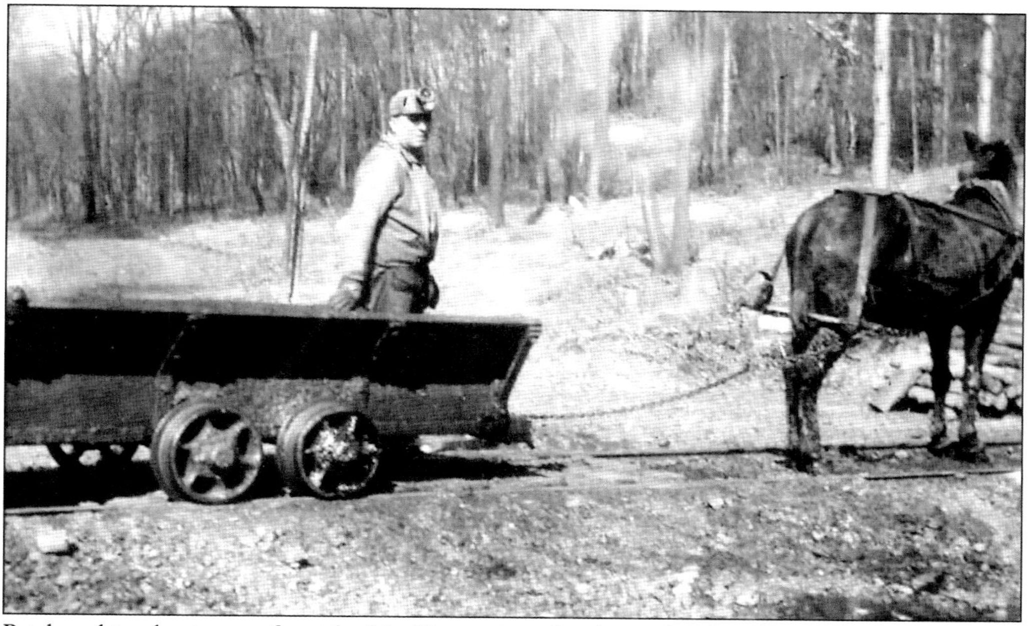

Brick-making businesses flourished in Kittanning, thanks to the abundance of local clay stores and their proximity to Pittsburgh area steel makers. Paul Morrow is credited with starting the first such business in 1806. As evidenced by these pictures, earlier mining processes used mule power to bring this commodity to the surface with the encouragement of tracks and human persuasion. What is not seen is the labor necessary to load the cart—a mining process, done chiefly by hand, even into the 20th century. (Courtesy of Richard Laube and family.)

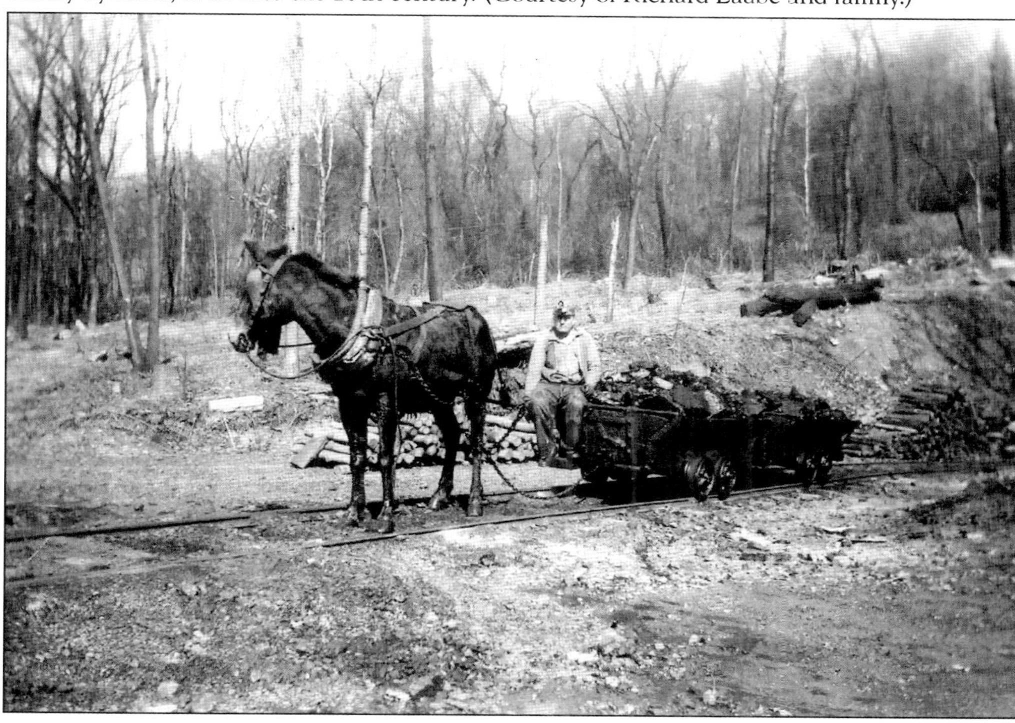

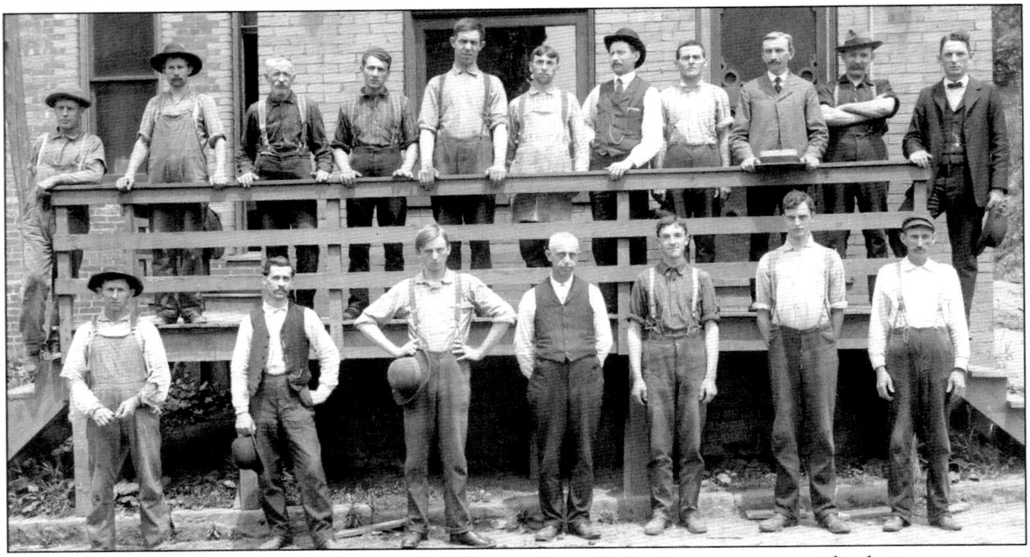

Employees of the American Planing Mill located on Oak Avenue pose with their supervisor W. A. Nicholson in this 1906 photograph. Nicholson, also seen as a teacher for the adult Bible classes of the First Baptist Church, is the gentleman dressed in the suit and tie at the top right of the photograph. Also pictured from left to right are (first row) C. Kunkle, O. C. Rairigh, Lee Patton, W. McMartin, Charles King, B. Gumbert, and W. Remaley; (second row) Ed Shotts, J. Geary, E. Shankle, J. Mechling, H. Hileman, H. Rupp, J. D. Williams, R. Kinnard, A. N. Wilson, R. M. McGregor, and Nicholson.

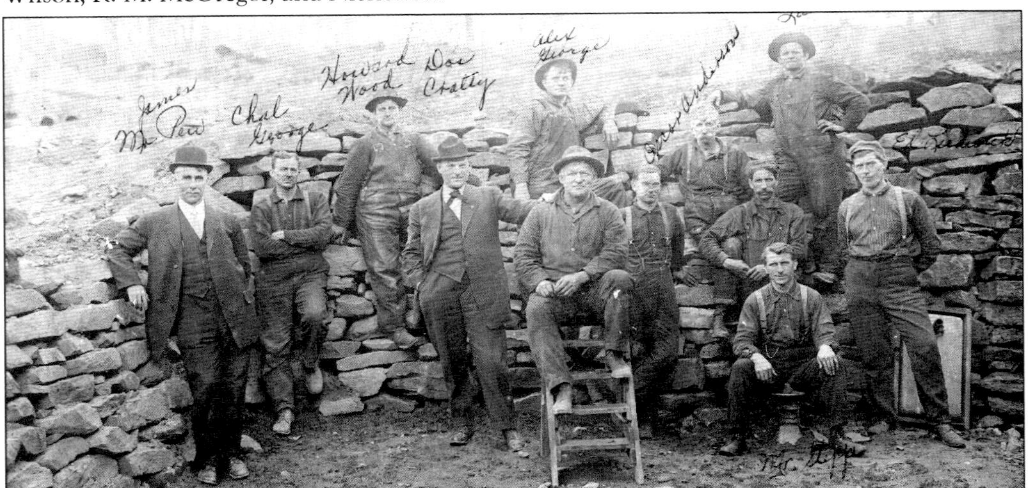

Natural gas provided local residents and businesses with a ready source of heat and capital. Ownership, whether private or through purchase of business shares, has been considered profitable and widespread among members of the business and professional community in Armstrong County. Prior to the use of fracturization, local gas wells were described as yielding about 100,000 cubic feet per day. Since then, it has not been uncommon for wells to produce three to four times that amount. The Peoples Gas Company employees are seen in this photograph, believed to be taken around 1910. Identified here are James Pew, Chal George, Howard Wood, Doc Cratty, "Uncle" Jake Siverling, Alex George, Oscar Anderson, Grant Lawson, Ed Ludwick, and Mr. Stepp.

3 Tys. Heilman has built, sold and rented,
Lots and houses contribute to his fame.
Fire is quenched, flame defied, loss prevented,
Harry Arnold and insurance mean the same.
With Arnold all loss is prevented ;
His insurance and Hose Company No 2
So protect you, when by fire you are tormented,
That they shield you like the red, white and blue.

CHORUS.

4 Our foundry is owned by John Marshall,
His wares, like his work, are up to date ;
The Clay Manufacturing Comp'ny
Make the best brick of any in the state.
For stoves, grates and back walls and hearthings,
For walls and for paving, these two,
The Brick Works and Foundry are owned by
The defenders of the red, white and blue

CHORUS.

5 Of mechanics whose work is abiding
John Rhodes is an expert in wood ;
J. L. Clark is a plumber so faithful
That the "biler" couldn't bust if it would.
Skilled workman, they say charged outrageous ;
Our answer to this is, 'taint true ;
Clark and Rhodes do good work for such prices
As give credit to the red, white and blue.

CHORUS.

6 Al. George fills you full when you're hungry,
Al. George sells you drink when you're dry ;
Louis Biehl sells the clothes that will warm you,
And Louie's prices never are too high.
The trade of these two men is booming,
Those who boom like these two men are few :
George and Biehl are old boomers from Boomtown,
And they boom for the red, white and blue.

CHORUS.

—8—

Even when there seemed to be little rhyme or reason to the verse, a concerted effort to spare no one seemed apparent in the full volume of skits and prose that comprised the jubilee celebration booklet from which this excerpt was taken.

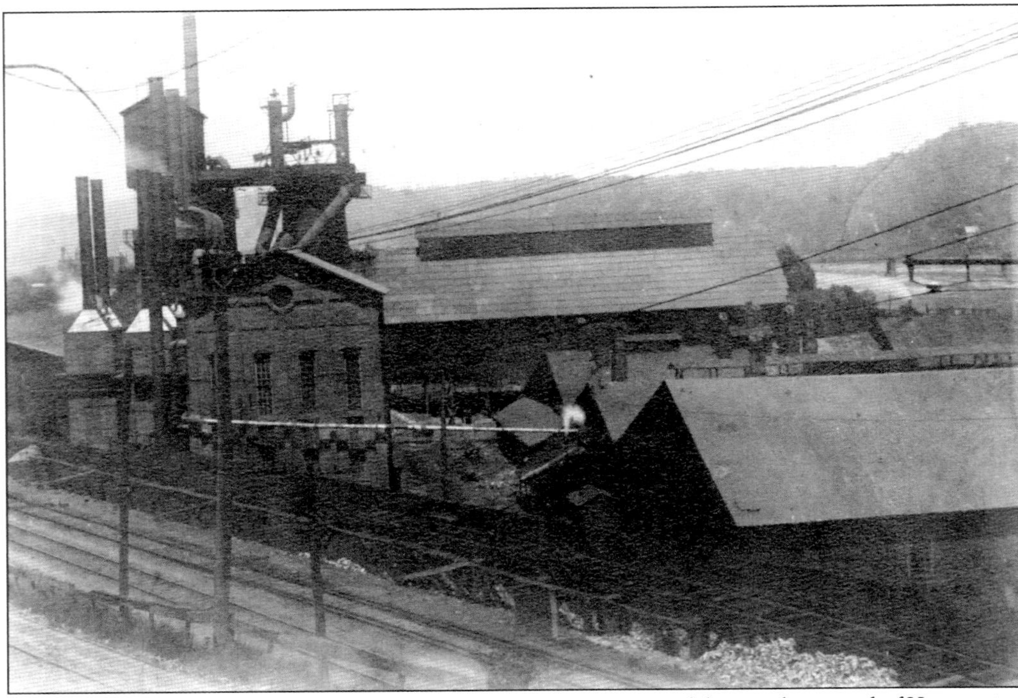

The Kittanning Iron and Steel Works occupied a large portion of the southern end of Kittanning close to the Allegheny River. Approximately 700 workers were employed either by the steel fabricator itself or the natural resource-related industries, such as coal mining, which were integral parts of the whole process. This mill was home to what was known as Rebecca Furnace, which was reported as operating with a four-hour casting procedure.

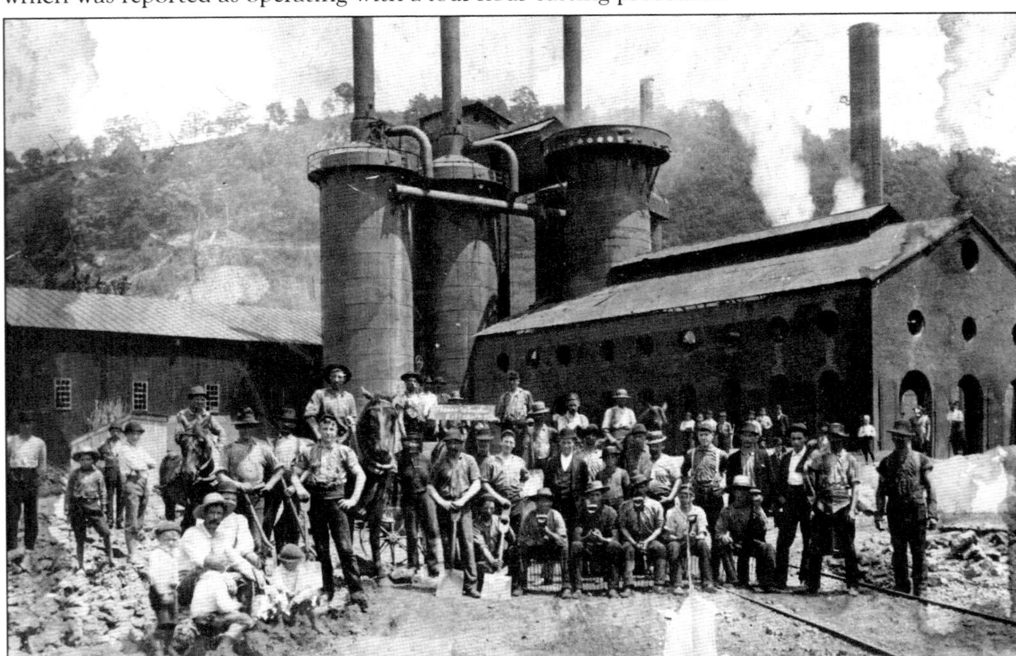

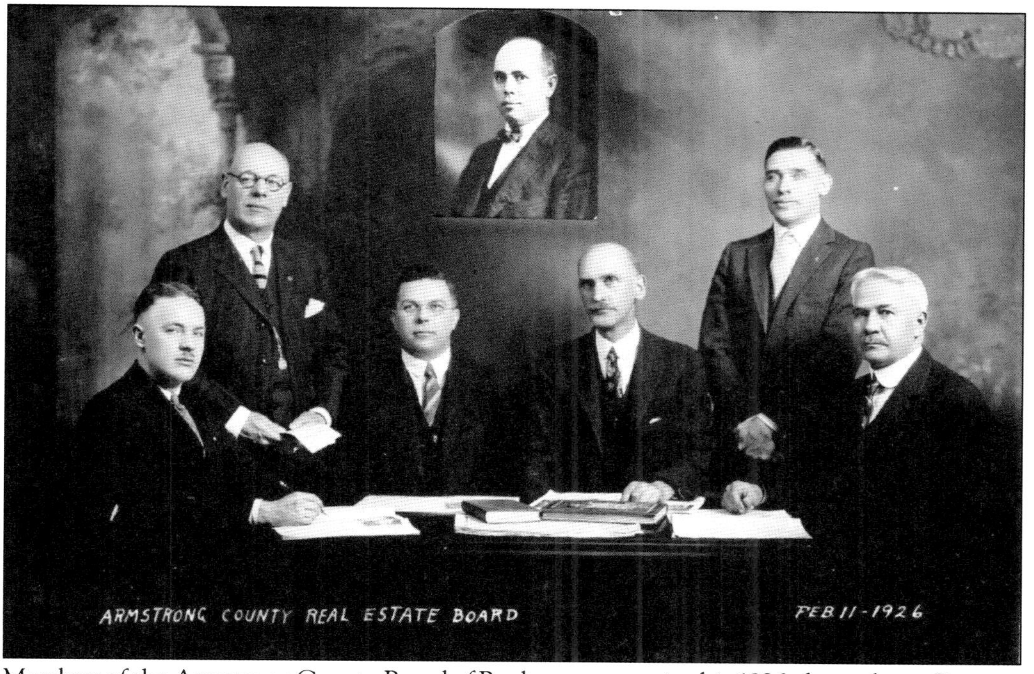

Members of the Armstrong County Board of Realtors are seen in this 1926 photo above. Because Kittanning is the home of the Armstrong County Courthouse, where land transactions are legalized and recorded, real estate businesses have been a presence in the town for any years.

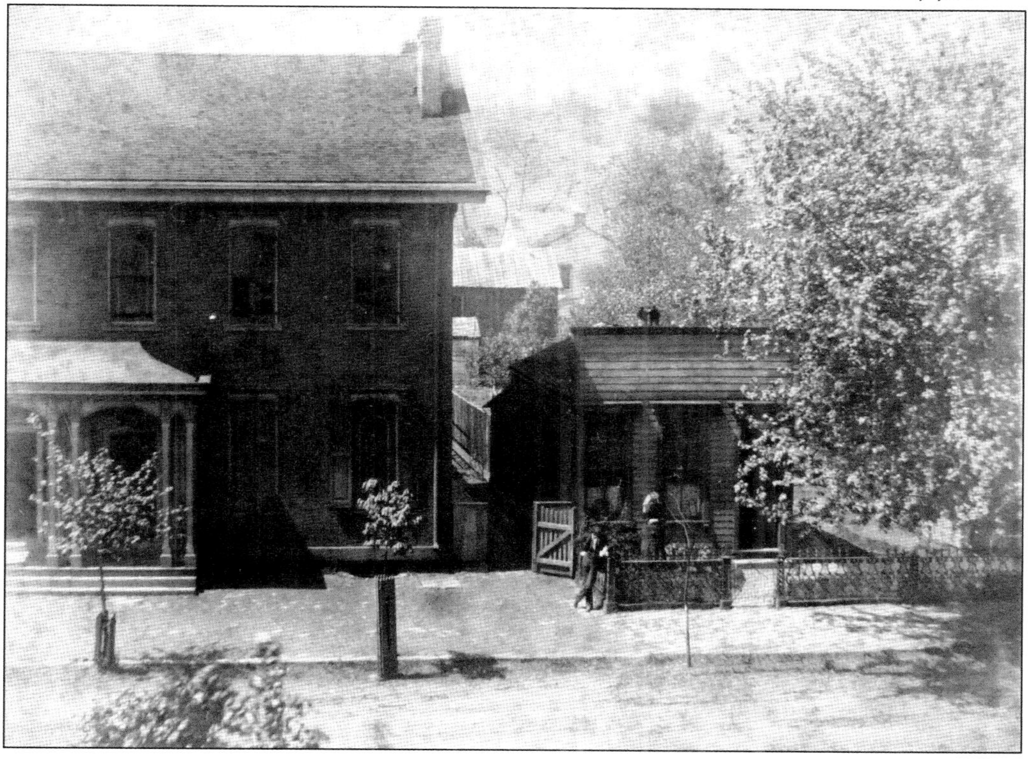

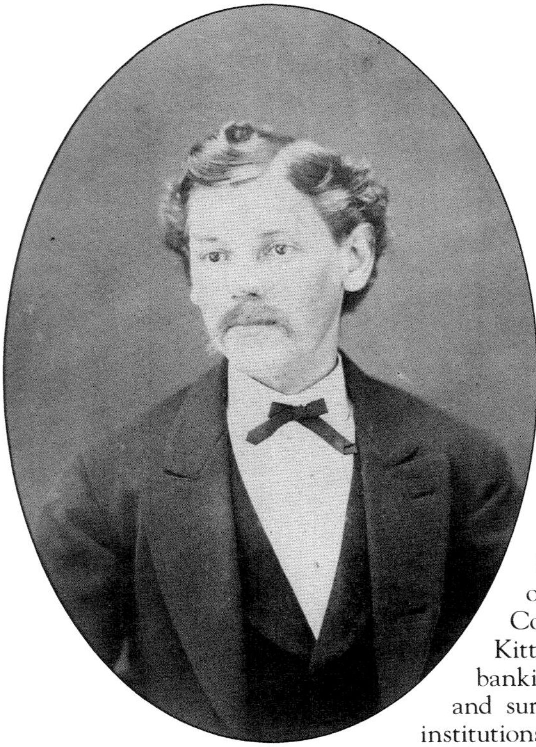

Pictured at left is J. A. Fox, a prominent member of Kittanning's banking community. Below is the business of money, as carried out by the Safe Deposit and Title Guarantee Company, of which Fox was associated with. Kittanning is able to boast of its solid history of banking, as the town entered the Great Depression and survived this time with the same number of institutions—four.

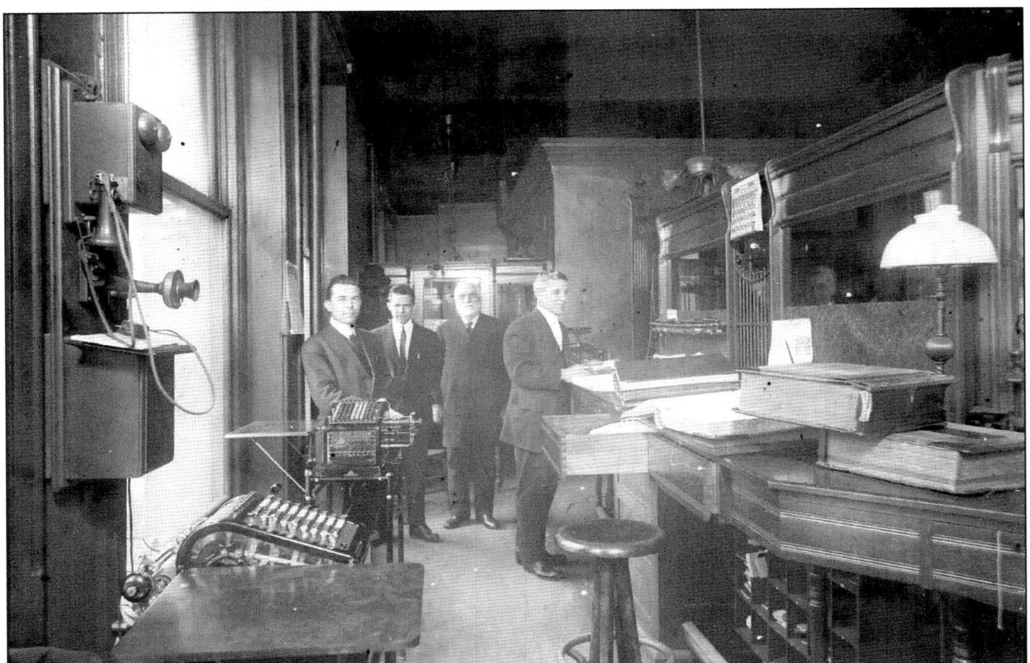

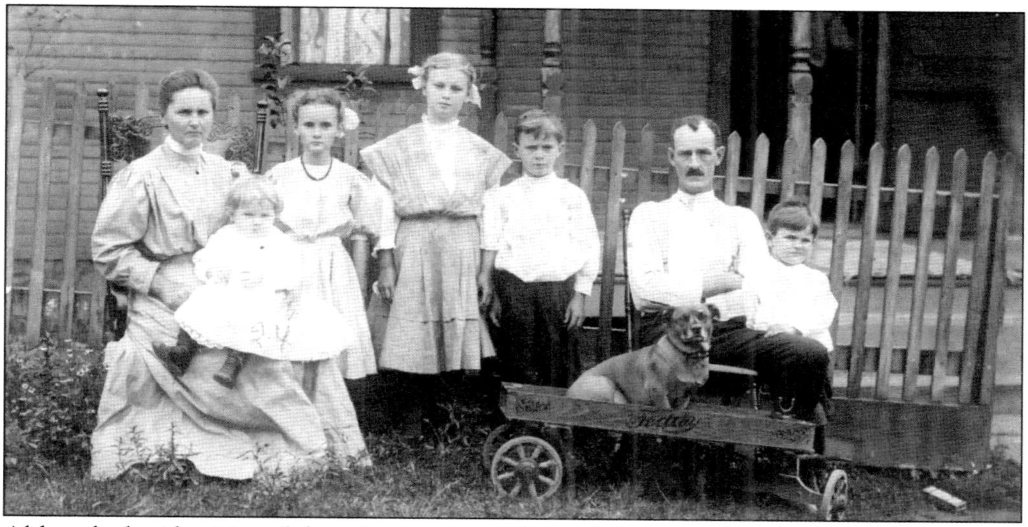

Although the identities of those in the above photograph are not known, it can be presumed that the woman in the picture is a wife and mother. For most of modern history, a man's home may have been his castle, but it was usually his wife or mother that made it livable. For their homemaking services rendered, most women, in all likelihood, did not receive monetary compensation. Employment outside of the home was frequently available to women in just a few traditional areas, such as domestic work, teaching, and nursing. Below, a group of piano students gather for a photograph taken at one of their recitals. While it is unknown if any fees were even charged, women with talents such as Mary Owens were able to use them for profitable ventures in their homes.

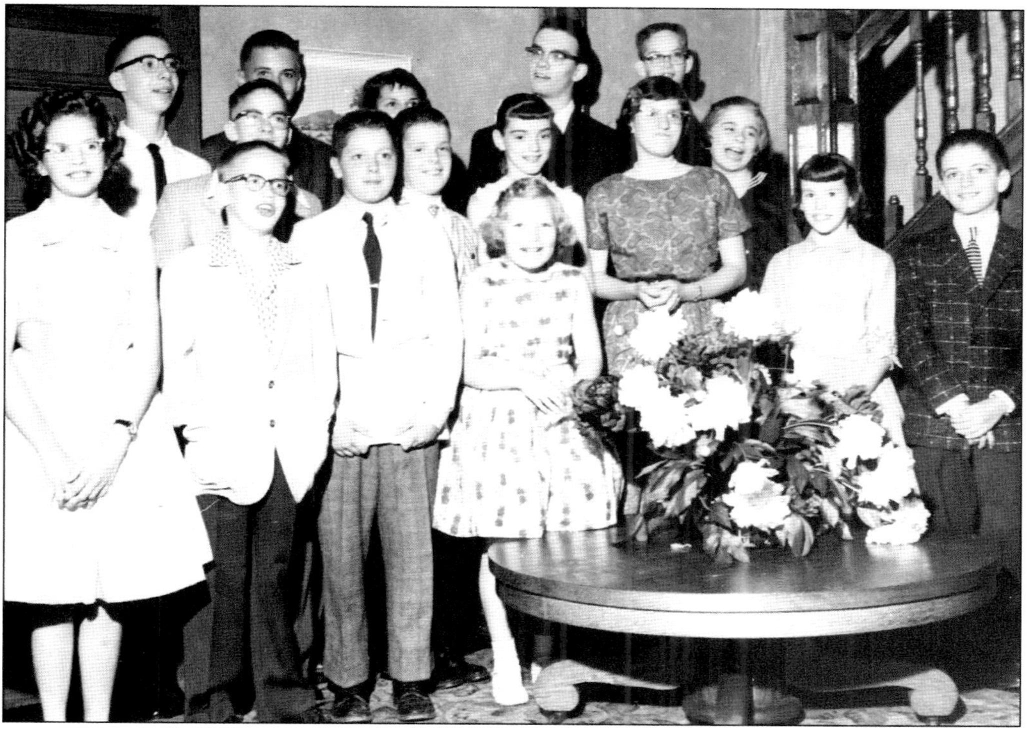

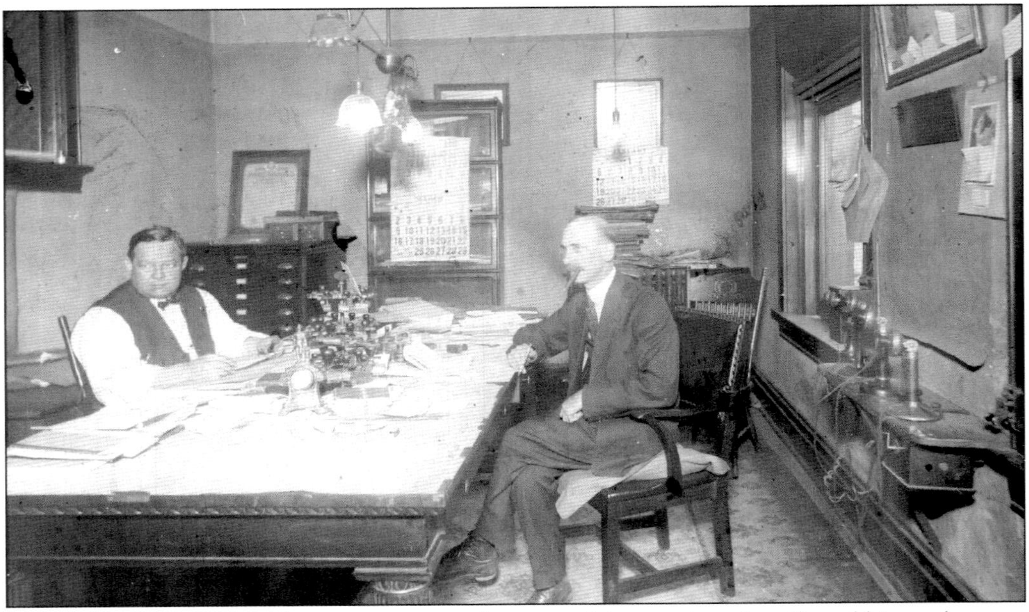

Roger Stone's business niche was insurance; however, this vocation also allowed him to become quite proficient in photography. Photographs of natural disasters were often useful to have, especially when widespread property damage occurred. It is not known what compensation, if any, was available over the years for victims, but Stone's ability to capture it with his camera certainly provides memorable images.

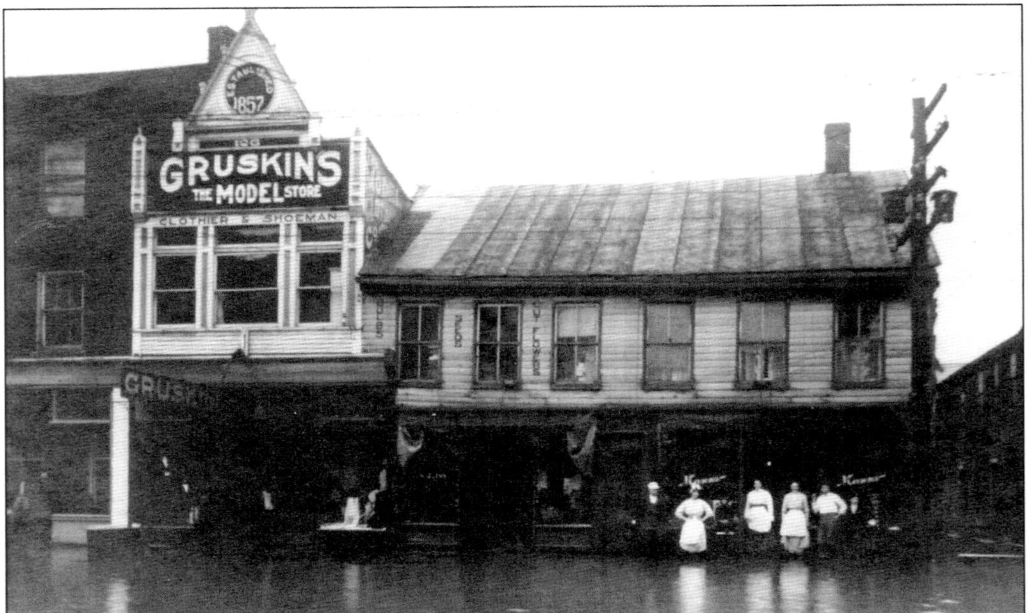

Before the advent of such government agencies as FEMA (Federal Emergency Management Agency), Kittanning's response to town flooding was for residents to roll their sleeves up and dig in. Appearing ready to bail out, these folks in front of Gruskins undoubtedly had a lot of cleaning to do once the floodwaters receded.

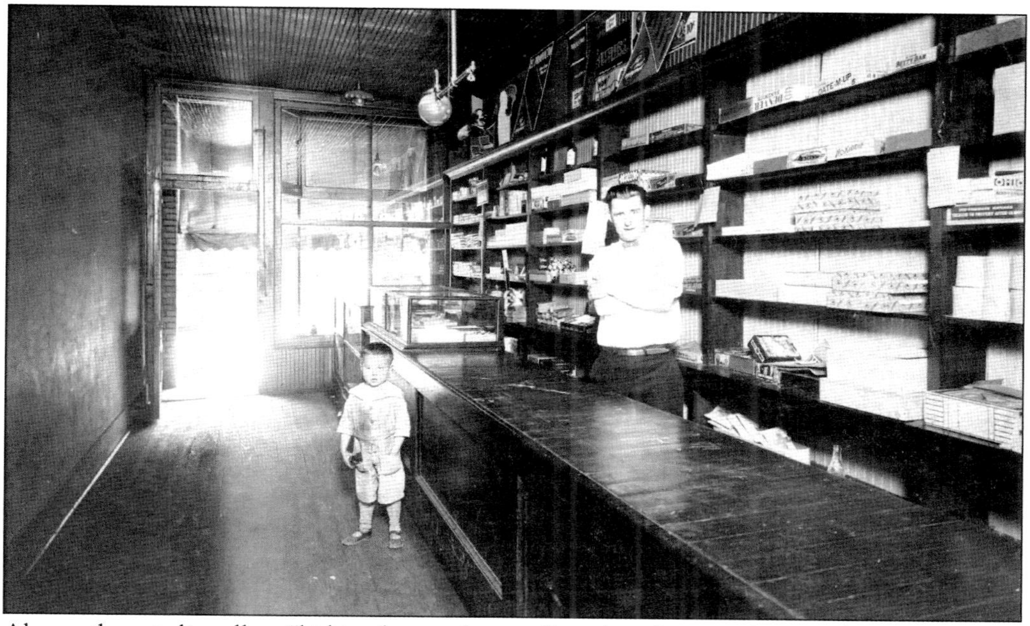

Above, there is literally a "kid in the candy store," as this photograph was taken inside Tarr's Candy and Tobacco Store, which was located on McKean Street. The storefront in the photograph below is identified as Paul Tibrak's Confectionary, seen around 1902. Both stores were well organized, with their wares neatly displayed. Of further note are the extensive patriotic buntings that hang from the exterior of Tibrak's. Even the watermelons appear to be standing at attention along the curb.

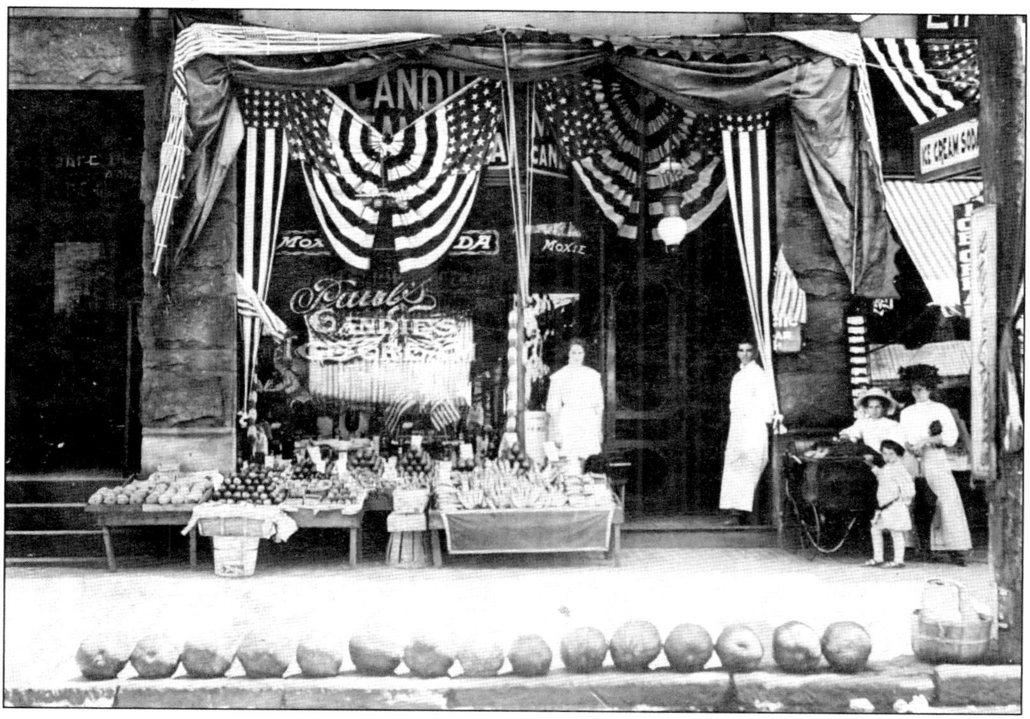

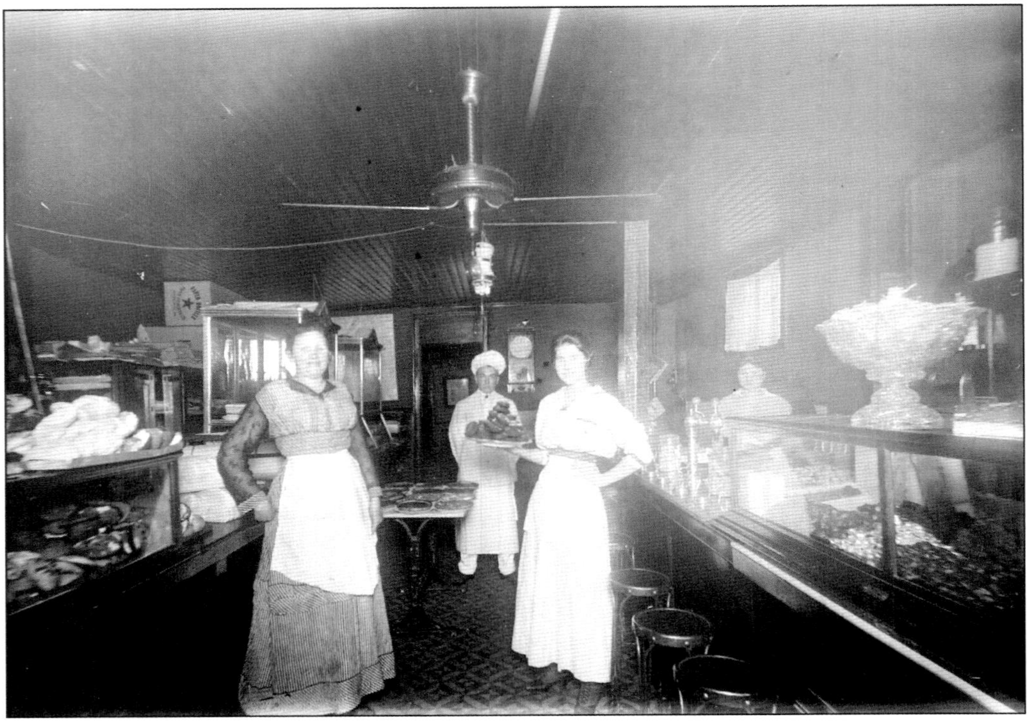

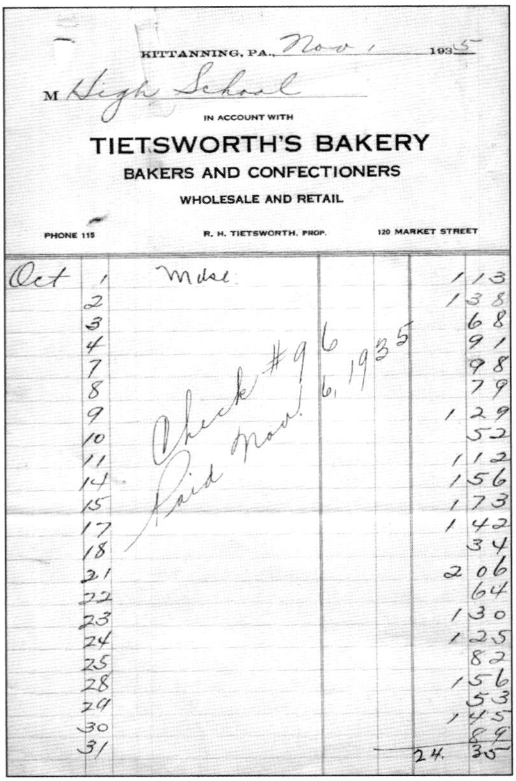

KITTANNING, PA., Nov 1 1935

M High School

IN ACCOUNT WITH

TIETSWORTH'S BAKERY

BAKERS AND CONFECTIONERS

WHOLESALE AND RETAIL

PHONE 115 R. H. TIETSWORTH, PROP. 120 MARKET STREET

Oct	1	Mdse		1 13
	2			1 38
	3			68
	4			91
	7			98
	8			79
	9			1 29
	10			52
	11			1 12
	14			1 56
	15			1 73
	17			1 42
	18			34
	21			2 06
	22			64
	23			1 30
	24			1 25
	25			82
	28			1 56
	29			53
	30			1 45
	31			89
			24.	35

Paid Nov. 6, 1935 Check #96

The Tietsworth's Bakery was located on the first block of Market Street, convenient for those who worked up an appetite for something sweet as they crossed the Allegheny River. Although the subjects in the photograph appear to predate the accompanying receipt, they still may have been involved in the preparation of other orders filled for the account holder, "High School." Note the phone number on the receipt's heading—115.

Here is the introductory page to the 1910–1911 program of the Kittanning Musical Club. Many such organizations have come and gone in Kittanning history. Their existence and success of their performances can now only be appreciated by the written records kept.

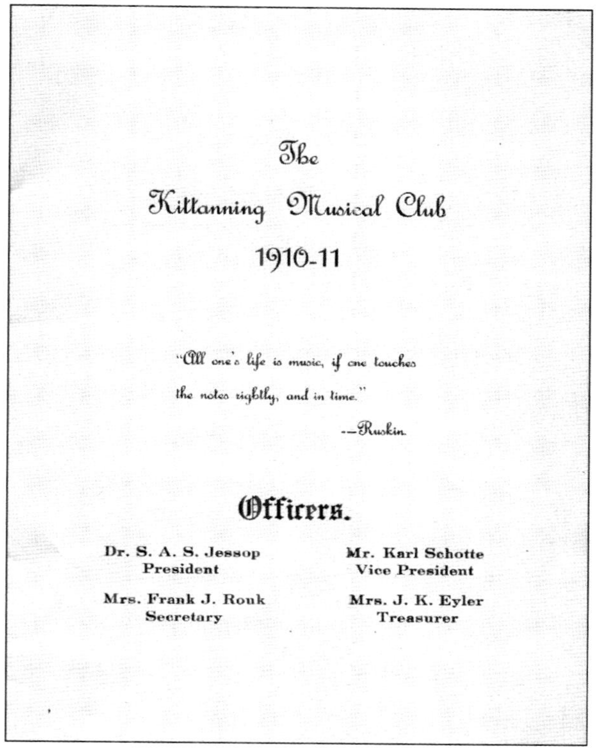

The

Kittanning Musical Club

1910-11

"All one's life is music, if one touches the notes rightly, and in time."

--Ruskin.

Officers.

Dr. S. A. S. Jessop President	Mr. Karl Schotte Vice President
Mrs. Frank J. Rouk Secretary	Mrs. J. K. Eyler Treasurer

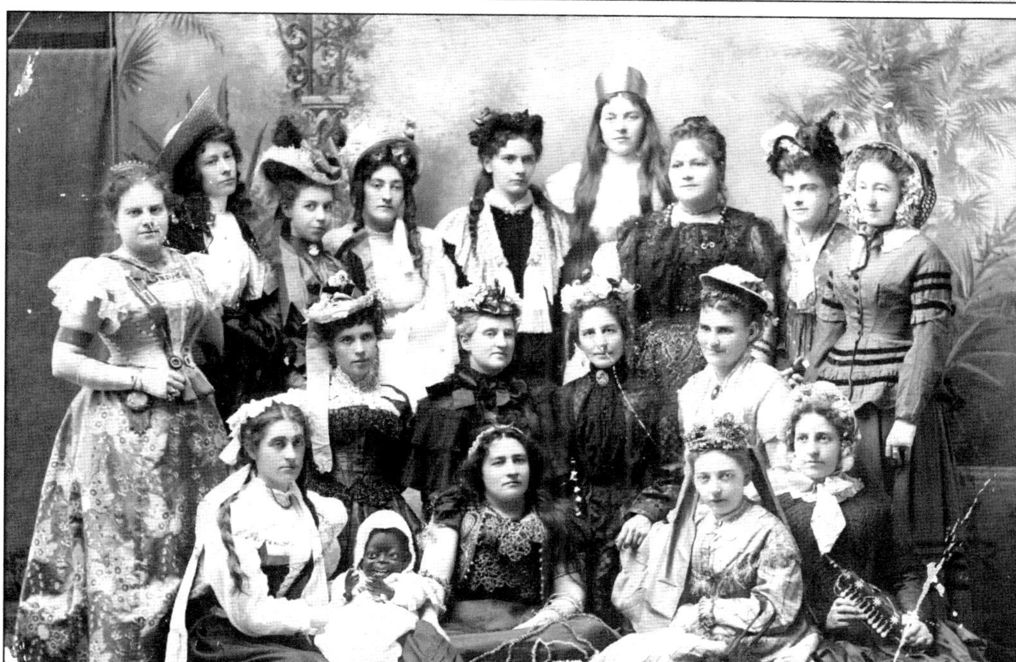

This photograph is identified as "the Spinster's Return" and is dated May 5, 1898. Apparently dressed in their theatrical costume, these ladies are ready to act. Their identities can be discovered with a visit to the Armstrong County Historical Museum.

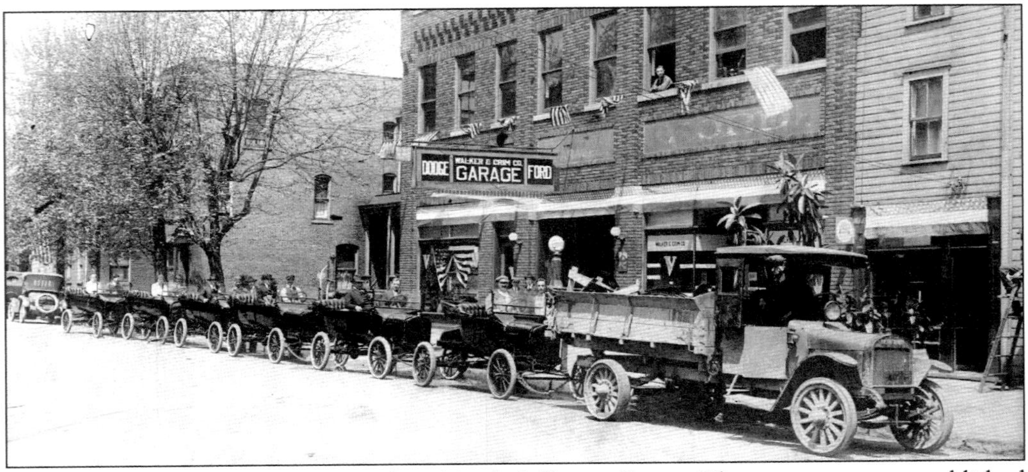

Walker Motor Company is pictured on North Jefferson Street. The company was established by a young Kendrick Walker in 1936. Walker, Armstrong County's first boy to earn an Eagle Scout badge, may have been young when granted the dealer authorization, but he was certainly not lacking in sales experience or initiative. After working for a family automobile business that failed during the Great Depression, he approached the Studebaker representatives in Pittsburgh about the possibility of starting his own dealership. Walker was denied immediately because of his age (20) and was advised to return home. Undaunted by the rejection, Walker did return home, but was able to presell new models, securing $900 in deposits. He returned to the auto representatives one month later with cash in hand. Unable to say no to this approach, Studebaker granted an official dealership to Walker, who apparently had aged overnight. (Courtesy of the Kendrick Walker family.)

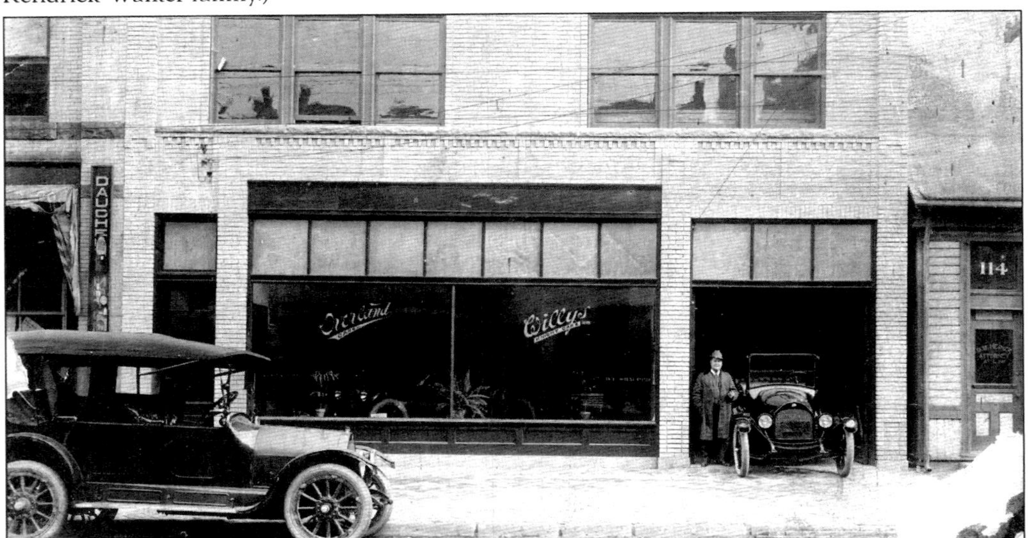

The Merritt (Mert) Schall family was also involved in the automobile sales and service business. Originally involved in Ford and Dodge dealerships around town, a local banker convinced Schall to consolidate his various operations. The result was a new structure built on South McKean Street. This move may have been prudent at the time of construction, but once the Great Depression hit, Schall lost possession of this building and business. Nevertheless, Schall, his sons, and their families remained in Kittanning as active members of the community.

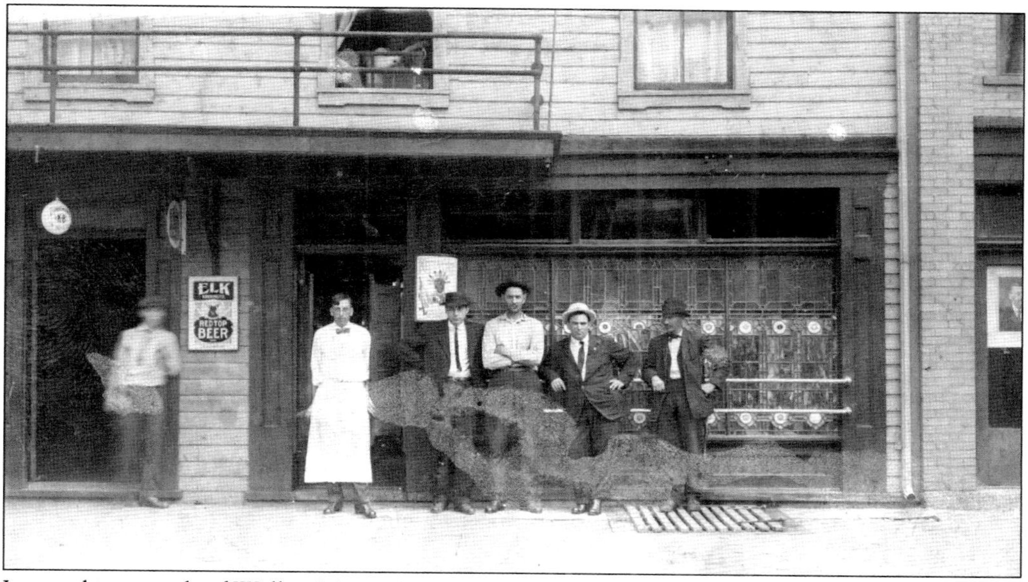

Located just south of Walker Motor Company on North Jefferson Street was the Nulton house, pictured in 1918. Although the hotel no longer stands, it was believed to have been established around 1830. The Reynolds house, also known as "the queen of Kittanning inns," stood close by on the corner of Market and Jefferson Streets. Authorization to construct and operate this establishment was granted to David Reynolds during the first court sessions, which were held in a log cabin in 1805.

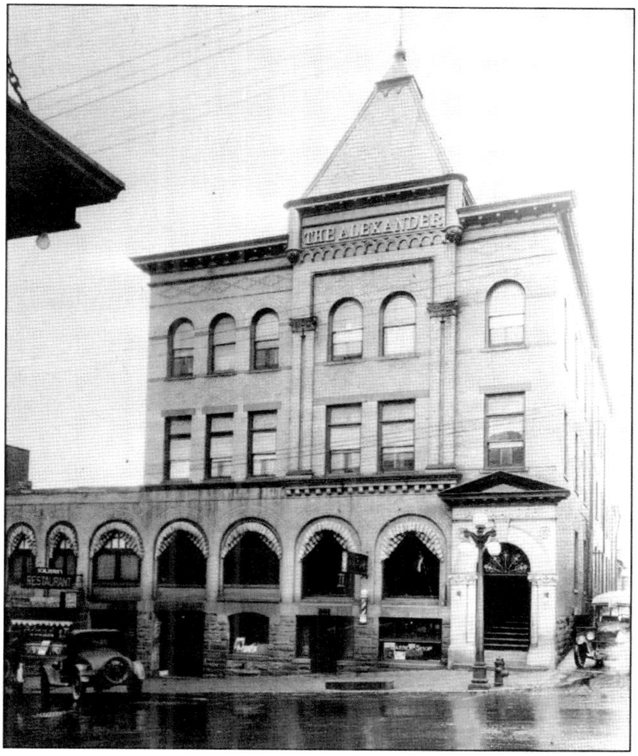

Hotel Alexander, one of eight hotels that prospered as way stations for travelers and visitors to Kittanning, is captured in this photograph, taken long before its demolition. The Hotel Alexander occupied a strategic location, just steps away from stores, businesses, and the hub of activity around the Armstrong County Courthouse at the upper end of Market Street.

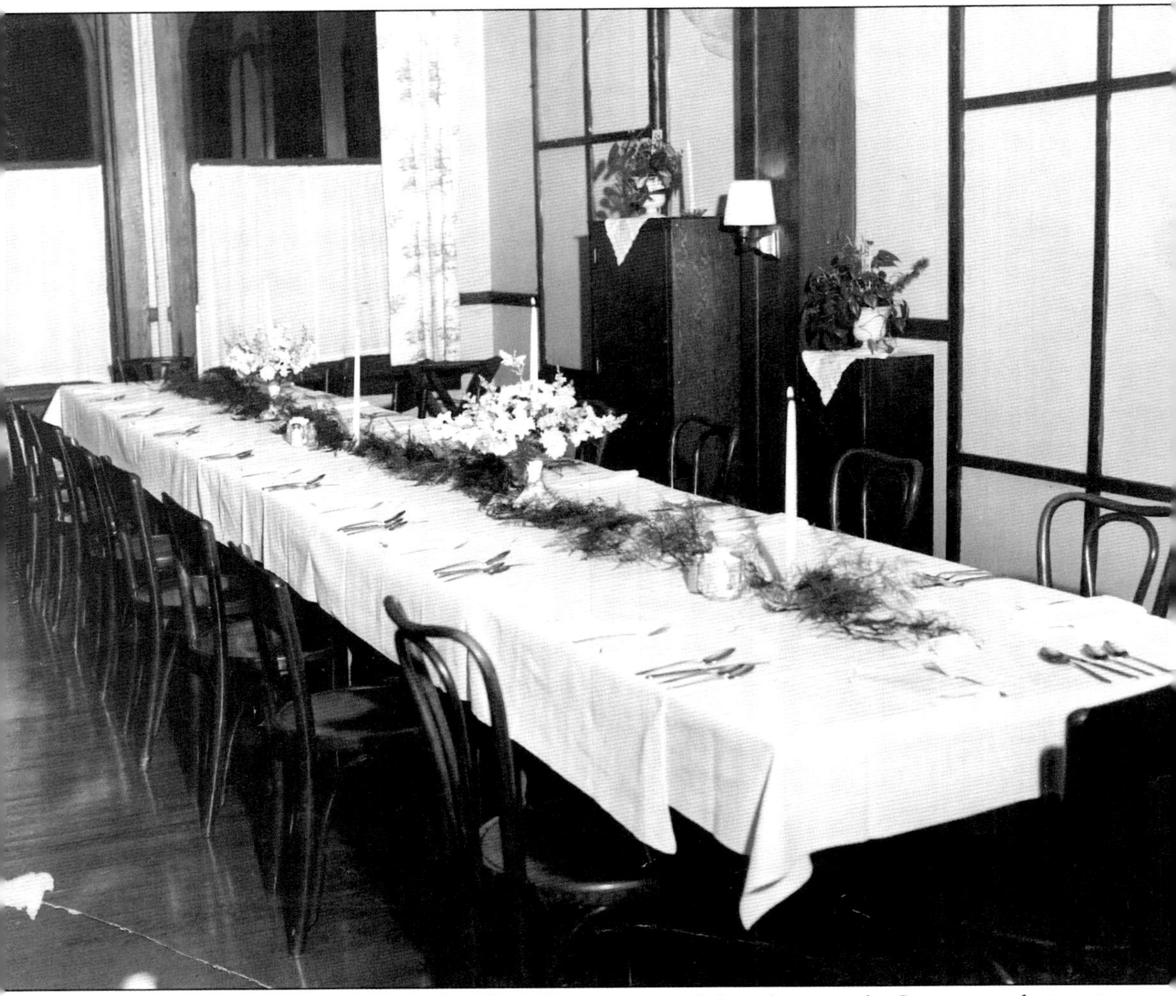

The interior of the Steim Hotel is the subject matter of this photograph. One can only imagine the conversations held at these tables and how they changed with the passage of time. The Steim Hotel, like others of its time, hosted riverboat and railroad crew members, customers that are much less frequently seen these days.

Five

Fame but not Always Fortune

Kittanning was home to many unique, talented people who did much to improve their surroundings. For some, their scope of influence extended far beyond borough and county boundaries. A few even elicited worldwide attention and acclaim, including Nellie Bly, Dennis Daugherty, Walter Wick, and J. Frank Graff Jr.

Although these four may have earned notoriety in different eras and in various ways, there are parallels that can be drawn from their individual experiences. None were exempt from difficulties, with more than one experiencing great loss early in life, such as the death of a parent during their youth.

All four had goals and usually viable plans to attain them. They were all resilient, determined people who were not easily thwarted. They were problem solvers and knowledge seekers.

The impact that these four had on their immediate world of Kittanning, as well as the world at large, may not have been readily apparent or sufficiently recognized; however, neither fame nor fortune seemed to be what they aspired to in the first place.

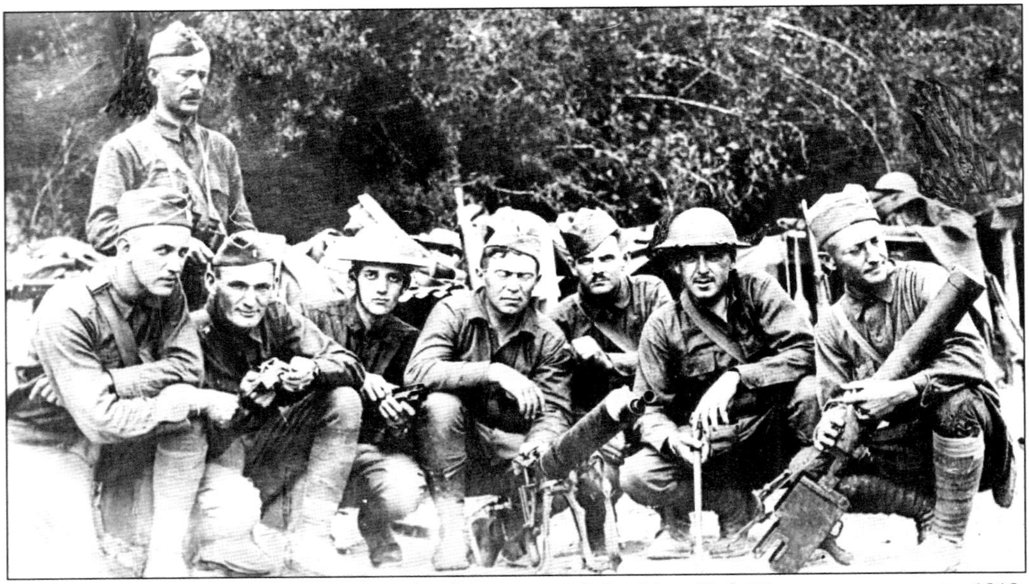

This photograph made its debut on the front page of the *New York Times* newspaper in 1918. It included Kittanning-area native J. Frank Graff Jr., a young lieutenant who distinguished himself while serving with the Company K of the 112th regiment. Graff received two battlefield promotions in France after he spontaneously took over command of the entire regiment when its commanding officer was killed. Graff is the soldier on the far left of the group. (Courtesy of the Peter Graff family.)

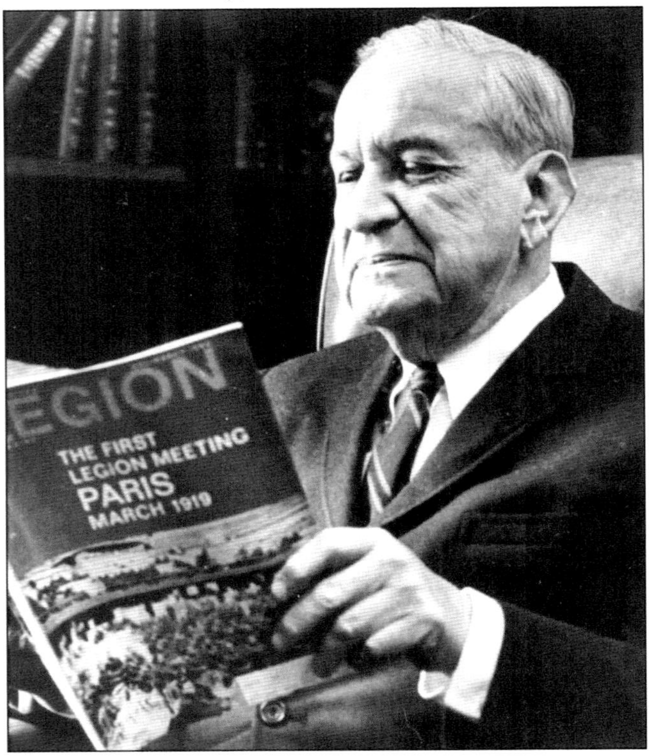

Although World War I interrupted the law career of Graff, he is seen in this photograph years later, reading an anniversary issue of the *American Legion* magazine. Graff remained in France at the war's end to attend the Paris Caucus of 1919, participating as a voting member in the organization of the American Legion. Graff returned to Kittanning, where he protected law then was elected to Armstrong County's highest judicial position in 1923. Judge Graff presided over a myriad of cases for nearly 59 years without interruption. Respected and consulted by his peers, Graff was known as the "Eighth Man of the PA Supreme Court." (Courtesy of the Peter Graff family.)

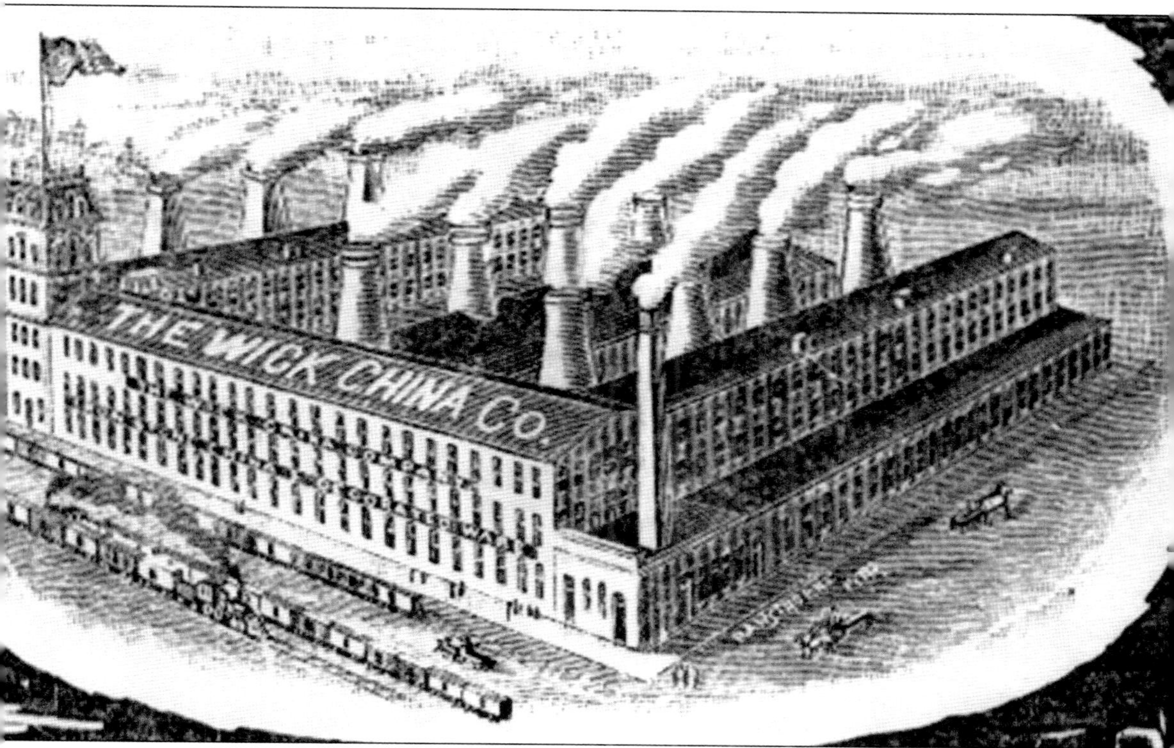

John Wick Jr. donated land to the immediate north of Kittanning for the Wick City China and Kittanning Plate Glass Companies, where hundreds of area residents were employed. Five different types of clay were used in the production of a variety of china tableware and ornamental vases. However, despite an abundance of local deposits of clay and several businesses that extracted them, Wick China Company turned to England and Florida for a large part of this clay. Organized in 1889, the first year of actual production for the Wick Chinaware Company was 1890. Due to demand for the products, rapid growth was experienced in a company that was plagued with employee and labor disputes and damages by forces of nature in 1913. Closed that same year, the company was bought by the George Pottery Company, who resumed china production with a variation in markings and design, permanently closing after World War II.

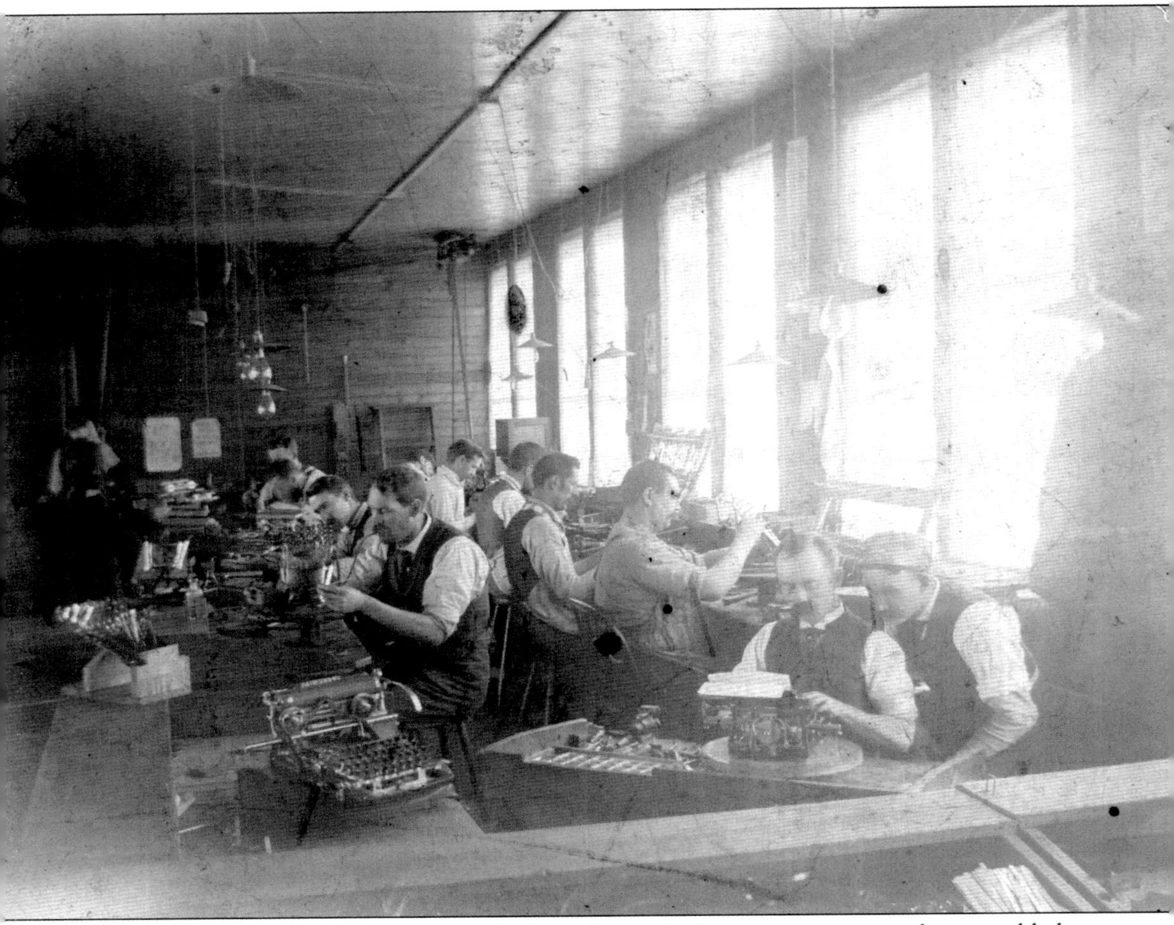

James "Denny" Daugherty was a gifted intellectual whose interest in machines yielded many patents, the most memorable being the Daugherty visible typewriter. Daugherty's innovations for this machine were the use of an ink ribbon and the ability to view typed letters while executing them. Daugherty did begin mass production of these typewriters but never saw the full potential of his genius. Still new to production, an erroneous decision that scrapped approximately 2,000 of the typewriters essentially abandoned the Daugherty visible typewriter for good. Daugherty's legacy, however, is still seen by millions on a daily basis. Located on the keyboard is the sequence of letters, "e r t y," which is not just a coincidence of this man who continued to improve the very machine that denied him fortune, at least the monetary kind.

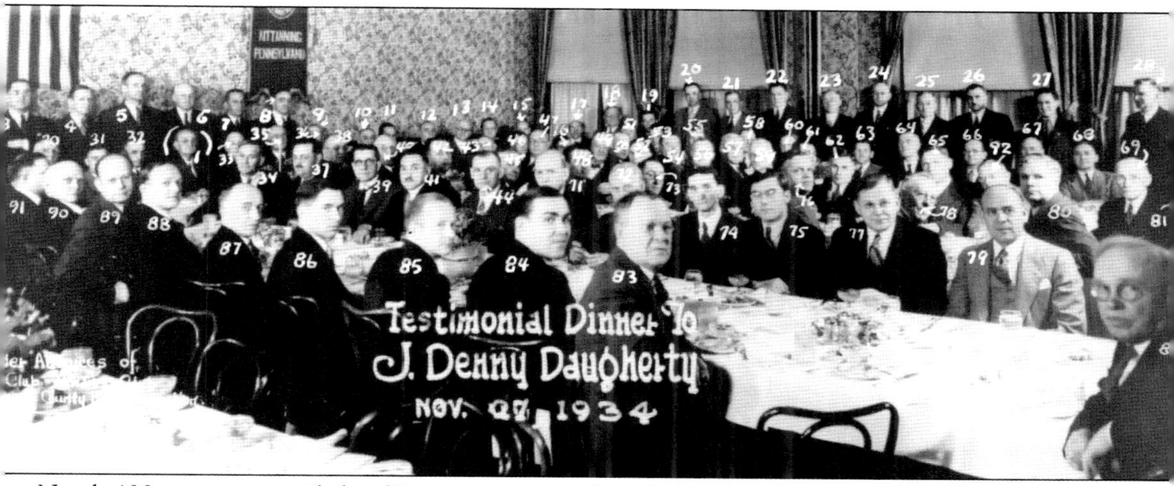

Nearly 100 guests, primarily local businessmen, are identified in this photograph of a testimonial dinner held in 1934 to honor J. Denny Daugherty. Daugherty did not financially succeed in the business world with his own manufacturing ventures. However, technical expertise and creativity enabled him to claim over 40 patents related to typewriters and business machines as a consultant to other larger typewriter manufacturers.

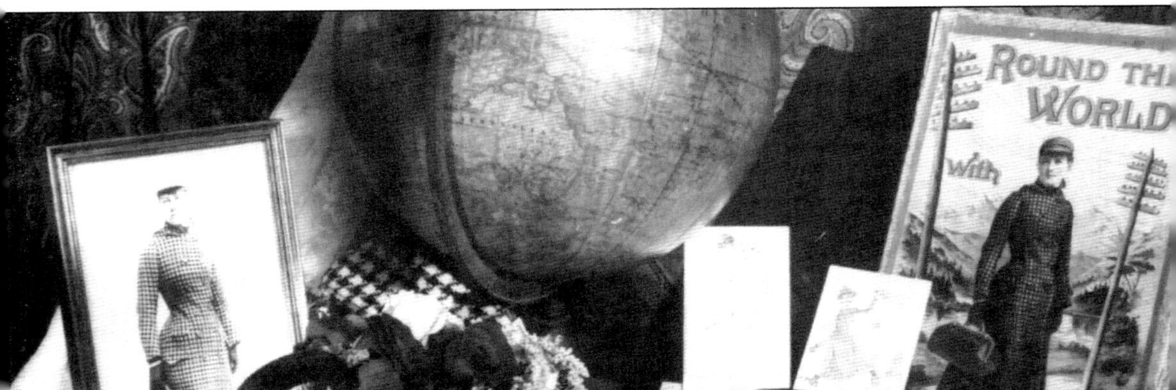

Known around the world as Nellie Bly, Elizabeth Cochrane Seaman was born in 1867. She spent her childhood in the Kittanning area until the death of her father prompted a move to the city. Finding her voice in writing, she was hired by the *Pittsburgh Daily Dispatch* after criticizing its stance on hiring women and was given the pen name Nellie Bly. A woman ahead of her times, Bly made her way to New York City, where she wrote about issues such as the treatment of the mentally ill. A recipient of the prestigious Pulitzer prize, Bly seemed unstoppable, especially when she bested the 80-day circumnavigation record of the Jules Verne character, Phileas Fogg. Bly found herself at the age of 28 earning an unheard of sum of $25,000 when she left the world of hard-hitting journalism for life with millionaire Robert Seaman. Following Seaman's death in 1904, Bly took up her pen for the *New York Evening Journal*. She died in 1922 at the age of 54 of pneumonia.

Six

Firemen and their Parades

Throughout its history, Kittanning residents took the responsibility of safety seriously. This small provincial city supported several fire companies to ensure this protection for all.

The purchase of a hand-operated fire engine in 1826 demonstrated the borough's sincerity on this matter. The price tag of $78.65 may seem inconsequential by today's standards; however, this was a sizeable sum of money in the early 19th century. With this equipment, Kittanning Fire Company No. 1 was a reality. Because of the growing population and improved engineering, fire companies either grew or were added. Prior to the consolidation of Wick Borough and Kittanning, Wick Borough had three of its own departments. After the public voted to merge the two communities, fire companies did the same.

Hand-drawn equipment was ultimately replaced with gasoline-powered engines, around the time of World War I. This was due in large part to the street surfaces. Soil-laden streets necessitated manual power until a combination of factors, such as automobiles replacing animals for transportation, enforcement of local health regulations, and advances in road-surfacing techniques enabled fuel-powered vehicles to do the job.

As determined as Kittanning was to work hard and smart to protect lives and property, residents also took the opportunity to use their service organizations to play hard.

In addition to the various social functions that grew out of the need for companies to raise funds and desire to join together for recreation, the entire community and much of western Pennsylvania has enjoyed and anticipated watching performances of the Kittanning Firemen's Band.

Organized in 1949, the Kittanning Firemen's Band has distinguished itself over the years through competition and public appeal. From its first competitions in 1949, this band, with its humble beginnings of 22 members wearing recycled World War II military uniforms, applied a lot of talent and collective effort to win over 100 competitions, including statewide titles.

Other musical groups have generated followings of their own, and samplings of some are seen here.

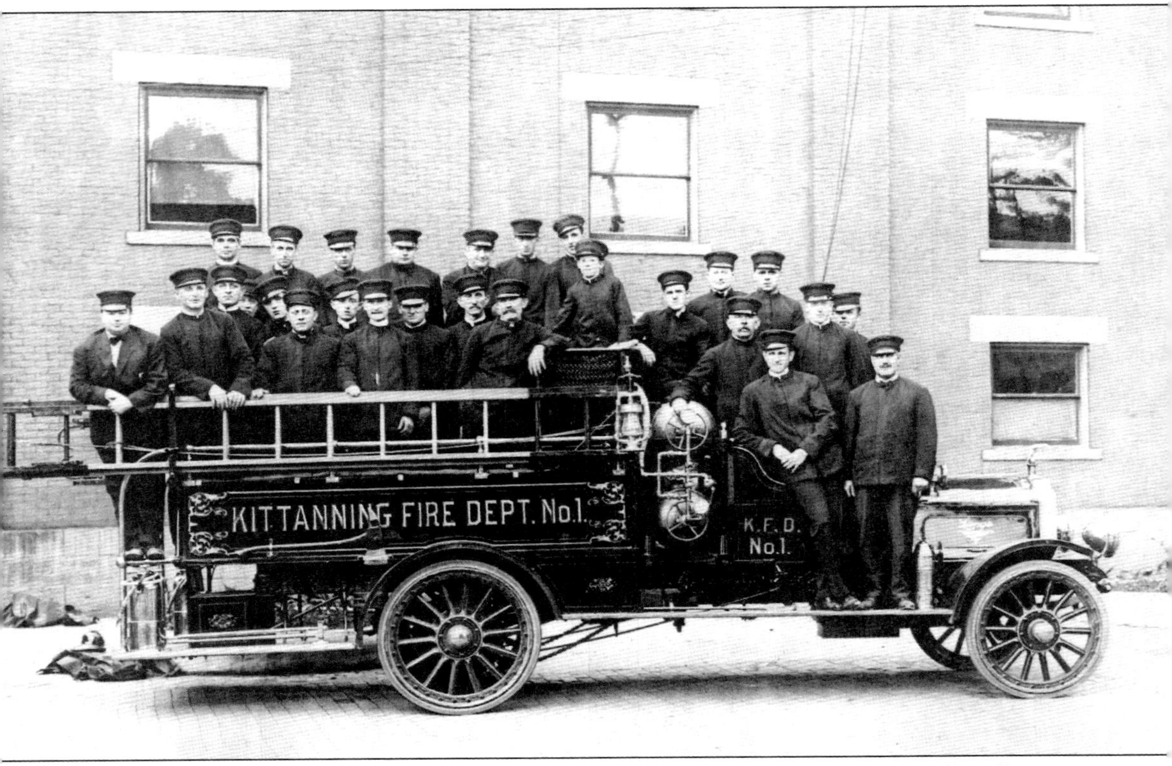

The firemen and the fire truck on which they stand belong to Kittanning Fire Department No. 1. Of special note is the youngest on board, John Lindeman, located above the "No. 1" of the insignia painted on the truck's side.

Assembled for the photographer are two fire companies of bygone days. At right, in formation in their fancy duds, are the members of hose company No. 3. Below, hose company No. 4 is pictured in this vintage engine. In a matter of moments, in the event of a call, all of these fine-looking men in suits could transform themselves into a unit of fine-tuned firefighters.

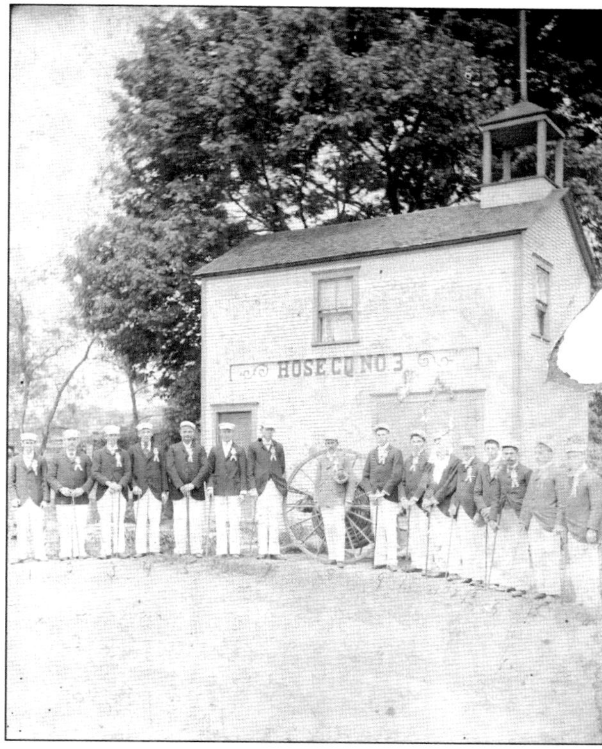

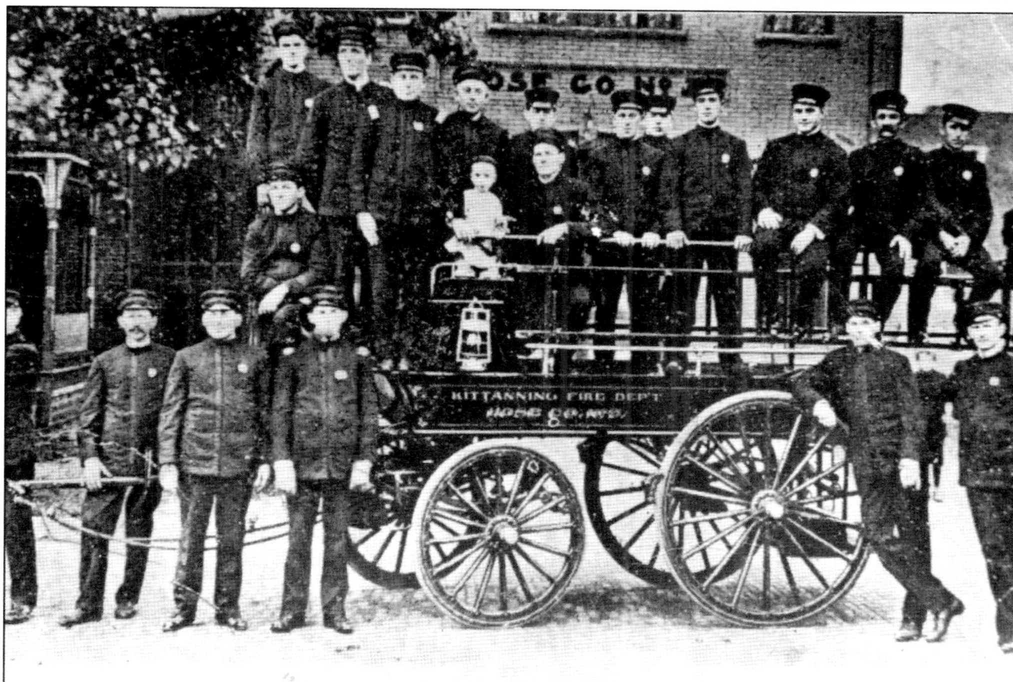

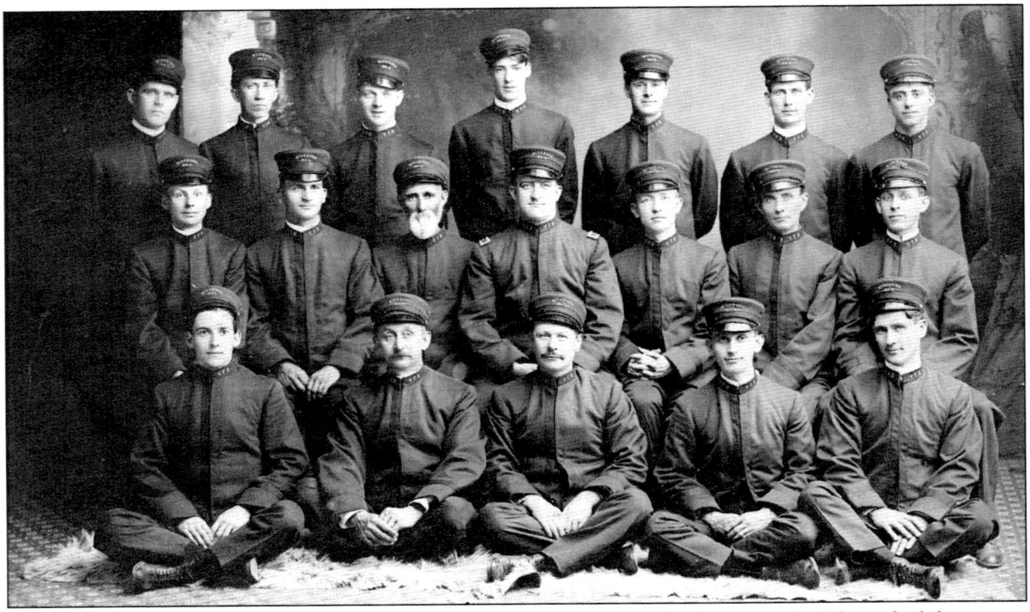

The Wickboro Hose Company No. 1 poses for this formal photograph. Identified here are James Simpson, Dan Berg, Harvey French, Charles Shaw, John Sedwick, Huv Sedwick, Virgil Crissman, Bill Bauer, Charles Morgan, John Story, Ellis Shaw, Charles Bowser, Ed Ritchey, Ed Lehner, Obe French, Ed H. Shafer, Charles French, Phil Olinger, and Charles Held.

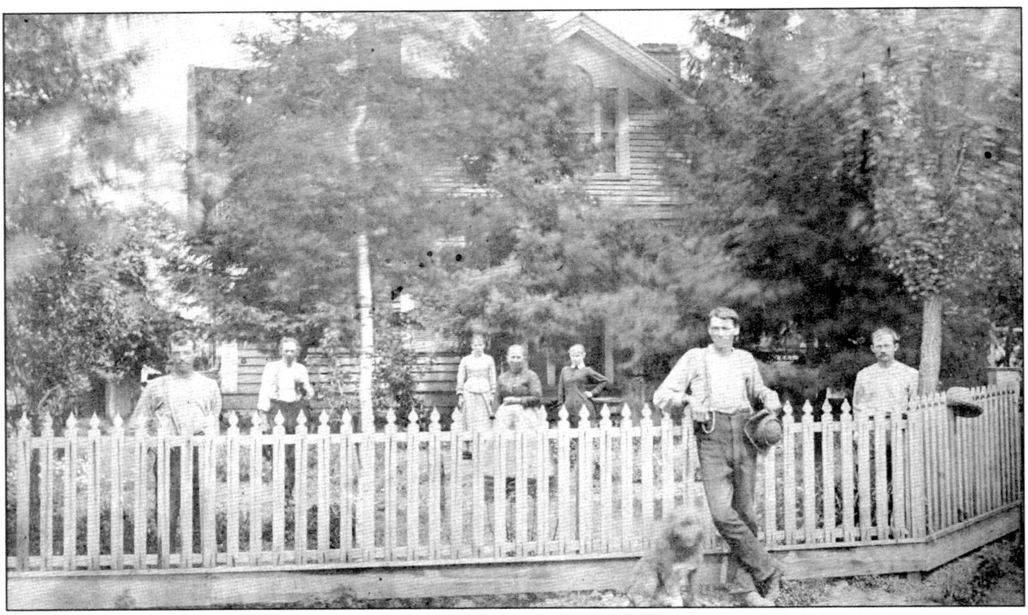

The classic "house with the white picket fence" is not necessarily for everyone nor does it look the same either. Kit-han-ne's long houses, residences of the Native Americans, destroyed in the 1756 battle of Kittanning can only be imagined now, and many of the other early Kittanning houses are long gone as well. No information could be found regarding the house shown in this picture, so its history and those of its inhabitants will in all likelihood remain a mystery.

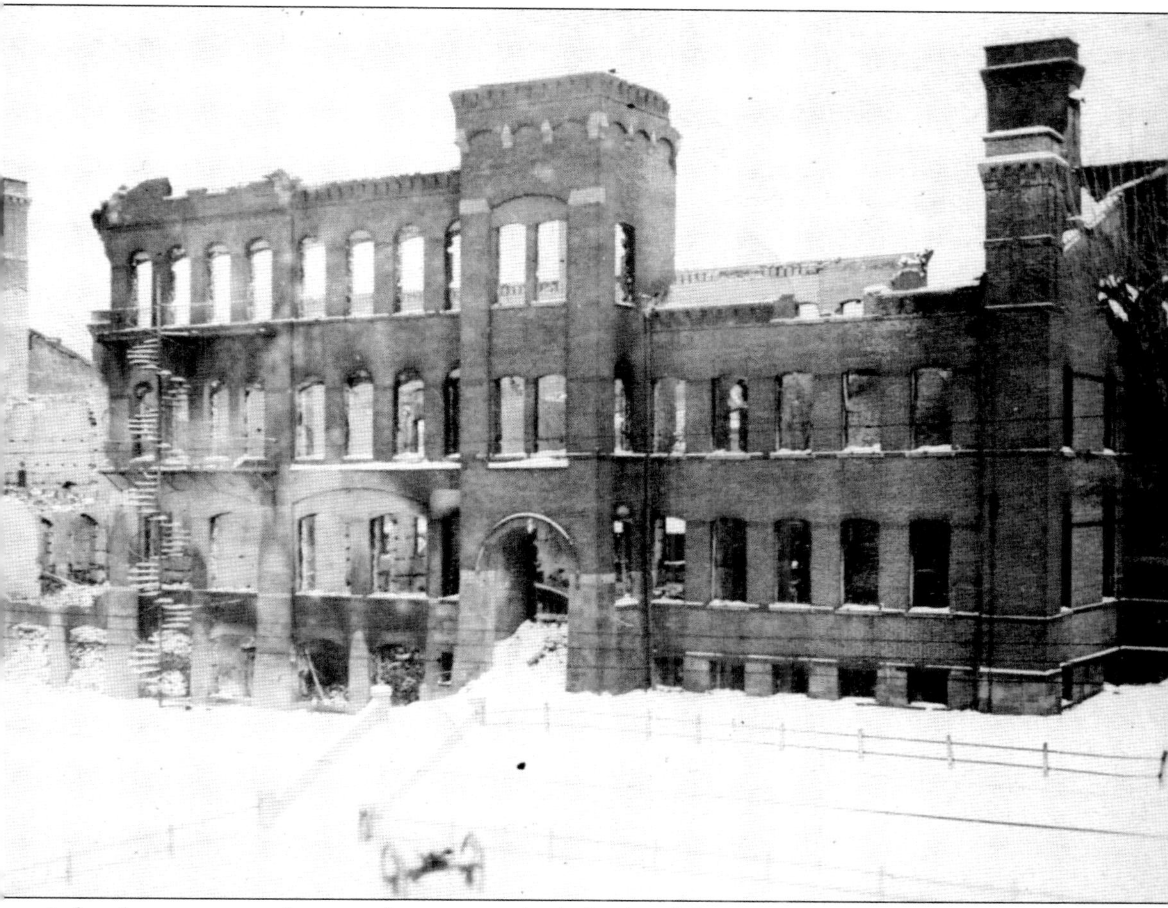

A fire that was never forgotten by anyone who helped to fight it or even witnessed it was the blaze that consumed Kittanning High School in 1919. However, good things came from bad, as a larger structure was built to replace it that was able to accommodate the growing student population at that time. It has served the school district in the years since. This building is now the Kittanning Junior High School.

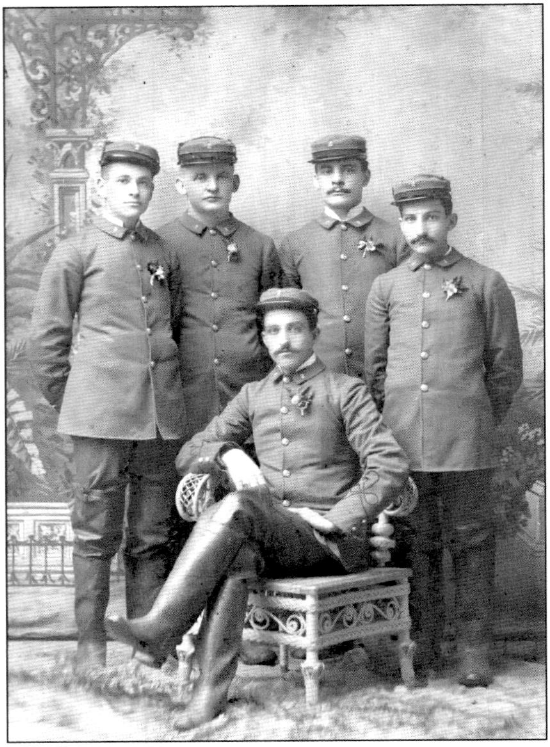

This photograph was identified by Mrs. James B. Kennerdell as, "First and Original Boys of Co. 7 Firemen." From left to right are James B. Kennerdell, Bird McClelland, Harry Hague, Henry Moesta, and Alex H. Taylor (sitting).

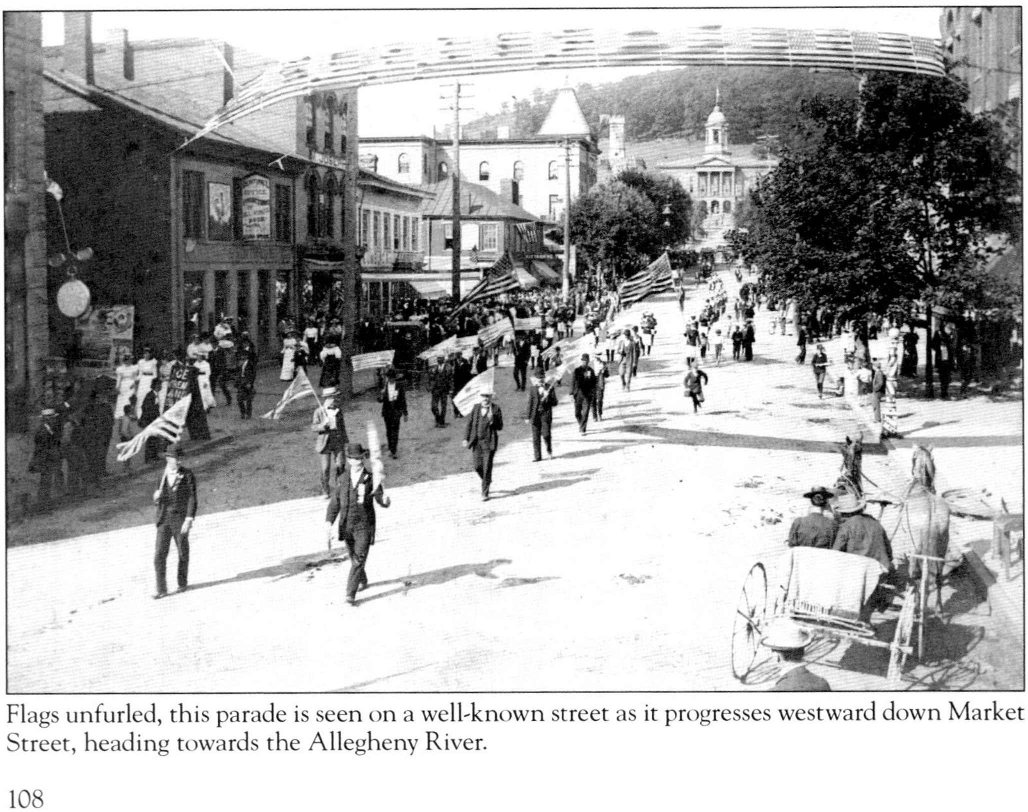

Flags unfurled, this parade is seen on a well-known street as it progresses westward down Market Street, heading towards the Allegheny River.

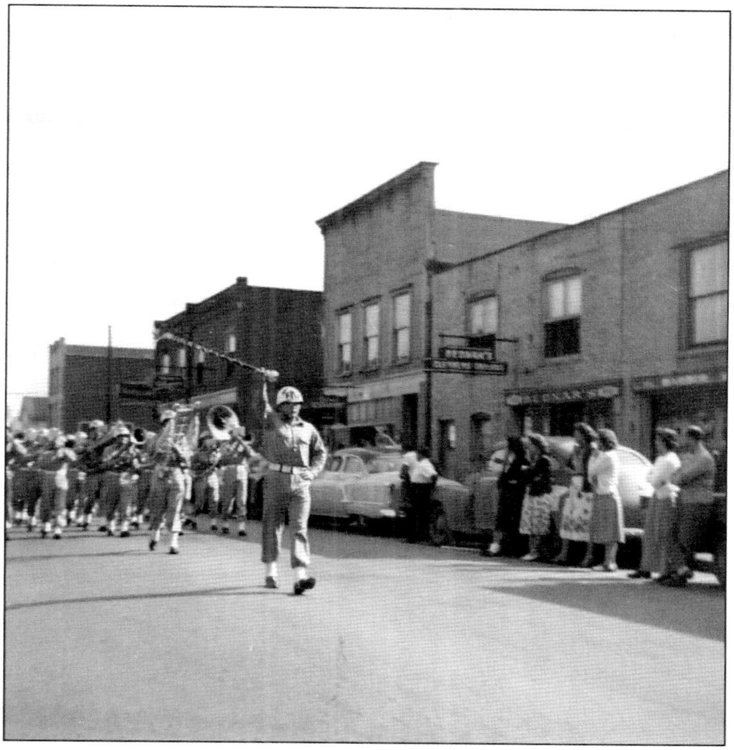

These candid photographs show the Kittanning Firemen's Band. Looking smart as they march in this parade, they undoubtedly sounded smart too. The popular firemen's band began with 22 members under the direction of Enrico Colonna and $25 worth of sheet music purchased with money donated by three Kittanning-based fire companies. (Courtesy of the Dave Linderman family.)

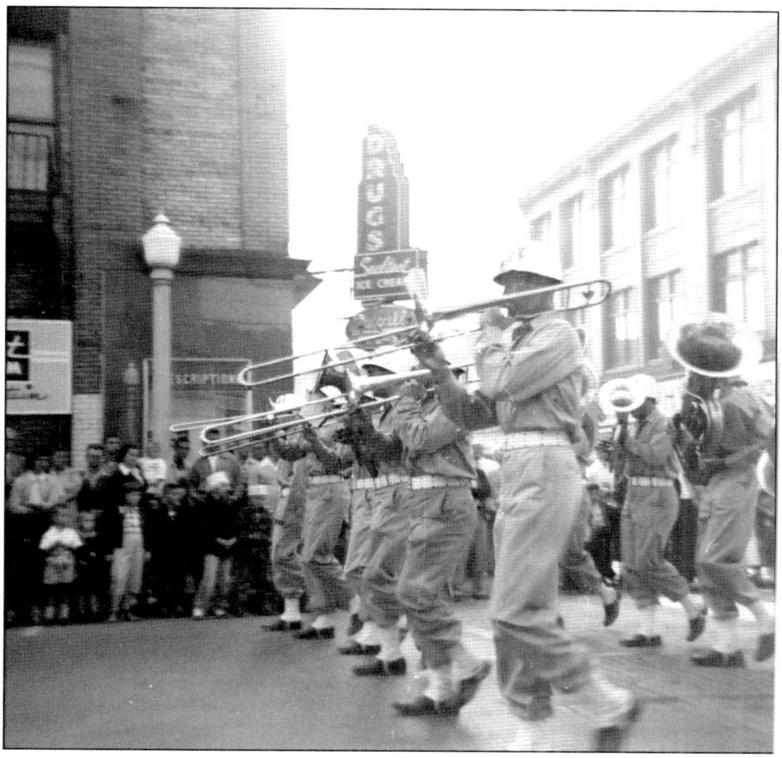

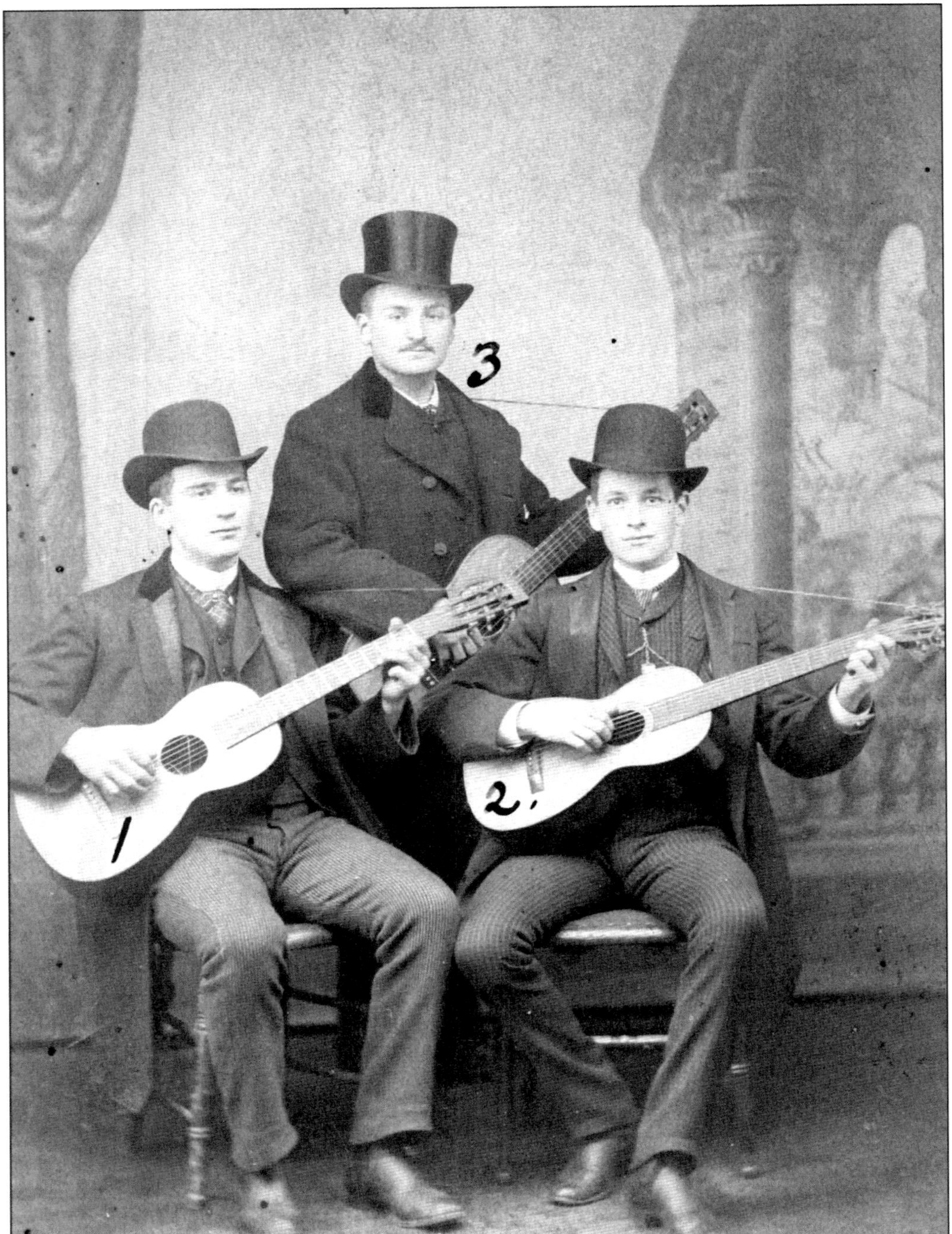

This undated picture shows Walter Hays (left), J. B. Kennerdell (sitting), and Harry Jack (standing). The group was known as Kittanning's famous Mandolin Club.

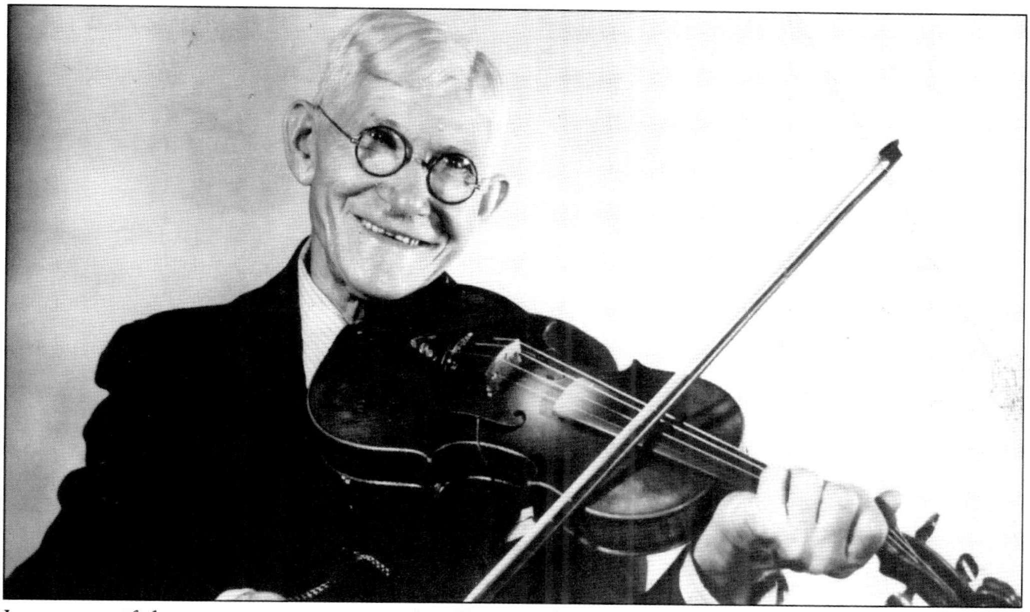

It seems as if there was entertainment for all musical tastes throughout Kittanning's history. Lee Wolfe, described as a "champion old time fiddler of Armstrong County," is seen above with fiddle in hand. Wolfe and James Vensel, an experienced "caller," were known to turn any occasion into lively square dance. If the music of the Country Band (below) did not capture one's attention, then their dress most certainly could have. These uniquely outfitted musicians posed for this photograph in 1904. Identified here are Frank Weylman, Alex H. Taylor, Henry Moesta, William Knoble, George Pecoo, and John Knoble.

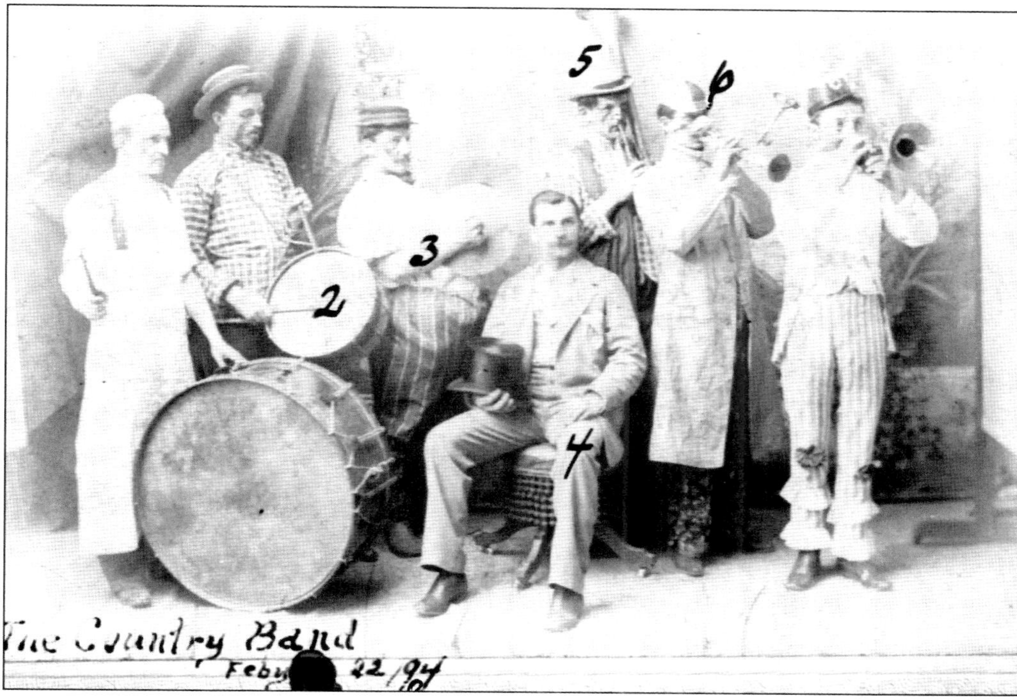

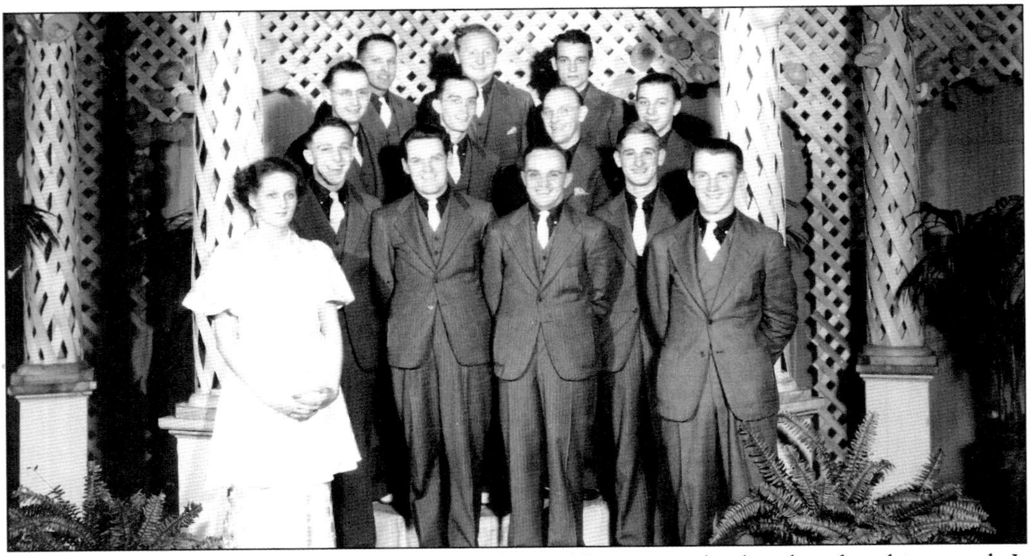

The Moon River Band established a name for itself as a popular band with a big sound. It kept a busy schedule of engagements at clubs, schools, colleges, and other community locations throughout western Pennsylvania. It was also a regular musical guest on a Greensburg radio station. Although its repertoire reflected the contemporary music of the 1930s and 1940s, the Moon River Band was also noted for performing original numbers composed by its own band members. With support from the Kittanning Elks fraternal organization, this band enjoyed almost a decade of play together.

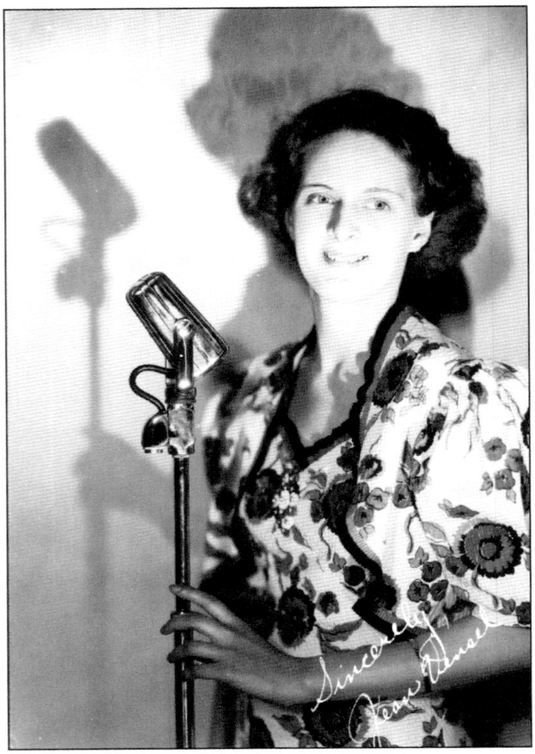

Jean Vensel Smart was the little lady with the big band. When asked to join the group, there was no hesitancy on Jean's part—it was her mother, Orpha Lasher Vensel, who had to be persuaded to allow the 17 year old to add her sultry tones to the band's musical mix. Her mother only consented if Jean's brother Leslie Vensel and Hap Fleming assured her that they would properly chaperone Jean. Apparently these two men were so effective that Jean never got the chance to even dance with anyone during those years. (Courtesy of Jean Vensel Smart.)

Seven

Forming a More Perfect Union

Since its days as Kit-han-ne, Kittanning has played an active role in the development of the nation as it is known today. When Col. John Armstrong marched his militiamen across rugged mountainous terrain to engage in battle with the Lenni-Lenape tribe, he did so with almost no advance information and certainly no assurances of victory. Nevertheless, he and his troops answered the call.

Armstrong's victory at this seemingly obscure wilderness village helped to turn the tide of the French and Indian War in America in favor of the British, with whom most European settlers sympathized. Although the 1756 battle of Kittanning ended the community of Delaware people living there, it seemed to set the tone for those that came later—other remarkable people who planted the roots of Kittanning and all those who helped to nurture its growth thereafter.

Although Kittanning never saw armed militiamen on its streets again, it sent many of its own to answer the call in all parts of the world. Military history indicates that Kittanning's response to the call for duty since then has been like that of the rest of western Pennsylvania, sending more of its sons and daughters (per capita) to military service than any other region in the country.

On the home front, Kittanning residents have individually and collectively given of themselves for the good of their town. The people of Kittanning have helped to maintain a sense of shared goals, shared purpose, and shared community in the three centuries since the Lenni-Lenape made this spot their home.

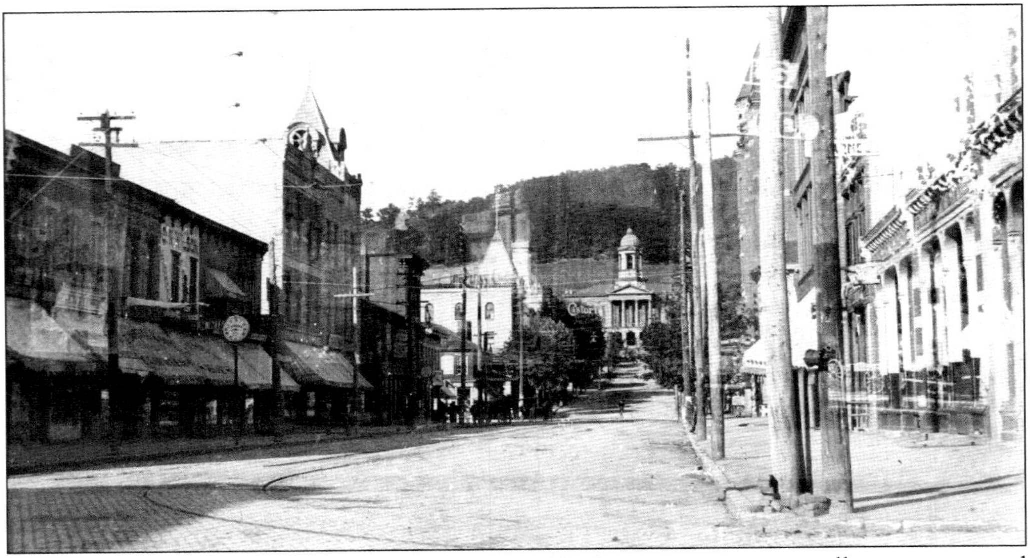

As late as the early 20th century, Kittanning's public hygiene, as in most villages, towns, and cities of those times, was lacking. By the early 1900s, the need for local ordinances was urgent, as Kittanning's usable water supply was deemed unhealthy, primarily from the contamination of unclean streets that were used by animals for transportation. In response, the borough facilitated the organization of a local board of health in February 1907. The board gave notice to all owners and occupants of buildings, both public and private, to put their property in sanitary condition. The board recommended disinfection with chlorate of lime. All cellars were to be whitewashed too. Original board members included James M. Hudson, Dr. L. D. Allison, W. A. Nicholson, James M. Heilman, J. P. Henry, and H. B. Stone.

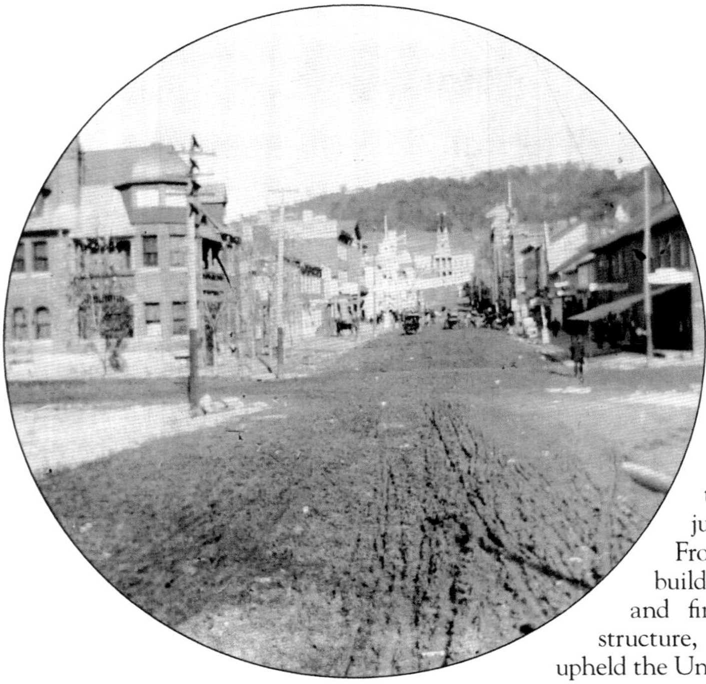

The picture seen here shows a street typical of the times before the ordinaces were passed. Built in 1858, the Armstrong County Courthouse's stately looking edifice is the third building to house Armstrong County's judicial branch of government. From its humble start in a log building to a bigger brick building and finally to this Greek revival structure, the county's judiciaries have upheld the United States Constitution.

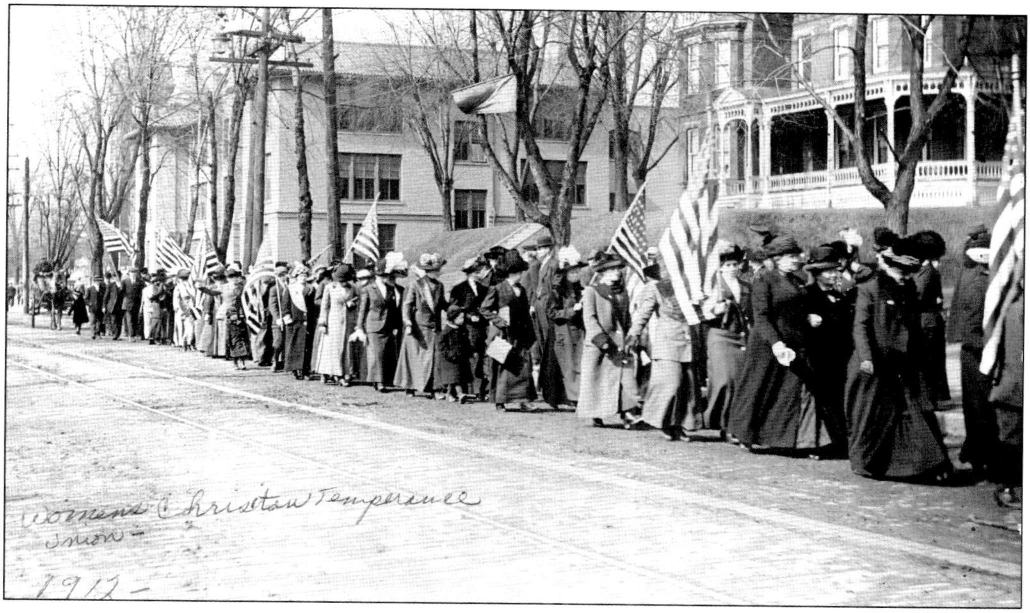

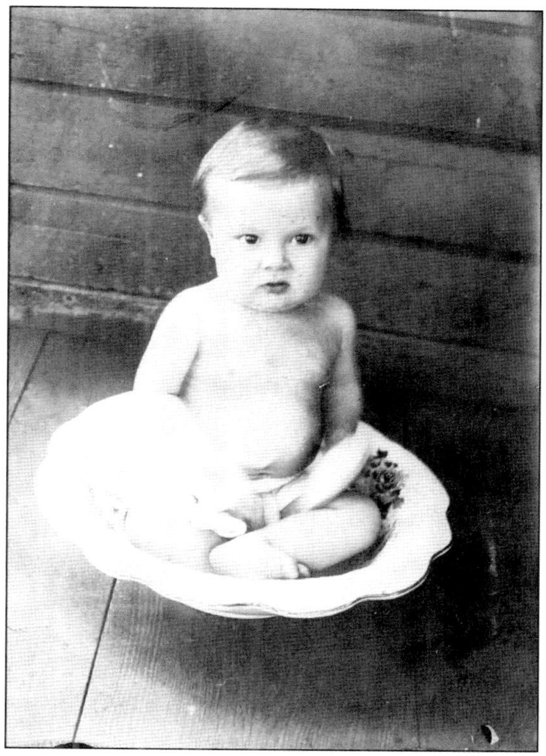

It is highly doubtful that the marchers pictured above had any notion of throwing the baby out with the bath water, unless the water happened to be bathtub gin. The 1912 photograph above is identified as that of a Woman's Christian Temperance Union march. Several temperance unions, groups dedicated to either the limitation of alcohol usage (usually for private or medicinal purposes only) or total abstinence from alcohol, formed in Kittanning over the years. The earliest of record was believed to be the Kittanning Temperance Society, organized in 1830. Supporters of this cause most likely thought that their wishes were fulfilled with the 1919 ratification of the 18th Amendment to the Constitution, but it was later repealed by passage of the 21st Amendment in 1933. As for the adorable babe in the basin, he or she shall go nameless.

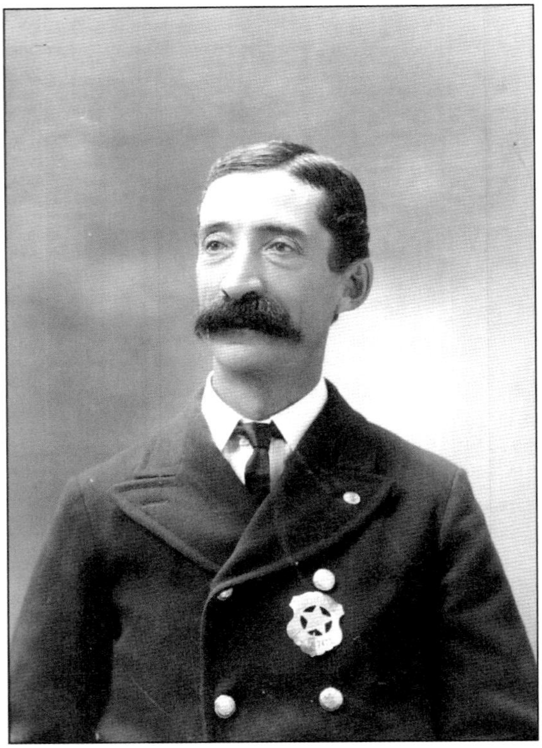

Laws are enforced on the streets primarily by those "in blue." Kittanning residents are protected from harm by men and women of the local police force, who put their lives on the line just as any other police or military member is asked to do. Pictured here is a former Kittanning chief of police. (Courtesy of Pete Harmon.)

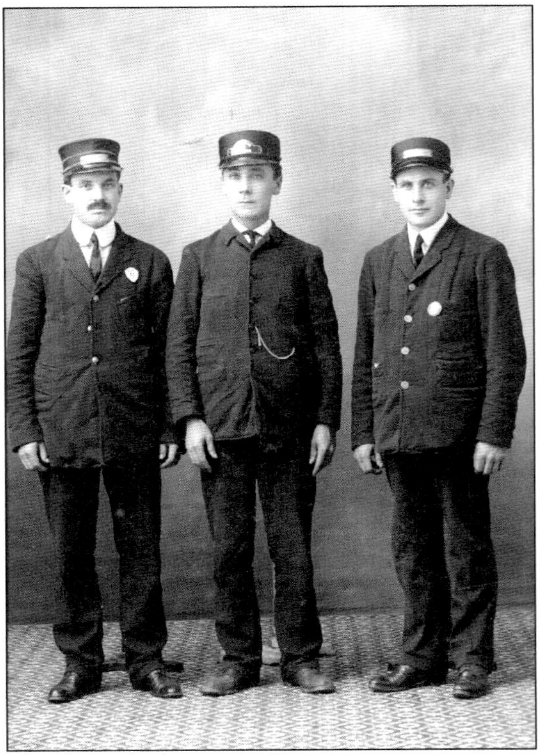

Since the Delaware Nation days of Kit-han-ne, Kittanning has probably had every means of conveyance on foot, hoof, or wheel used within its boundaries. Seen here are three employees of Ford City and Kittanning Street Railway Company. The Pennsylvania Railroad also double tracked through town, providing two passenger trains per hour as public transportation.

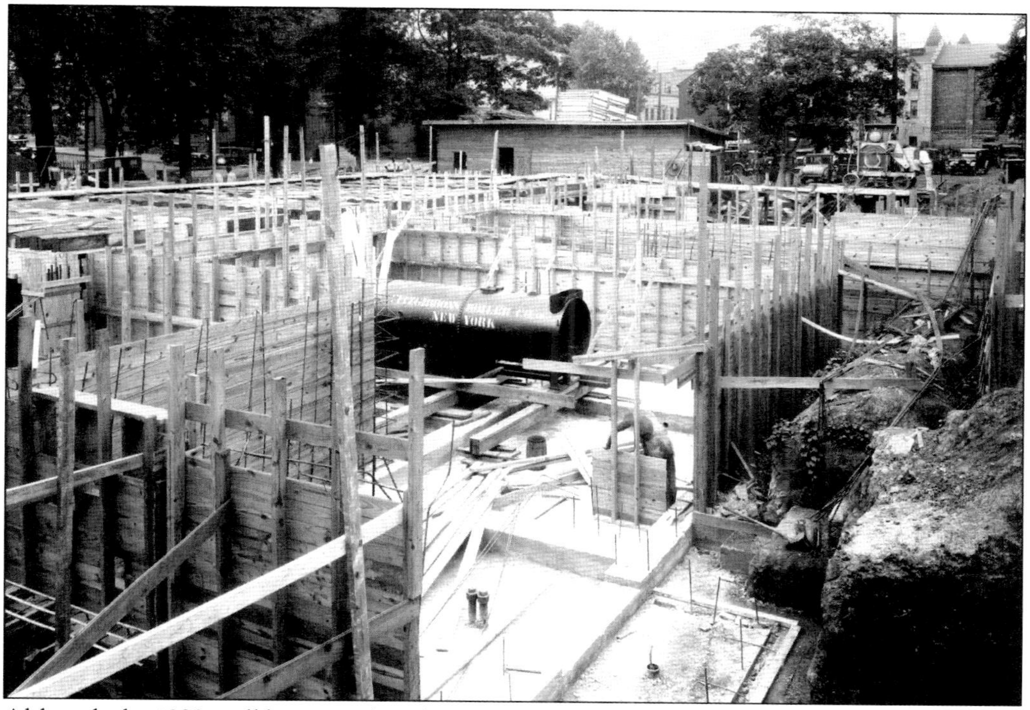

Although the 1930s will be remembered as the Great Depression, it was a time of growth as well. These photographs show the Kittanning Post Office in its rough and later more finished states. More photographs like these can be seen at the Armstrong County Historical Museum.

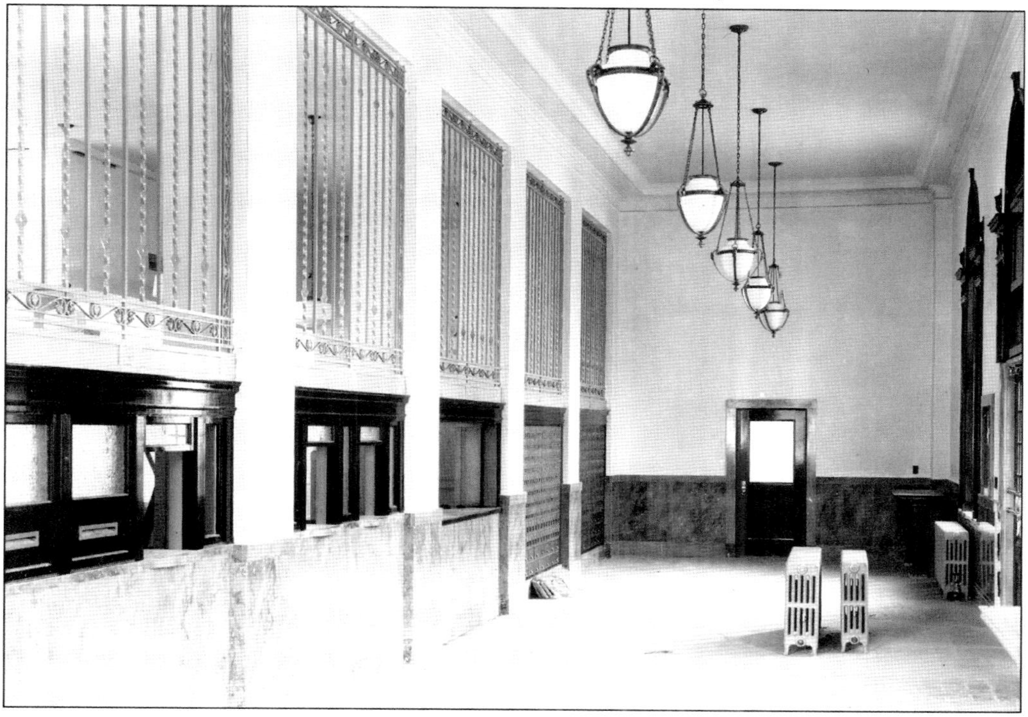

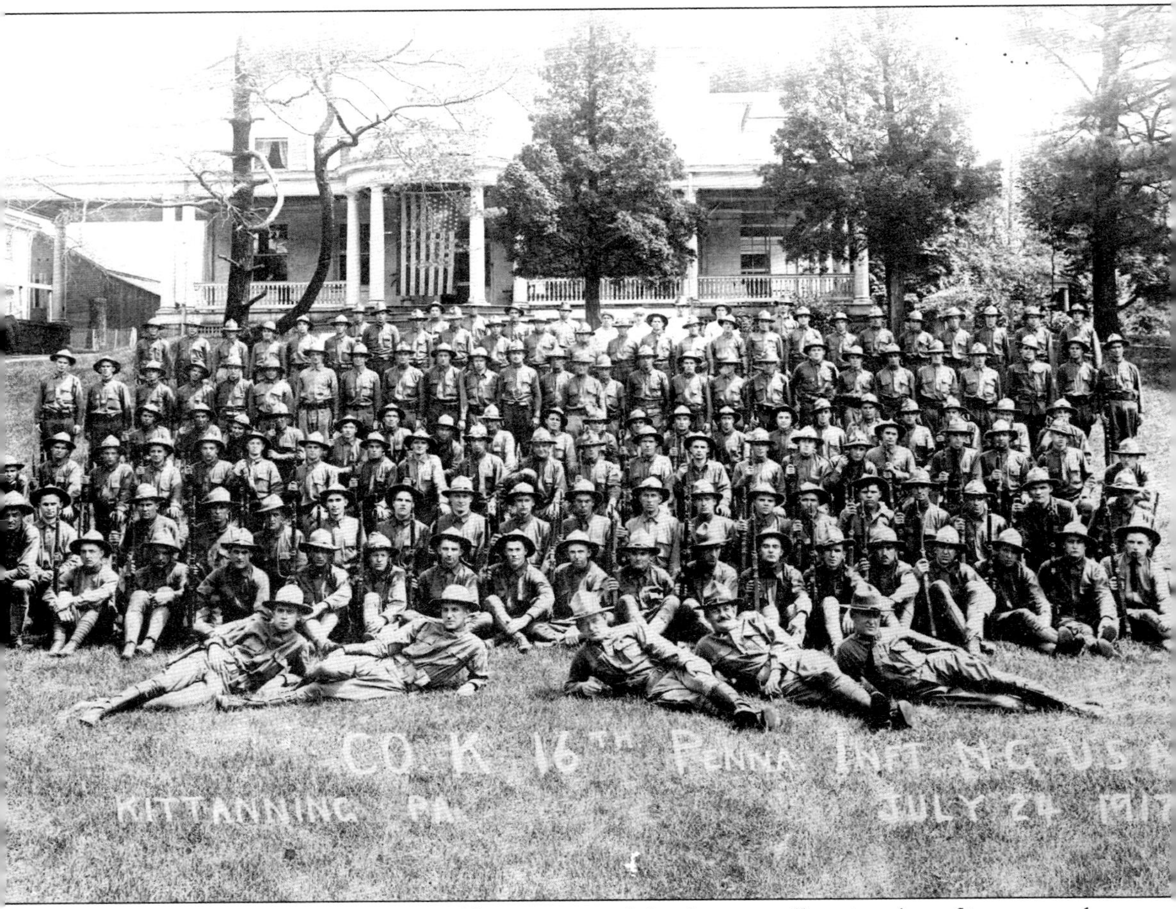

Kittanning has been represented by its sons and daughters in all national conflicts, even those that predate the formation of the United States. A tribute to those who gave the ultimate sacrifice, their lives, can be seen on the exterior of the Armstrong County Courthouse annex building on Market Street adjacent to the courthouse.

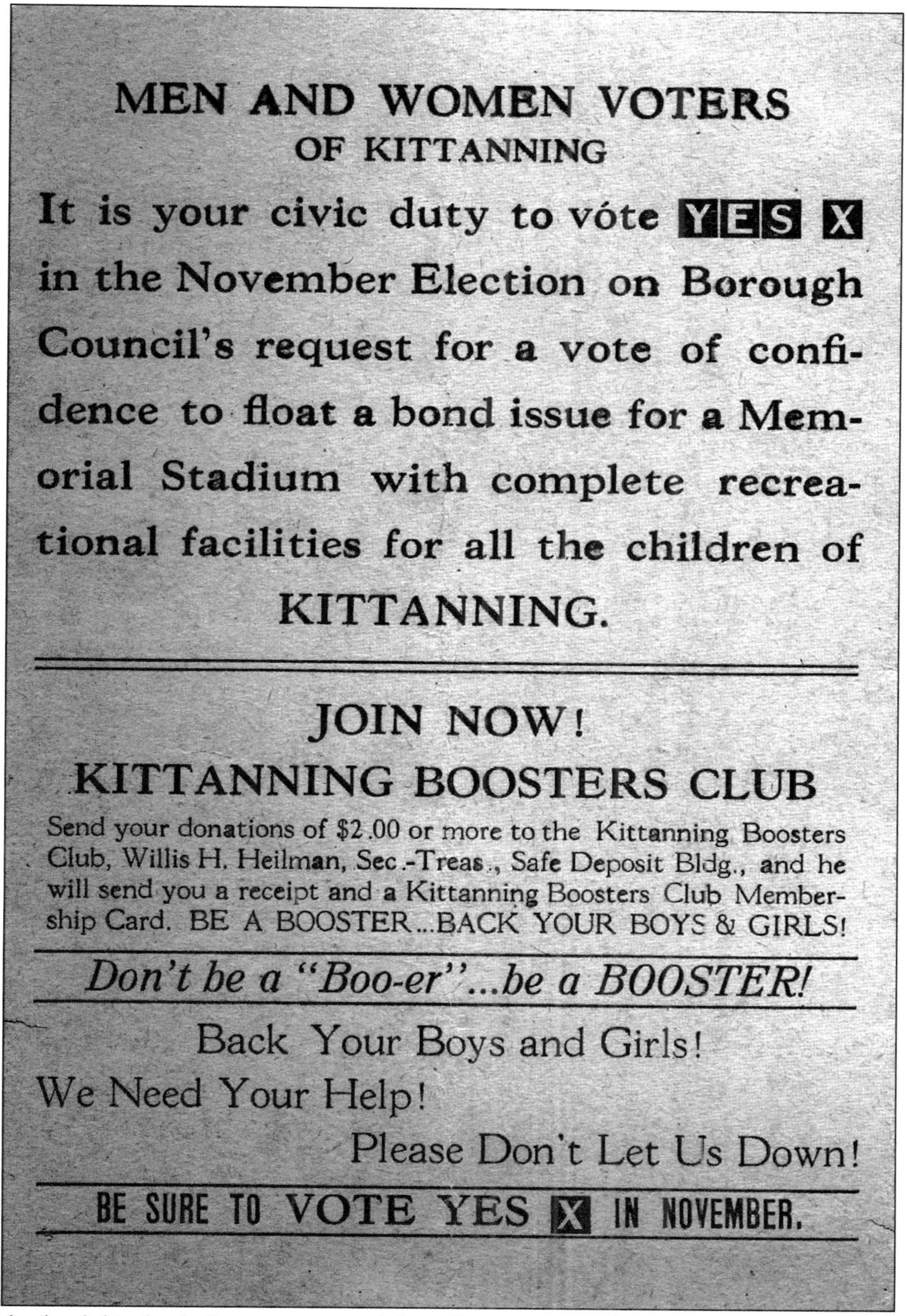

MEN AND WOMEN VOTERS
OF KITTANNING

It is your civic duty to vóte YES X in the November Election on Borough Council's request for a vote of confidence to float a bond issue for a Memorial Stadium with complete recreational facilities for all the children of KITTANNING.

JOIN NOW!
KITTANNING BOOSTERS CLUB

Send your donations of $2.00 or more to the Kittanning Boosters Club, Willis H. Heilman, Sec.-Treas., Safe Deposit Bldg., and he will send you a receipt and a Kittanning Boosters Club Membership Card. BE A BOOSTER...BACK YOUR BOYS & GIRLS!

Don't be a "Boo-er"...be a BOOSTER!

Back Your Boys and Girls!
We Need Your Help!
Please Don't Let Us Down!

BE SURE TO VOTE YES X IN NOVEMBER.

The back of this football program, saved from Kittanning High School's September 26, 1947, game against Grove City High School, encourages men and women to vote "yes" in the upcoming election concerning the completion of Memorial Stadium. Participation of every adult resident in government is ensured with the right to vote, and Kittanning has been known for an active citizenry in the electoral process.

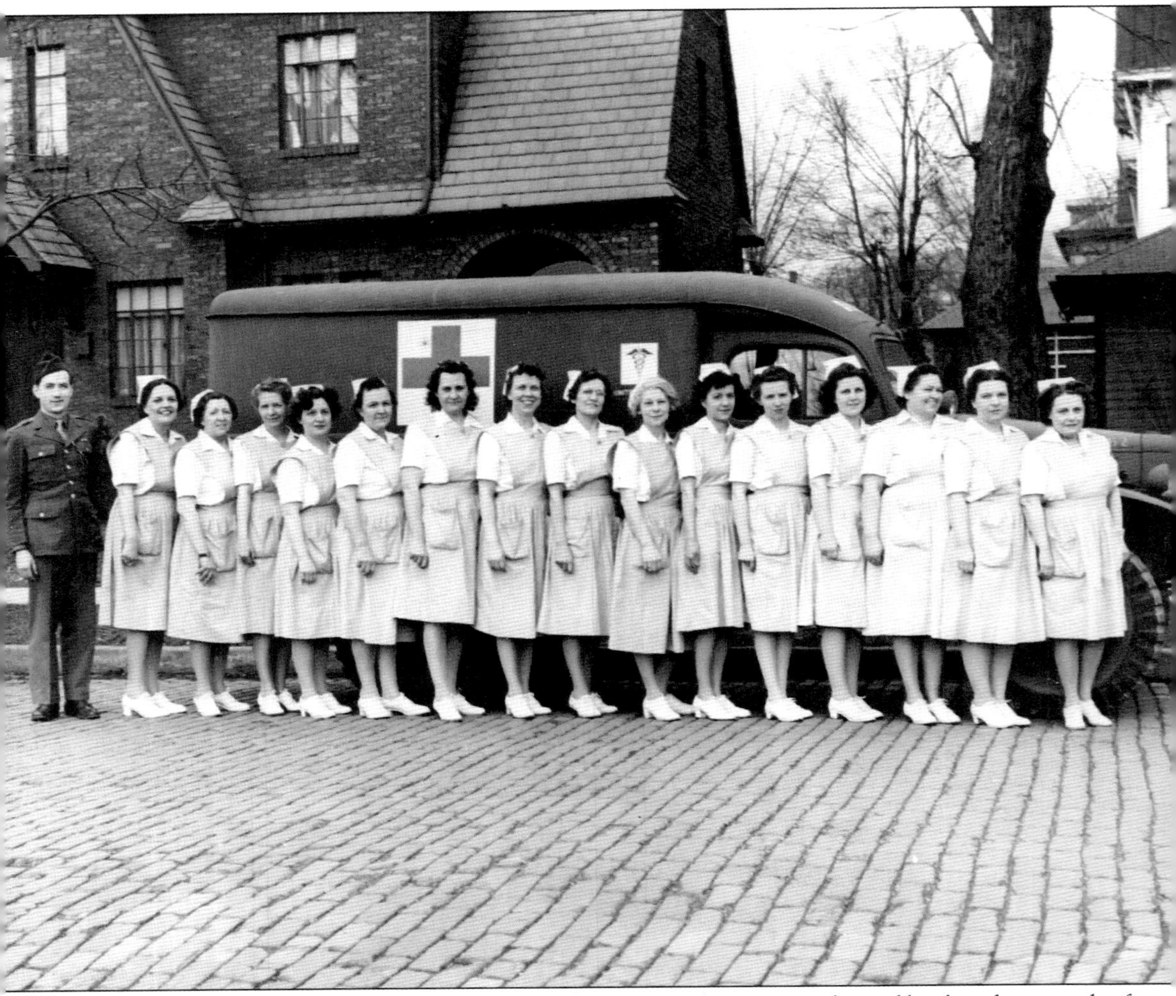

Service to the country in time of trial can take on many forms, as evidenced by this photograph of World War II Red Cross nursing volunteers. As difficult as it is to ensure the adequate recognition of known military troops, it is even more difficult to identify and thank the countless others who contributed in lesser-known ways, such as these women.

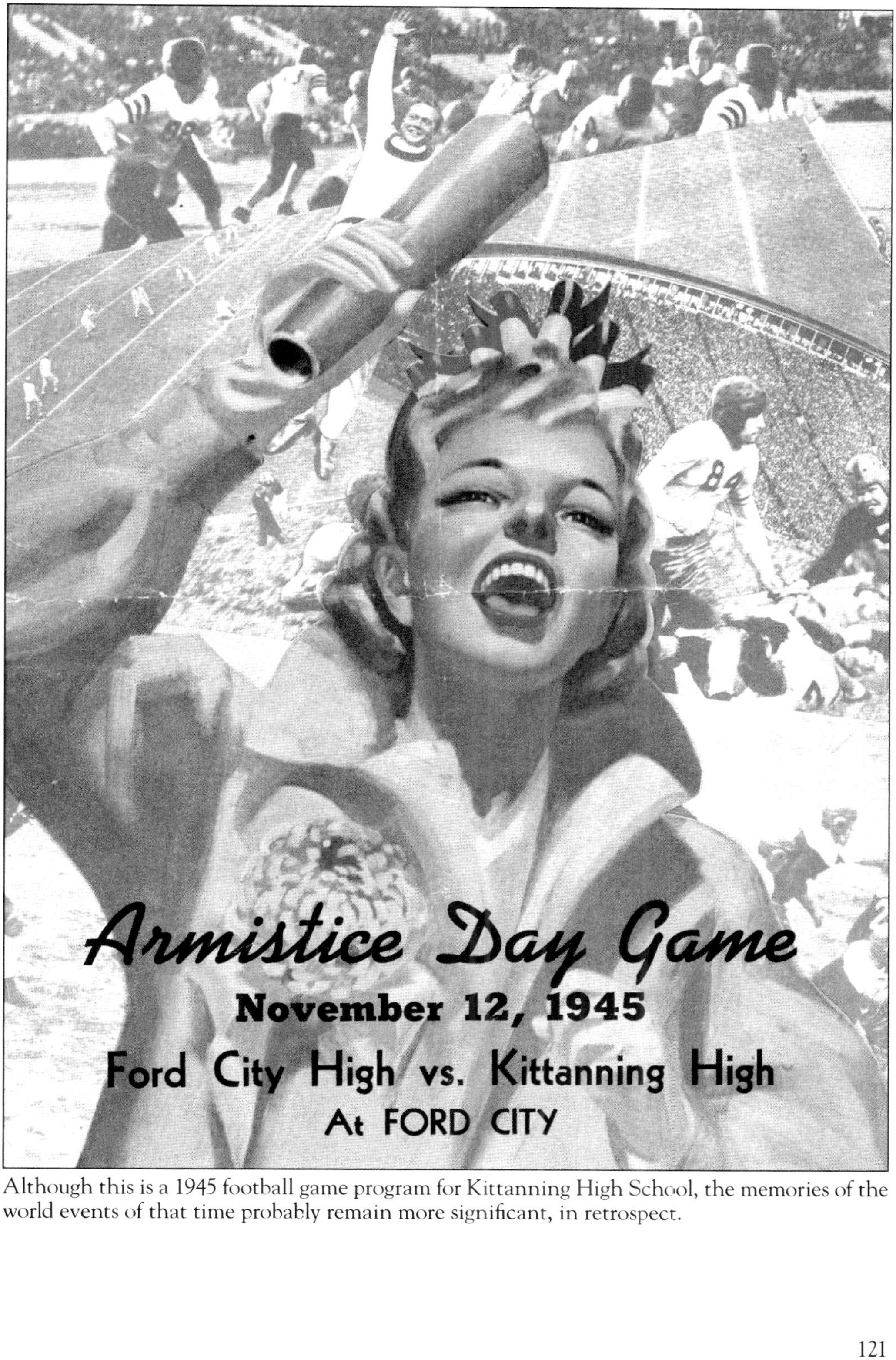

Although this is a 1945 football game program for Kittanning High School, the memories of the world events of that time probably remain more significant, in retrospect.

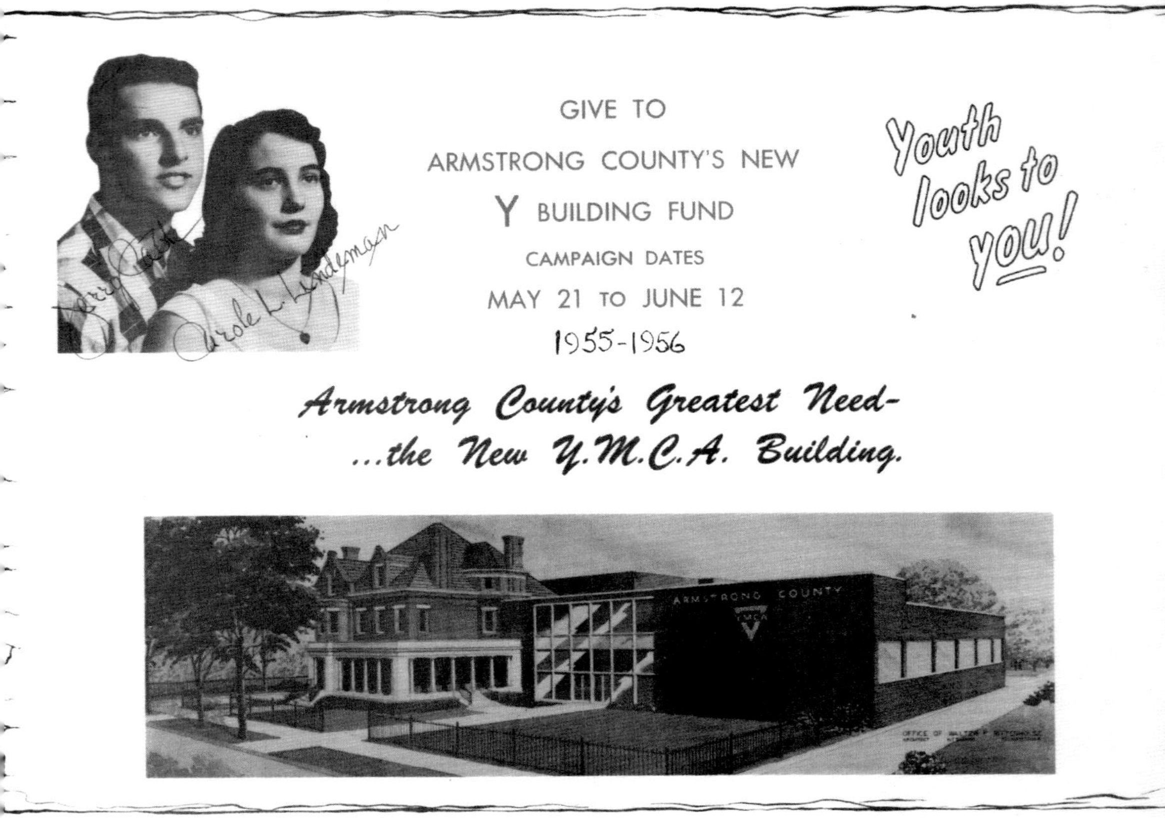

The Kittanning of 1956 was certainly not the same village that Col. John Armstrong and his militiamen marched into in 1756. While some things remain the same, such as the principles that guided those first residents as they established local government, schools, churches, and businesses, many changes were necessary for Kittanning to evolve into a contemporary town. The Kittanning High School class of 1956 was notable for several reasons. They would be the first to graduate from the newly-constructed high school, located on Orr Avenue, which is still used today. This group of industrious youths was also instrumental in expanding and modernizing another Kittanning institute, the YMCA. Thanks to the money earned by these teens through student-led dances, dinners, and other activities, in addition to a generous donation from the Crane family, the Armstrong County YMCA was well on its way to becoming the facility that thousands have enjoyed since then. This photograph collage poster was used to spark interest in this project in the community, with Carole Lindeman and Jerry Cable representing their peers.

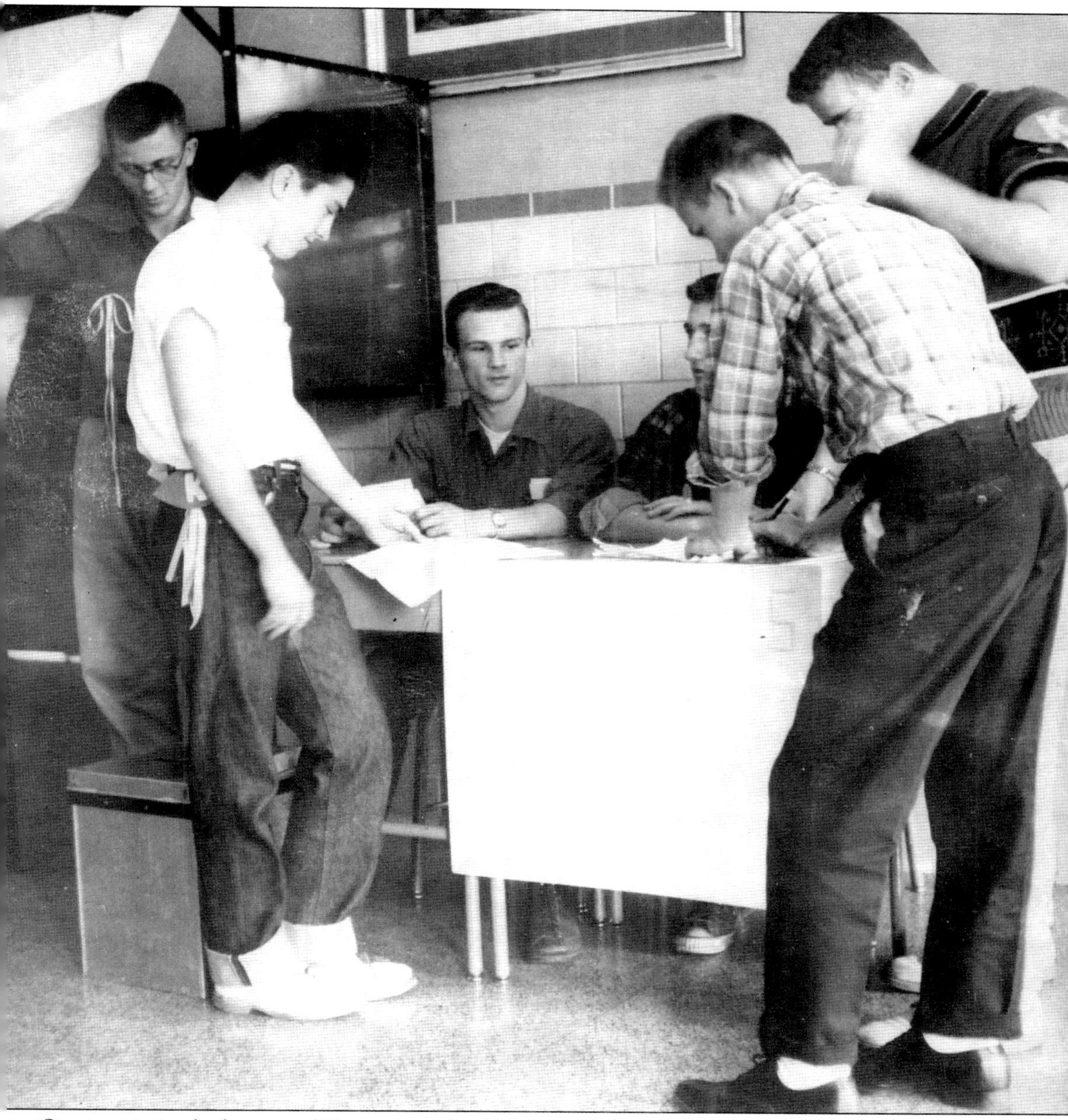

Once again in the history of Kittanning, the 56th year of the century seemed to be a significant one. In this case it was 1956 in the 20th century. Kittanning's newly-built high school, located on Orr Avenue, became operational. Although it was just a trial run for students, the electoral process was put in motion with a mock election, as seen in this photograph taken at the high school. The mock election's results were not known, but the nation reelected Pres. Dwight Eisenhower to a second term of office. The class of 1956 would have to wait four more years before their votes would be recognized outside of these high school halls.

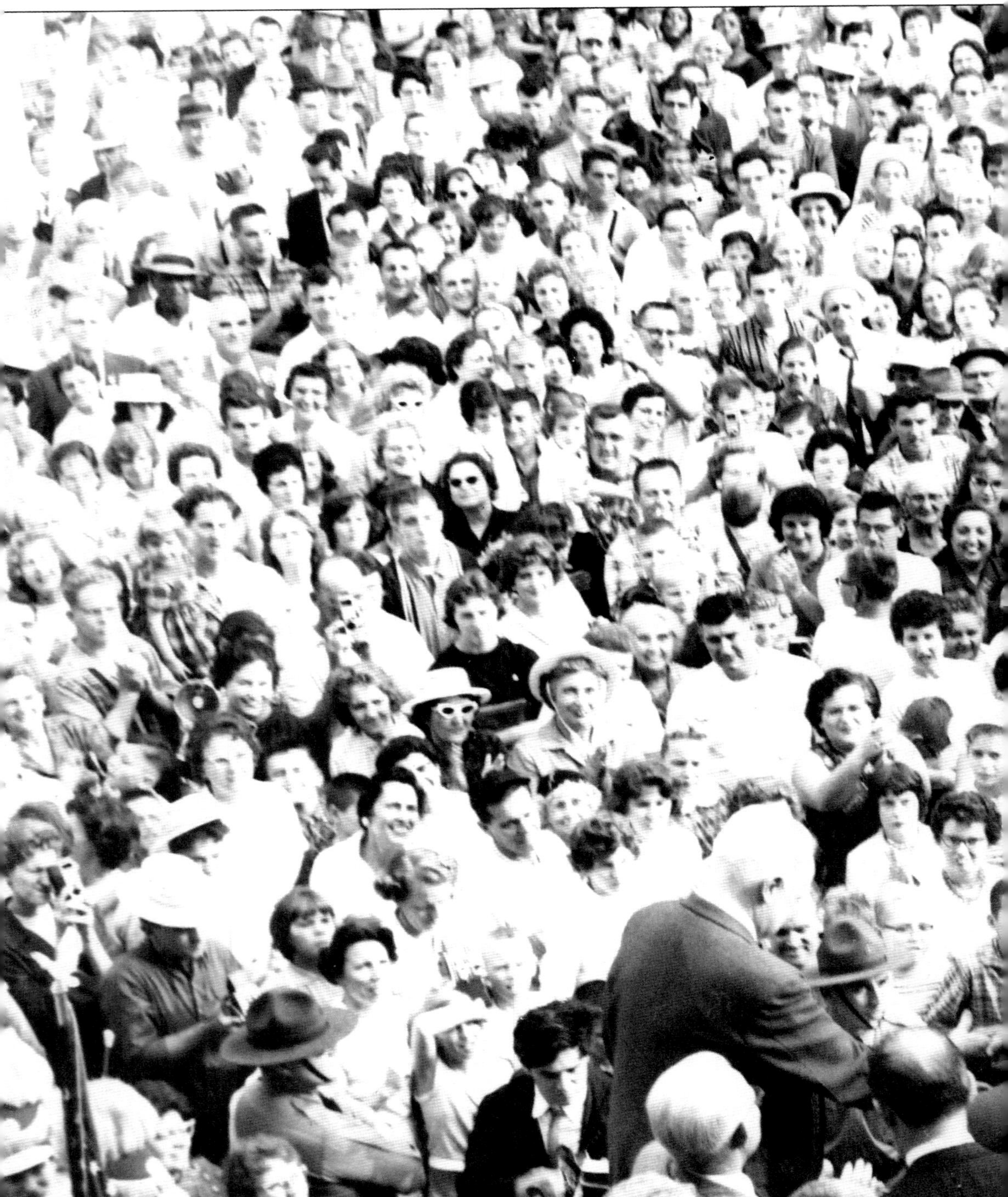

A rising political star, Sen. John F. Kennedy Jr. is seen here as he prepares to address the crowd gathered to hear his campaign speech on Market Street. Typically conservative in their political expressions, Kittanning residents appear to be a captive audience for this young congressman.

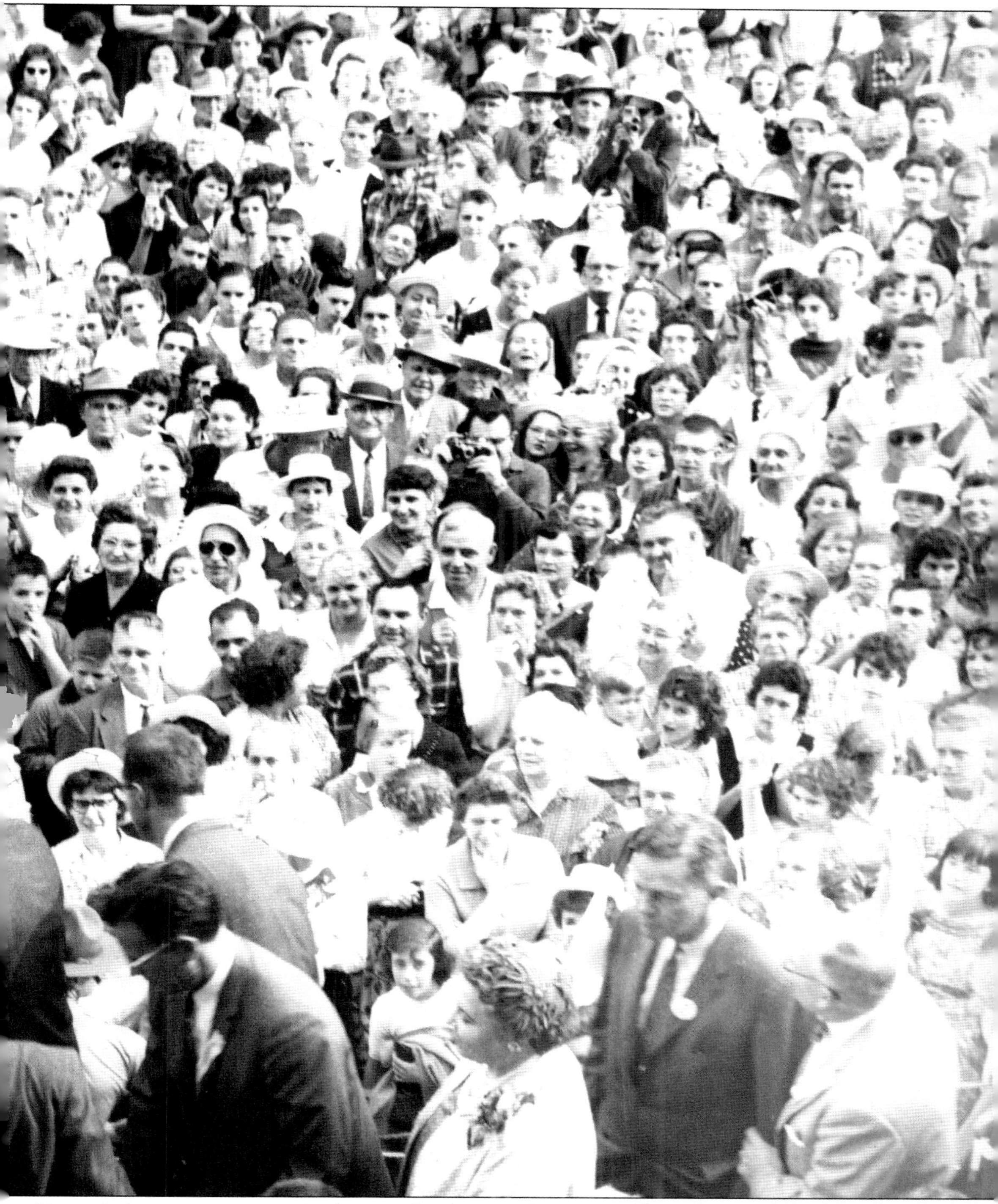

Kennedy later went on to win the race for the presidency, possibly with some help from the Kittanning High School class of 1956, who were able to exercise their right to vote in their first national election.

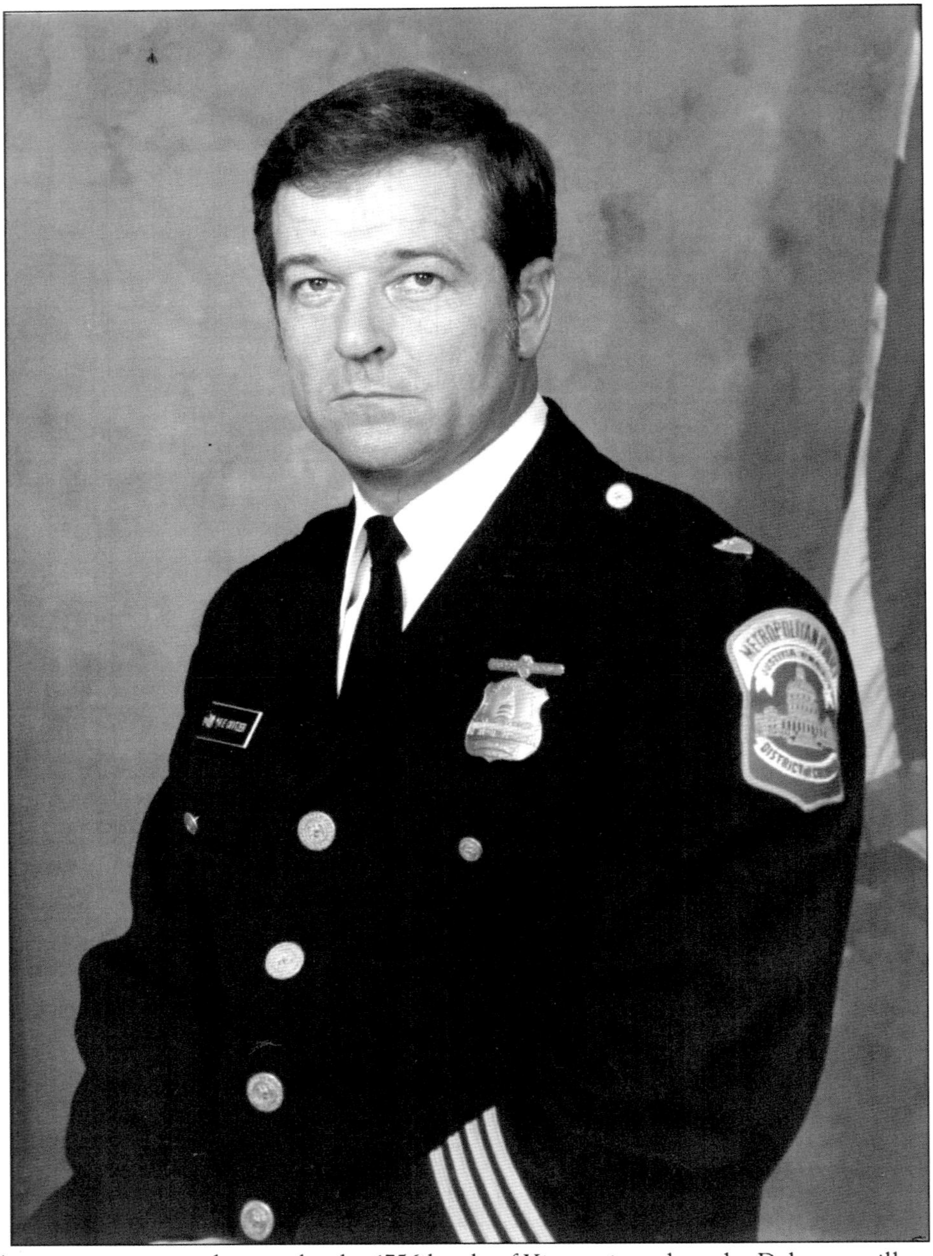

Kit-han-ne was put on the map by the 1756 battle of Kittanning when the Delaware village was set ablaze and the ensuing explosion was heard as far away as Pittsburgh. Years later, Kittanning was again in the midst of another significant event in U.S. history. At that time, Ron Crytzer, current Armstrong County Historical Society officer and member of Kittanning High School class of 1956, was living in Washington D.C. and working as a metropolitan police officer. Crytzer was asked to join 19 of his fellow officers to lead the funeral procession of Pres. John F. Kennedy as it marched the streets of the capital city. Crytzer remembers this opportunity as a truly great honor. Kittanning was honored and well represented by him and his service to the fallen leader.

About the Armstrong County Historical Society

The Armstrong County Historical Society calls 300 North McKean Street in Kittanning home. The museum, which contains a varied collection of artifacts from Kittanning history, is located in the McCain House. The building's carriage house lays adjacent to it and holds Armstrong County's largest collection of genealogical information in the Mildred Lankerd Thomas Genealogical Library. Hours of operation vary, however, private museum tours are available.

The society welcomes visitors and volunteers to help preserve and share in the county's rich history. Contact the society at 724-548-5757 or visit its Web site at www.armstronghistory.org.